Fifty Key
Television Programmes

Fifty Key
Television Programmes

Edited by Glen Creeber

ARNOLD

First published in Great Britain in 2004 by
Arnold, a member of the Hodder Headline Group,
338 Euston Road, London NW1 3BH

http://www.arnoldpublishers.com

Distributed in the United States of America by
Oxford University Press Inc.,
198 Madison Avenue, New York, NY10016

British Library Cataloguing in Publication Data
A catalogue record for this book is available from the British Library

Library of Congress Cataloging-in-Publication Data
A catalog record for this book is available from the Library of Congress

ISBN 0 340 80943 4

1 2 3 4 5 6 7 8 9 10

Typeset in 9.5/12.5 New Baskerville by Charon Tec Pvt. Ltd, Chennai, India
Printed and bound by Bath Press Ltd., Bath

What do you think about this book? Or any other Arnold title?
Please send your comments to feedback.arnold@hodder.co.uk

This book is dedicated to David Lewis

Acknowledgements

I would first like to thank Lesley Riddle at Hodder Arnold for originally coming up with the idea for this book, and Abigail Woodman for taking over responsibility for it at a later stage of development. Although I would like to thank all my friends at Cardiff University (particularly John Tulloch and John Hartley), finishing this book coincided with my appointment at Aberystwyth. I would therefore like to thank all my friends, colleagues and students there for helping me get through the first frantic year, especially Kevin Donnelly, Jamie Medhurst, Elan Closs Stephens and Ioan Williams. I would also like to thank all my contributors for doing such an excellent job, but particularly Brett Mills and Matt Hills, who not only produced more than their fair share of contributions but also helped me with the original conception and development. Finally, I would like to thank everyone in The White Lion and The Black Lion pubs, Talybont, above all, John and Mo for always keeping a welcome in the hillside! And, of course, special thanks, as always, to Catrin.

Contents

Note: to aid cross-referencing, when a programme appears in bold in the main text it indicates that it has a chapter to itself elsewhere in the book.

Notes on Contributors

Dr Rod Brookes is a Lecturer in Media and Cultural Studies at Cardiff University. His current research interests are on the media, sport and globalisation; the representation of the public in the media; and images of global politics in popular media fictions. He is the author of *Representing Sport* (London: Arnold, 2002), and has also published a number of chapters and articles on the media and health scares and the media and national identity.

John Corner is Professor in the School of Politics and Communication Studies at the University of Liverpool. His latest book is the edited collection *Media and the Restyling of Politics* (with Dick Pels) and he is currently working with colleagues on a history of the current-affairs programme *World in Action*. He is an editor of the journal *Media, Culture and Society*.

Dr Glen Creeber is a Senior Lecturer in Film and Television at the University of Wales, Aberystwyth. He is the author of *Dennis Potter: Between Two Worlds, A Critical Reassessment* (London and New York: Macmillan, 1998) and editor of *The Television Genre Book* (London: British Film Institute, 2002). He is currently writing *Previously On: Television Drama in the Age of Serial Fiction* and editing *Studying Television: An Introduction*, both with the British Film Institute.

Dr KJ Donnelly is a Lecturer in Film and Television at the University of Wales, Aberystwyth. He is author of *Pop Music in British Cinema* (London: British Film Institute, 2001) and editor of *Film Music* (Edinburgh: Edinburgh University Press, 2001). At present he is writing a book about film and television music for the British Film Institute.

Gary R Edgerton is Professor and Chair of the Communication and Theatre Arts Department at Old Dominion University. He has published five books, more than 50 book chapters and journal articles on a wide assortment of media and culture topics, and is co-editor of the *Journal of Popular Film and Television*. He was selected recently to receive the 2004 American Culture Association Governing Board Award for Outstanding Contributions to American Cultural Studies.

Peter Goddard is a Lecturer in Communication Studies at the University of Liverpool. His research interests include media history and institutions and documentary, news, current affairs and politics on television. He is currently completing a book on *World in Action*.

Dr Matt Hills is a Lecturer in Media and Cultural Studies at Cardiff University. He is the author of *Fan Cultures* (London and New York: Routledge, 2002) and *The Pleasures of Horror* (Continuum, forthcoming). He has also recently contributed to *The TV Studies Reader* (Routledge, forthcoming) and *Red Noise: Buffy the Vampire Slayer and Television Studies* (Duke University Press, forthcoming).

Dr Ros Jennings is Director of Research for Arts and Humanities at the University of Gloucestershire, where she also contributes to teaching Film Studies and postgraduate research methods. Her own work is currently concerned with ideas of crossing cultures and narratives of identity in relation to film and television. She is writing a book on the reception and meaning of Australian television programmes in the UK.

Dr Jason Jacobs is Senior Lecturer in the School of Arts, Media and Culture at Griffith University. His publications include *The Intimate Screen: Early British Television Drama* (Oxford: Oxford University Press, 2000) and *Body Trauma TV: The New Hospital Dramas* (London: British Film Institute, 2003).

David Lavery is Professor of English at Middle Tennessee State University in the US, where he teaches courses on literature, popular culture, film and television. He is the author of over 60 published essays and reviews and author/editor/co-editor of *Late for the Sky: The Mentality of the Space Age* (Southern Illinois University Press, 1992), *Full of Secrets: Critical Approaches to Twin Peaks* (Detroit: Wayne State University Press, 1994), *Deny All Knowledge: Reading The X-Files* (Syracuse UP, 1996), *Fighting the Forces: What's at Stake in Buffy the Vampire Slayer* (Lanham, MD: Rowman and Littlefield 2002), *Teleparody: Predicting/Preventing the TV Discourse of Tomorrow* (London: Walflower Press 2002) and *This Thing of Ours: Investigating The Sopranos* (New York: Columbia University Press, 2002). He co-edits the e-journal Slayage: The Online International Journal of Buffy Studies.

Justin Lewis is Professor of Communication at Cardiff University. He has written several books about media, culture and society. Among his recent books is *Constructing Public Opinion: How Elites Do What They Like and Why We Seem to Go Along With It* (New York: Columbia University Press, 2001).

Dr Brett Mills lectures in Media and Cultural Studies at the University of Glamorgan, where he teaches, amongst other things, a course on film and television comedy. He is the author of *Television Sitcom* (London: British Film Institute, forthcoming).

Robin Nelson is Professor and Head of Department of Contemporary Arts at Manchester Metropolitan University. He has broad research interests in the arts and media and his publications on TV drama include *Boys from the Blackstuff: The Making of a TV Drama* (London: Comedia, 1986) and *TV Drama in Transition: Forms, Values and Cultural Change* (Basingstoke and New York: Macmillan and St. Martin's Press, 1997).

Catrin Prys is a Lecturer at the University of Wales, Aberystwyth, teaching through the medium of English and Welsh. She is currently finishing her doctoral thesis on

'Dennis Potter: An Investigation into the Styles and Aesthetics of Television Drama'. Her other main research interests revolve around television drama and Welsh and European theatre.

Dr Jane Roscoe is Head of Screen Studies at the Australian Film, Television and Radio School, Sydney, Australia. She has taught screen studies in the UK, New Zealand and Australia. She has published extensively in the areas of documentary, mock-documentary, audiences and new television hybrids. She is the author of *Documentary in New Zealand: An Immigrant Nation* (Palmerston North: Dunmore Press, 1999) and she is co-author (with Craig Hight) of *Faking It: Mock-Documentary and the Subversion of Factuality* (Manchester: Manchester University Press, 2001). She is currently completing a book on documentary and performance entitled *Flickers of Authenticity*.

Dr Jamie Sexton is Lecturer in television and news media at the University of Wales, Aberystwyth. He has recently been working on an AHRB-funded project at Cardiff University, studying audiences of cult media, and previously worked at the AHRB Centre for British Film and Television Studies, Birkbeck, researching technological change and aesthetics in British television of the 1960s and 1970s. He is currently co-editing a book with Laura Mulvey, *Experimental British Television*.

Introduction

What is interesting is always interconnection,
Not the primacy of this over that.

Michel Foucault

When [Arnold] first approached me with the idea of editing a book called *Fifty Key Television Programmes* I was a little unsure as to whether it was something I really wanted to be involved with. As an academic in the area of television studies I was concerned that such a book would be seen as an attempt to build a 'television canon' i.e. a list of the 'best' and most 'important' television programmes ever made. I have always been suspicious of 'canons', distrusting the reason why certain 'texts' are chosen while others are frequently and inexplicably excluded. It always seemed to me that canons tell us more about the people who construct them than about the texts themselves, and I didn't want to help take television studies down the canonical road (some might say, cul-de-sac) already travelled by literature and film.

Deriving from the Greek word *kanon* (meaning to measure or rule), the term was originally applied to certain texts of the Bible or to actual 'canonised' theologians. It was later transferred to literature when the notion of a 'canonised' text became an essential part of assembling – what the English literary critic FR Leavis famously referred to as – 'the great tradition' (Leavis, 1948). However, the very notion of a 'canon' is clearly problematic, always depending on a set of criteria whose judgement is inevitably open to bias and prejudice. Yet despite its inherently subjective nature, a canon tends to gradually solidify into an unquestioned authority, something like a 'natural truth' which, by very definition, becomes both self-perpetuating and dangerously removed from criticism. As Peter Brooker has recently put it (2002, 23), although the notion of a canon

> *…clearly implies a process of judgement and discrimination, it is a circular and self-ratifying one, since the truly great are deemed unquestionably great and, in this respect, beyond judgement. Their canonic status is self-evident and you either recognize it or you don't. What such an orthodoxy depends upon of course is authority: the 'unspoken authority', as we say, of canonic texts and their expert interpreters.*

In fact, the problems of defining television in canonical terms seemed to me to be one of the field's greatest strengths. In contrast to literature and even film studies, television studies seemed to me to be refreshingly democratic and egalitarian. Simply in terms of the sheer variety of programmes offered by television it is frequently difficult to make justifiable comparisons across genres. For example, how do you compare the textual aesthetics of a quiz show with a documentary, or a reality game show with a news bulletin, or a cartoon with a party political broadcast? Such comparisons reveal just how complex the study of television (and, in particular, the notion of 'quality' and 'judgement' in television studies) actually is (Jacobs, 2001, 430). Indeed, Raymond Williams' original notion of television coming to us in an endless 'flow' (rather than as individual works of 'art') seemed to suggest a medium that did not easily allow itself to be examined in isolation, organised authorially or arranged canonically (Williams, 1974).

Added to this, recent audience research has further problematised the very notion of judgement in film and television studies. What one viewer may regard as quintessential 'quality television' another may view as unadulterated rubbish. The huge investment that some fans put into shows such as **Doctor Who** (BBC, 1963–89), **Star Trek** (NBC, 1966–9) or **Big Brother** (Endemol, 1999) certainly suggests that judgement and taste is not something that is universally shared by audiences as a whole. While many critics and social commentators regarded the American soap opera **Dallas** (CBS, 1978–91) as second-rate escapist melodrama, Ien Ang famously revealed audiences' passionate investment in the drama, constructing a form of 'emotional realism' that made it a crucially important and an aesthetically sophisticated text for many of its loyal and devoted fans (Ang, 1985). As Paul Willis puts it, 'TV watching is, at least in part, about facilitating a dialectic between representation and reality as a general contribution to symbolic work and creativity. The audience is not an empty room waiting to be furnished in someone else's taste' (1990, 36).

Similarly, what passes as 'quality' television may well change from one historical period to another. A programme that was hugely popular in one age – *Miss World* (BBC, 1951–79) or *The Black and White Minstrels Show* (BBC, 1958–87) may be regarded as tedious or downright offensive in another. In contrast, a programme that was regarded as generally 'trashy' or banal in one era – **Charlie's Angels** (ABC, 1976–81) or *Thunderbirds* (ITV, 1965–6) – may be regarded, with hindsight, as an enduring classic. Such discrepancies may also occur from country to country or from culture to culture. While Australia may take little notice of their home-grown soap operas like **Neighbours** (Grundy, 1985–) and *Home and Away* (Network Seven, 1989–), they are passionately watched and adored in the UK, and while **Dallas** took most of the world by storm during the 1980s, it was an unanimous flop in Japan.

However, as I thought more about the concept of this book so I slowly began to see how difficult it is to ever fully disconnect oneself from the notion of a canon. From the food we eat and the clothes we wear, to the films we watch, the books we read and the programmes we watch on television, we are unconsciously making choices and judgements which, if recorded and listed, would no doubt construct a personal 'canon' of sorts.

And no matter how much we may dislike it, every time we talk or write about TV, as students and teachers, we are making *judgements.* Whether it is an entirely personal judgement or one that tries to follow a strict academic agenda and methodology, every time we choose to look at or discuss a programme we are implicitly categorising and evaluating it. Simply by choosing to mention it at all we are putting it on the agenda and selecting it as somehow 'worthy' of our time and scrutiny. This may lead others to look at it or argue about our particular perspective, thus creating a self-perpetuating circle that inherently chooses and excludes at will.

Seen in this light, canons (of a sort) are simply inevitable, a way in which we all organise the world around us and discuss particular arguments and debates. We all (either consciously or unconsciously) build canons; they are the way in which we come to organise difficult and sometimes complex information and structures of knowledge. To pretend that this does not happen (and to pretend that you can completely avoid canon construction) is simply to deny the way that knowledge is collated, distributed and understood. As the editors of *Canonic Texts in Media Research* (Katz, Peters, Libebes and Orloff, 2003, 4) have recently put it:

> *For pedagogical purposes, some principle of selection and organization among the vast amounts of print is indispensable. No such principle will ever be sociologically neutral, but no scholarly or artistic institution will be able to operate practically without one either. Canons are editing devices, search engines in a world in which intelligent editing is one of the most crucial needs and scarcest resources.*

If canon construction is inevitable, then would it not be more helpful if we were to talk about their construction and influence openly, discuss how and why they have been constructed and who has constructed them? In that way perhaps we could help prevent them solidifying into a *natural law* and finally reveal them as the fluid, subjective and inherently biased categories that they clearly are. Indeed, if we dispense with them completely, what will we be left with? If we are not careful, the fear of making any comparative judgements may disable us from examining or discussing a number or group of texts in any detail at all. In the end, one of the central cores of television studies (i.e. the programmes themselves) will be erased from all critical debate. I am not saying that we should therefore create rigid hierarchical categories of judgement, only that if categorisation *is* an intrinsic way in which knowledge in the arts and the humanities is assembled, then would it not be better if we were to accept that and bring it out into the open for all to see and discuss? As the television academic Charlotte Brunsdon has put it, 'I am not arguing that we should rewrite our syllabuses to re-install evaluative criticism as our central concern, but I do think we should pay attention to the concealed ways in which we are teaching evaluation...' (1997, 129). As she concludes, 'Judgements are being made – let's talk about them' (ibid., 147). With this in mind, I decided that a book such as this could actually provide the ideal opportunity to help put both the text and the notion of critical judgement back on the agenda of television studies where I believe it belongs.

So for the sake of transparency, let me explain first how I came up with the final fifty programmes. At least, then, the reader may get a greater sense of *how* and *why* this particular list was put together. Ideally, I felt that each programme had to:

- *Be extremely popular with audiences and widely recognisable to potential readers.*
  We concluded that there was not much point trying to illustrate a general theme or issue in TV studies by choosing a programme that very few readers were likely to be familiar with.

- *Raise important issues surrounding TV, particularly in areas of construction, production and consumption.*
  This would normally be backed up by programmes where further (usually academic) reading is already possible.

- *Represent an array of genres.*
  We couldn't afford to permit predominance of a single genre such as soap opera or sitcom if the book aimed to address issues across the board of television as a whole.

- *Represent newer genres.*
  Contemporary, often hybridised genres such as 'reality TV' are being invented and reinvented all the time. It was important therefore that the generic changes in the historical development of television were represented by actual examples.

- *Represent as broad an historical spectrum as possible.*
  We didn't want all the programmes to be derived from a limited historical period – particularly the contemporary – thereby neglecting other important periods in television history.

- *Be readily available.*
  Students clearly need to follow up their work with reference to the actual programmes. There was no point in choosing a whole host of programmes potential readers would be unable to obtain on video or DVD.

- *Abide by the publisher's demands.*
  It would be misleading to suggest that there was no pressure from the publisher to look at certain programmes above others. For example, America is a huge market for British academic books and publishers almost always prefer the selection of television programmes that both British and American readers will be familiar with.

- *Attract a contributor who was qualified to write about a particular programme.*
  Contributors had to write on a number of programmes, a fact that inevitably influenced our final selection.

Of course, not all the programmes chosen here fit neatly into all of the above categories. For example, the availability of a programme to readers sometimes had to be waived if we felt it was still important enough (for a variety of the above reasons) to include – see, for example, *Marty* (NBC, 1953) or *Heimat* (SFB, 1984). Similarly, although TV events such as the moon landing or the television coverage of September 11, 2001 are not easily available to readers (and are not even properly 'programmes' in their own right), I still felt that they needed to be included for the important issues and debates that such global televised events inevitably raise. Although it is important that the book should include programmes already addressed by earlier academic books and articles – such as ***Dallas, The Singing Detective*** (BBC, 1986) and ***The Cosby Show*** (NBC, 1984–92) – sometimes I felt the book also had a responsibility to include a number of programmes which, to this date, have been partially ignored by the academy – see, for example, ***Brass Eye*** (Channel Four, 1997–2001), ***The Monkees*** (NBC, 1966–8) or ***The Benny Hill Show*** (ITV, 1968–89). Finally, when a number of potential programmes expressed similar styles and themes – such as ***Big Brother***, *Survivor* (Planet 24, 2000–) and *I'm a Celebrity Get Me Out of Here!* (ITV, 2002–) – I felt that only one should be chosen so as to allow other styles, themes and issues to be adequately represented elsewhere in the book. In this sense, one programme is frequently meant to be representative of a whole genre or sub-genre of programmes, although in an ideal world more examples would have been welcomed.

However, my contributors and I have done our very best to ensure that the vast majority of the 50 programmes chosen are familiar to our readers, representative of both historical and generic spectrums, raise important issues concerning TV and media studies and are generally widely available on video and DVD. In doing so, we aim to offer a wide variety of television programmes that reflect and hopefully illuminate discussions and debates central to the study and analysis of television as a whole. The choice of programmes will not satisfy everyone, but we intend to offer a sufficiently broad spectrum of texts and debates that will hopefully inspire and instigate the discussion of television for many years to come.

If it is a solid and elite 'canon' of television you are looking for then I hope you will find this volume ultimately disappointing. However, if you are seeking a varied selection of issues and debates about and around television – investigated, examined and exemplified through the analysis of the programmes themselves – then read on. We do not pretend these are the 'greatest' television programmes of all time (nor do we want them to solidify into something of a 'natural law'), but I hope you will find their analysis interesting and revealing, whatever your personal view of the programmes themselves or the means by which they were selected. If canons are inevitable, then I suggest we discuss them, dissect them and explore them, but continually keeping in mind, of course, that they are always built on sand and never set in stone.

Glen Creeber, Aberystwyth, 2003

Chapter One

24

Rod Brookes

Production Details

(Fox Broadcasting, 2001–)

Main Director: Stephen Hopkins
Creators, main Producers and Writers: Robert Cochran, Joel Surnow

Cast includes (first series only):

Jack Bauer (Kiefer Sutherland)
Teri Bauer (Leslie Hope)
Kim Bauer (Elisha Cuthbert)
Senator David Palmer (Dennis Haysbert)
Sherry Palmer (Penny Johnson)
Nina Myers (Sarah Clarke)
Victor Drazen (Dennis Hopper)

Series one of *24* recounts the longest day of agent Jack Bauer's life as he strives to prevent the assassination of African-American presidential candidate Senator David Palmer and rescue his kidnapped wife Teri and daughter Kim, while exposing a mole in the Counter Terrorist Unit (CTU) where he works. The show has been critically acclaimed as stylistically innovative in its storytelling techniques. First, as Jack's voice-over reminds us at the beginning of the each of the first few episodes, 'events occur in real time'. When a Serbian terrorist warns Jack that he must deliver a cellphone for Senator Palmer to answer at 10.45 exactly or his daughter will be killed, this phone call will happen 45 minutes into the episode (or at least it does if US advertising breaks are taken into account – otherwise each hour of story time equals about 42 minutes of screen time). Second, the show makes extensive use of split-screen, partly as a conventional means of showing the facial expressions and reactions of the participants in the many cellphone calls that are central to the narrative, but also to depict characters performing the same actions from different camera angles or distances, or to depict different characters performing different actions simultaneously, in a style which is central to the distinctive look of the show. Additionally, hand-held camerawork and editing is used to heighten realism and tension, a convention that is now established in a number of US police series.

1

Precedents in the use of real time and split-screen from popular cinema can be identified easily. For example, the duration of the film *High Noon* (Kramer, 1952) – 85 minutes – approximated the same continuous stretch of time in its characters' lives (Bordwell and Thompson, 1986, 88). Director Stephen Hopkins – responsible for *24*'s pilot and 12 episodes, including the key opening and closing ones of the first series – has identified *The Boston Strangler* (Fryer, 1968) as one of the main sources for his adoption of the split-screen technique (Talen, 2002). However, whereas both techniques are used to heighten tension, neither involves a break with conventional television narrative structure.

It maybe useful to compare *24* with the experimental film *Timecode* (Figgis, 2000). *Timecode* bears certain similarities to *24* in its use of real time, split-screen, hand-held camerawork and a digital clock display in the titles. However, in *Timecode* the division of the screen into four quadrants is rigidly maintained all the way through the film. Each quadrant shows footage from one of four cameras as they follow the main characters in a semi-improvised drama based on a series of events involving a film production company in Los Angeles, and the footage in each of these quadrants consists of one continuous take. Characters are shown performing the types of mundane activities that characterise everyday life but don't feature in television or film fiction unless they are associated with significant action – waiting around, walking, smoking a cigarette and, yes, visiting the bathroom. The viewer's attention is directed towards the quadrant that is currently showing the most significant events only through the use of sound. By contrast, *24* assimilates split-screen, real time and hand-held camerawork within a drama that utilises continuity editing techniques (i.e. shot/reverse shot, etc.).

The premiere of *24* took place in the US on November 5, 2001, two months after the attacks on the World Trade Center and the Pentagon (an immediate consequence of this was that a shot showing the plane exploding in episode one was cut). It earned favourable reviews in the US and the UK, and in 2002 picked up a respectable number of nominations and awards at the Emmys and the Golden Globes. And even though *24* was the 'lowest-rated drama on the four major networks to win renewal', the show rated well with those segments that advertisers want to attract but are perceived as more elusive: the affluent men and young adults (Werts, 2002). Is it significant that in the year following the events of **September 11, 2001** a series featuring counter-terrorism was acclaimed by many critics as the most important new show? Does *24* typify in some way the cultural, political and social context of the US under the presidency of George Bush?

The first series of *24* certainly rehearsed many of the themes identified by Knight (2002) as constituting the 'conspiracy culture' that has developed in the US since the 1960s. Its plot appeals to anxieties relating to the effects of accelerating globalisation on nation states: the movement of people, money and information across national boundaries. First, threats to national security are represented as *external*. The CTU is involved in identifying the movement of assassins, monitoring communications and tracking money transfers that transcend the borders of the US. Second, the nation itself is represented as unstable and vulnerable to *internal* threats that may be connected with racial tensions. In the opening episode, CTU head, Walsh, briefs his agents that the threat to Senator Palmer comes from a 'lone shooter from overseas' probably funded by a 'domestic hate group'. Walsh confides in Jack the importance of this: 'If Palmer gets hit, the first African-American with a shot at the White House, it will tear this country apart' – although as the plot develops it becomes apparent the assassination threat has nothing to do with Palmer being black.

But conspiracy culture since the 1960s is not just about external and internal threats to the nation, but also about distrust of the ability of the state, government or the political process itself. *24* features a number of different conspiracies. First, there is the conspiracy concerning Palmer's campaign itself. Concerned that his Los Angeles campaign-backers might be prepared to sanction murder in the light of revelations from his son's therapist, Palmer confronts his former advisor, Carl. To Palmer's surprise, Carl reveals that he never worked for Palmer, that he and Palmer 'always worked for them'. Later, Palmer would turn over to the Justice Department a tape implicating his backers in murder. But the backers' motives are left unclear. Why would a group of wealthy white businessmen have such a high stake in Palmer's election that they would be prepared to go to such lengths?

Second, there is a Department of Defense conspiracy. A major storyline in the later episodes is that the government have taken Serbian warlord Victor Drazen alive and have been moving him around by helicopter between secret prison facilities at night, while both Palmer and Jack believe Jack to have killed Drazen on a Palmer-approved covert mission in Serbia. And there is the main conspiracy – the identity of the CTU mole and who that mole is really working for. Revealed as the mole by the final episode, CTU agent Nina shoots Teri Bauer after Teri discovers Nina talking on the phone to her employers in German. Later Nina appeals to Jack not to kill her: 'If you kill me, you won't know who I work for. You think I work for the Drazens, but I don't'. But this is as much of the conspiracy as the first series gives away: no motives and no clues to the identity of the real conspirators. That the threat might come from Serbian terrorists is perhaps understandable given recent US armed intervention in Serbia, but when the threat is finally revealed to come out of Germany – which makes little sense in the real world – what does this mean?

It is interesting how little detail is provided in *24* on the various conspiracies involved and the motives behind them. It seems enough just to evoke a vague sense of conspiratorial menace. And whereas many of the contemporary popular cultural texts Knight (2002) discusses as typifying conspiracy culture adopt an ironic, postmodern approach by featuring in-jokes and intertextual references (for example, *The X-Files* [Fox, 1993–2002]), *24* plays it absolutely straight. Perhaps this is how *24* can be related to its historical, cultural, political and social context – in its very lack of specificity about the origins and motives of the conspiracies featured, it appeals to a generalised paranoia that it is the whole world – not only outside the nation's boundaries, but also inside – that is inherently unstable and unpredictable.

If *24* is about the danger posed by conspirators to the safety of the US nation and its citizens, the utter inhumanity and evil these conspirators embody is repeatedly signified by the violence they inflict on female characters. *24* is distinct from other conspiracy spy thrillers in integrating the main character's domestic life as a key element of the plot. Jack not only has to protect Palmer's security; he also has to try to keep his wife Kim and daughter Teri safe. From the moment when first Kim and then Teri are tricked out of their safe suburban Santa Monica home into downtown Los Angeles, fraught with dangers, the main narrative role that these characters perform is that of victims.

The tension of key scenes in the series is often based on the sadistic depiction of threatened or actual violence against Kim and Teri. After Jack has apparently failed to follow the instructions given to him by Gaines, the head of the kidnap gang, Gaines orders his henchmen to 'kill the wife and kid'. Kim and Teri are dragged kicking and screaming to the edge of an open grave. They are forced to kneel and handguns are levelled at the back of their heads. Just in time, Gaines makes the call that they are to be kept alive after all, and they are dragged away sobbing.

As victims, the narrative role played by Kim and Teri ensures that they are repeatedly in need of rescue, that their own unaided attempts to resist or escape are unsuccessful or incomplete. In episode 13, the one that could have been the last had Fox decided not to commission the whole projected series, Jack has freed his wife and daughter from their captors' compound. He then stays behind to delay their pursuers by deliberately blowing up their crashed van, thus giving Kim and Teri a head start in setting out for a reservoir by which they will be rescued by helicopter. But Kim and Teri still manage to get lost in the woods, even though Jack has given Teri a map of the area on a PDA. Hence Jack arrives at the rendezvous first, and much of the tension of this key episode is based around him having to go back and rescue them – *again*.

The series has been praised as a stylish and innovative spy thriller show featuring excellent performances by a likeable cast. By contrast, the actual content of the show has so far escaped much serious analysis or criticism. But how significant is it that a show that appeals to paranoid anxieties about potential threats posed by the outside world should be so highly acclaimed at this particular historical moment? And is it inevitable that the sense of tension so successfully built through its innovative narrative techniques should be based on threatened or actual violence against the main female characters in the show? While its status as a 'key' or stylistically innovative series is assured, these are questions that future criticism of the drama will certainly need to explore.

QUESTIONS TO CONSIDER

- Do you think *24* would have been possible if the events hadn't occurred in 'real time'? How does this technique help create much of the suspense and tension of the drama?

- How does *24* compare in its treatment of the conspiracy theme with other films and television shows (for example, *Enemy of the State* (Scott, 1998) or **The X-Files**)?
- In contrast to the show's innovative look, the role played by female characters in the narrative structure tends towards the stereotypical. Would you agree?
- Do you think the events of **September 11, 2001** explain the popularity of the show? What elements of the drama would you classify as explicitly reflecting the George Bush presidency?

RECOMMENDED READING

Rothkerch, Ian (2002), 'A day in the life', www.salon.com, February 5, an interview with creator, producer and writer of *24*, Joel Surnow.

Sangster, Jim (2002), *24: The Unofficial Guide*, London: Contender.

Topping, Keith (2003), *A Day in the Life: The Unofficial and Unauthorized Guide to 24*, Tolworth: Telos.

Chapter Two

An American Family and *The Family*

John Corner

Production Details

An American Family

(US Public Broadcasting Service, January–April 1973. 12 episodes. NET: national educational television)

Producer: Craig Gilbert
Directors: Alan Raymond, Joan Churchill
Sound: Susan Raymond

The Family

(BBC1, April–June 1974. 12 episodes. BBC television)

Producer: Peter Watson
Director: Frank Roddam
Camera: Philip Bonham-Carter
Sound: Peter Edwards

An American Family (USA) and *The Family* (UK) were both landmark television documentaries. Above all, they were exercises in the observation of domestic living and were pioneering moments in the development of documentary form and in the relationship between television and 'real life'. Although they differed in their approach, and in the nature of the family life depicted, they both combined what is essentially an anthropological project (looking closely at how a particular social group works) with an entertainment project (linking some of the pleasures of social voyeurism with the established satisfactions of soap opera). This combination is particularly significant given later developments in 'reality television', including the emergence of a wide range of 'docusoap' formats and the kind of detailed surveillance of behaviour introduced in programmes such as ***Big Brother*** (Endemol, 1999) and ***Popstars*** (Screentime, 2001–).

Both the American and British documentaries were grounded, socially, aesthetically and technologically, in the tradition of observational film and television. A key strand of this tradition is often referred to as 'direct cinema', following US precedents, and the European strand is often labelled 'vérité', although this can be misleading given the different conventions employed (Winston, 1995). Broadly speaking, observational work of this kind explores the possibilities of portrayal and knowledge that follow from sustained filming, over a period which may extend to months, of a subject area quite tightly limited in its space, time and participants. The intensity and duration of the engagement that results are thought to provide a new, deeper documentary experience. In particular, the absence of strong directorial control in the shooting process (the crew simply wait for things to happen, as it were) is pointed to as a way of letting a new degree of honesty into the filmic record and a new freedom into the exercise of audience judgement.

Apart from the developing tradition of observational film-making, there had been a number of US television programmes taking a 'close look' at the family by the time Craig Gilbert formulated the idea for the series. Alan King's *A Married Couple* was filmed in 1969, and portrayed ten weeks in what was described as a 'marriage in crisis'. Gilbert, who had worked on a number of documentary projects, including a study of the anthropologist Margaret Mead, was attracted by the kind of loose, spacious observationalism which King displayed. The family finally chosen by Gilbert, after much deliberation and searching, were the Louds, a quite wealthy, middle-class family (mother, father, sons and daughters) living in Santa Barbara, California. Santa Barbara offered the advantages of closeness to excellent post-production facilities and a climate that allowed extensive shooting with available light in the garden and patio areas of the house. It might be noted here how the choice of a prosperous family makes for a quite distinctive projection of 'ordinariness' within the American social setting, a factor which has implications both for viewing relationships and the kind of social comment the series provoked.

The crew produced their material after a seven-month shoot, involving almost daily visits to the Louds' home to follow the routines of their domestic life and occasional short trips away with members of the family. Jeffrey Ruoff (2002) offers a superb account of how the eventual form and look of the programme emerged from a mixture of conscious influences and intentions and simply the 'way things fell out'. Formally, it is significant to note, given later developments in this vein, that the series contained no interview material and included no voiced-over commentary save for a prologue to the first episode and occasional references to times and places. Some sections of first-person narration by the participants, over the filmed action, occurs at times. The viewing experience was offered predominantly as an exercise in onlooking and overhearing (the British phrase 'fly on the wall' is apt), largely unbroken by any direct verbal mediation or by an attempt to bridge between the realm of viewing and the realm of the observed in the way that occurs within interview formats. Thirty years later, when reality television of all kinds often comes extensively packaged and presented, it is perhaps easy to overlook the real rigour and excitement of this kind of practice. An exception to the dominant observationalist aesthetic was the title sequence, which, presenting each member of the family in turn and freeze-framing them to upbeat signature music, not surprisingly drew its references more from popular series drama.

In terms of its formal system, *An American Family* had to take account of the fact that (unlike in most fictional series) the family events and circumstances it depicted were in some cases already known to the viewing public through newspaper reports well in advance of screening. Filming finished at the end of 1971 and the first episode was screened in January 1973, allowing a full year's gap. Perhaps the most significant fact to emerge prior to transmission, giving a strongly retrospective mood to many scenes, was that the Louds had separated during the period that the film was made (for reasons that they claimed had nothing to do with the filming itself). In fact, Gilbert starts the first episode of the series with a sequence shot on the last day of filming, noting as soon as Pat Loud appears on-screen that 'this New Year will be unlike any other that has been celebrated at 35, Wooddale Road … Pat Loud and her husband, Bill, separated four months ago after twenty years of marriage'. As Ruoff (2002) suggests, this imparts to many of the earlier scenes a special kind of significance (we know the outcome, the participants do not). To a degree, the series was trailed as being about a family 'in crisis' in a way that overtook the provisional design and is not strictly fair to what we see and hear in the twelve episodes.

Another feature of the formal design of the series is the extensive use of parallel shooting and editing, whereby scenes shot in different locations are intercut with each other to show, or to suggest, simultaneous action and occurrence. The series employs this device in order to track individual family members. Significant here is Lance Loud, the gay son, whose distinctive approach to the film-making (he acknowledges the presence of the camera throughout) and whose self-consciously camp performance were important in the impact and appeal that the series had with some audiences.

The series received intensive publicity and review on its transmission, with a wide range of related newspaper commentary and the now familiar shift to temporary 'celebrity' status for the Louds themselves. Above all, the documentary raised a number of interesting questions. How far had the film-makers behaved ethically and without implicit biases of their own? What kind of general information about American family life could be gleaned from the episodes? Had the family members been too self-conscious and strategic in their 'performance' to the cameras? Critics reached different decisions on the strengths and weaknesses of the series but most recognised its powerful and problematic originality.

As well as the direct precedent of the US series, Paul Watson also had the work of Roger Graef, in his series *The Space Between Words* (BBC, 1972), from which to take his bearings in devising *The Family*. Graef had attempted to explore the inner life and tensions of a family by the use of the observational method, framing his film quite clearly as a 'communication experiment' and making contact with emerging ideas of family therapy. Watson also saw his project as a serious analytic exercise, stressing particularly the placing on-screen of precisely the kind of people who he thought did not get properly represented on television at the time. Watson's chosen family, the Wilkins of Reading, were working class and this gives *The Family* a distinctive character when it is compared with its precursors. It also has consequences for the kind of response the series received within a country notoriously anxious about issues of class taste and class bias.

Watson's approach was, again, an extensive period of shooting, with the crew letting themselves in to the house with a key early in the morning and often leaving after the family had gone to bed. Using faster film stock than the US series, Watson and his team were able to do interior shooting with natural light and thus to operate with a freer brief as to what to shoot and when (this did not stop the criticism of 'badly lit' appearing in some reviews).

A key feature of *The Family*'s communicative design was the idea of transmitting earlier episodes while still shooting others. So episode one went out while episode four was being shot and this relationship continued throughout the three-month run. The family were even filmed watching themselves in earlier episodes, but this material, with its nervous laughter, was felt not to work well within the screened programmes and was not used. Nevertheless, the impact of being self-conscious television stars at a national level (the series drew an audience of 7 to 10 million viewers) was widely seen as exerting an additional distorting effect on the kind of 'performance' that some family members gave. In *The Family*, this suspicion was compounded by the degree to which the series was taken, not to be just a specific piece of observation (*these* people in *these* particular circumstances) but a portrait more generally of working-class family life or even of aspects of British family life.

Graef (1974) thought the main problem in negative responses was the uncomfortable nature of the viewing experience for many people who identified all too strongly with what they saw on the screen and then variously had to 'deny' the truth coming through. My own view is that this explanation may underrate the extent to which class and regional differences strongly informed perspectives on the series, whatever the sense of recognition around some of the aspects of family life depicted. The Wilkins also had a family profile that it was rather hard to pass off entirely as 'ordinary' in 1974. One of the children was fathered by Mrs Wilkins' lover during a separation from her husband; the eldest daughter had a live-in boyfriend; and the eldest son was living in the house with his wife, whom he had married at sixteen because she was pregnant.

Regarded in terms of their episodic design, the programmes have a relaxed, spacious approach and an engagement with the inconsequential, with the expanded durations of domestic time, that now looks quite bold. The intermittent conversational exchanges are a long way from the crafted dialogue of soap opera or the more con-ventionally articulate and extensive conversations sometimes to be found in observa-tional glimpses of middle-class life. Voice-over is hardly ever used, although occasional and brief exchanges between crew and family members occur. Fade-outs to black are used to signify shifts in time, and the viewer quite quickly gets used to the initially 'odd' forms of watching and listening that the programme rather uncompromisingly offers. The quiet and subtle title sequence, working transformations on a 'family photograph', placed in a frame on a mantelpiece, with the family eventually gathered around it, makes the connection both with popular fiction and the series' more serious sociological ambitions.

QUESTIONS TO CONSIDER

- Do the problems of being 'true to reality' in family observation series outweigh any potential for new kinds of understanding?
- Where do you judge each series to be placed in relation to the interplay of 'knowledge values' and 'entertainment values'?
- In what ways do the two series differ in their handling of domestic space, time and ways of speaking?
- Compare and contrast the conventions and viewer appeal of fictional characterisation with those of 'real-life characters'.

RECOMMENDED READING

Graef, Roger (1974), 'Skeletons on the Box', *New Society,* June 27, 1974, 772–3.
Ruoff, Jeffrey (2002), *An American Family: A Televised Life,* Minneapolis: University of Minnesota Press.
Young, Colin (1974), 'The Family', *Sight and Sound,* Autumn, 206–11.

Chapter Three

The Benny Hill Show

Brett Mills

Production Details

(ITV [Thames], 1969–89)

Writer: Benny Hill
Producers/Directors: John Robins, David Bell, Keith Beckett, Peter Frazer-Jones, Mark Stuart, Ronald Fouracre, Dennis Kirkland

Performers:

Benny Hill
Jenny Lee-Wright
Henry McGee
Nicholas Parsons
Bob Todd
Rita Webb
Jack Wright

The Benny Hill Show is the greatest comedy success story in the history of British broadcasting. Running for two decades while other comedy shows faltered and failed, it made a huge star of its eponymous writer and performer. Simultaneously, it not only cracked the impenetrable American television market, but also became an international phenomenon, sold to hundreds of countries. It seems odd, then, that it is now a series that is reviled and, while not forgotten, is remembered in complex and contradictory ways. The story of *The Benny Hill Show* is certainly one that encapsulates the fickle nature of broadcasting and the relationship between cultural politics, social change and television.

The series' origins are similar to those of much television comedy. Alfred Hill, born in 1924 in Southampton, spent much of his early career performing songs and jokes around Britain in music halls, changing his name to Benny in homage to the American stand-up, Jack Benny. After appearing as a supporting performer in many television variety shows of the 1950s and 1960s, the first of his shows for which he wrote all the material was *Hi There!* (BBC, 1951). Following this, the first incarnation of

The Benny Hill Show appeared on the BBC from 1955 to 1968; from here the series migrated to ITV, where it ran for twenty years. It is this latter series which is most commonly remembered.

The comedy in *The Benny Hill Show* revolves around simple recurring characters (such as the lisping idiot, Fred Scuttle and the linguistically challenged Chinaman, Chow Mein) interspersed with a wealth of visual gags and, importantly, material centred heavily on male lust for women. To this end, the series contained 'Hill's Angels', a dance troupe of 'bikini-busting, boob-bouncing beauties' (Lewisohn 1998, 319), who, in speeded-up sequences, chased Hill to the strains of the music most associated with the show, 'Yakety Sax'. In this way, the series continued the long-standing British tradition of 'seaside postcard saucy smut' (Novick, 2000, 96), in which women are reduced to ageing harridans or buxom young beauties, while the men desire nothing other than to satisfy their own carnal pleasures. It was the successful use of such traditional forms of humour that led to *The Benny Hill Show*'s success, with ratings up to 20 million (Novick, 2000, 84); unfortunately, it was Hill's inability to move on from such material which would lead to the show's later infamy.

It is simplistic, though, to see the series as relying solely on smutty, sexist gags. Indeed, at the time, the programme was often lauded for its sophisticated understanding of the genres and possibilities of television and audiences' relationships with it. Pre-empting such self-aware fare as *The Kenny Everett Video Show* (ITV, 1978–81), *The Benny Hill Show* consistently parodied television series and blockbuster films, while also relying on the tricks of editing, television's ability to hold tight close-ups on Hill's leering reactions, and the inherently visual nature of the medium to develop comedy which, while music hall in origin, was certainly television in expression. In addition, the movement of the programme from being broadcast in black and white to colour helped highlight the blue of Hill's childish and childlike eyes, resulting in a performer at once both adult and immature in appearance, the most common representation of masculinity seen in all forms of British and American comedy (King, 2002, 77–92). This seamless synthesis of traditional material and a new medium made Hill 'the world's most popular comedian in the television era' (Lewisohn, 2002, ix).

What was even more astonishing was the success of *The Benny Hill Show* in America, a country which it has long been assumed just doesn't get the British sense of humour, or, indeed, is not particularly interested in culture from other countries (Lewisohn, 1998, 319). Throughout the 1970s Hill's programmes were offered to the American networks, who repeatedly refused to buy them. Yet in 1978, with *The Benny Hill Show* such a massive hit in Britain, the struggling station WTAF in Philadelphia agreed to buy special episodes, as long as they were edited to remove all references that were specifically British, to make the programme as comprehensible as possible to an American audience. While this had long been a stumbling block for British comedy, it actually functioned as a liberating force for *The Benny Hill Show*, as what was left was 'top-heavy with Hill's inspired mime performances' (Ross, 1999, 126). The episodes soon gained a cult following and, as the series was never properly syndicated, it was left up to individual stations to buy the programme and screen it as they wished. By never becoming uniformly scheduled, the programme thus appealed to diverse audiences spread across America, each of which thought they had found the programme of their own accord.

The Benny Hill Show managed to be successful in America partly because its visual nature was able to travel well, but also because the series' theatrical background meant the joke content and performance style were easily understandable to American audiences whose comedy still displays its vaudeville origins. Furthermore, American audiences admired the ways in which the show revelled in its 'bad' humour and smut level, something unheard of in much American broadcasting, but which, with a society increasingly at odds with the demands of feminism, was due for a comeback (Lewisohn, 1998, 319). The programme's success, then, 'can be attributed to both the carnivalesque nature of his humor and the retrograde, "antifeminist" shift in American television's signification of women' (Miller, 2000, 232). It is not insignificant, of course, that American audiences found it more comfortable to see a foreign comedian portraying women and using comedy subjects in a less liberal manner, even if they did quite quickly follow suit. Indeed, Halliwell (1987) argues that *The Benny Hill Show* was the kick-start American comedy had been waiting for, and that contemporary sitcom matter, in which *Will and Grace* (CBS, 2000–) effortlessly portrays gay lifestyle and **The Simpsons** (Fox, 1989–) combines quick-fire visual gags with satiric wit, can all be traced back to *The Benny Hill Show*. In fact, the programme achieved such popularity and influence the world over that Hill gradually managed 'global recognition unparalleled since Charlie Chaplin' (Ross, 1999, 80).

Contemporary analysis of *The Benny Hill Show* reduces the programme to little more than 'lots of slap and tickle with sexy bimbettes, and treatment of women as brainless sex objects' (Lewisohn, 1998, 319). That is, changes in forms of comedy deemed acceptable within British society in the 1980s – particularly those deemed acceptable for broadcast – centred around a raft of 'alternative' comedians who attempted to adhere to a strict no-sexist, no-racist manifesto (Wilmut and Rosengard, 1989, 3). Within these politically drawn battle lines, Hill's programmes became symbolic of all that the new comedians felt was wrong, offensive and dangerous about forms of humour which had entertained British audiences for decades. The most public anti-Hill tirade came from Ben Elton, a British stand-up comedian famous for his 'motormouth' delivery of politically informed, politically correct satirical comedy. In an interview with the music magazine *Q*, Elton argued that while 'Benny Hill is chasing naked women about the park I could say "fuck" a thousand times on telly and I wouldn't be nearly as offensive as that' (quoted in Lewisohn, 2002, 368). Certainly the series is often quoted when the analysis of women in comedy is outlined, and it is found seriously wanting (Porter, 1998).

While there is a clear argument that Hill was no worse in any of his representations than virtually all comedy at the time (and quite a bit of it since), it was the depiction of women in his series that contributed significantly to their decline, not only in terms of ratings but also as regards the public's affections generally. The fall from grace experienced by Hill is one almost unmatched within British broadcasting history (at least, before Michael Barrymore), and no one was more shocked than he when it was announced by Thames in 1989 that they were terminating his contract (Ross, 1999, 151). So, while Hill remained an international superstar, with his series continuing to play in over 100 countries, social and political changes in Britain rendered his comedy not only offensive, but, in the end, simply old-fashioned. In the final series of the show Hill took such criticism on board, attempting to rework the ways in which he portrayed women, including getting them to perform 'more operatic things' (Novick, 2000, 114). However, this simply removed the potency and rationale behind his comedy and the programme limped along until its end, when swathes of the British public, as well as many people at Thames, could put the whole embarrassment behind them.

All of this was symbolic of the final years of Hill's life. While he continued to make a number of programmes and his success in America was relatively undimmed, he was all but forgotten by the British public and television industry. He died in 1992, at the age of 68, alone in his house in Southampton; it was two days before his body was discovered.

The role and content of comedy in Britain has changed since then, and, while *The Benny Hill Show* has not received the reappraisal afforded to many programmes, some assessment of Hill's skills purely as a writer and performer is beginning to emerge. Housham outlines the difficulty in making sense of the conflicts between 'traditional' and 'alternative' comedy, and wonders 'whether the sexism, homophobia and racism evinced in British comedy in the old days should now be weighed as inconsequential traits against the more admirable and considerable grasp of stagecraft, timing and delivery displayed by Hill' (1994, 10). More significantly, Neale and Krutnik argue that the reliance on jokes about sex, bodily functions and rude words means that the content of the routines of many 'alternative' comedians 'unconsciously allies them with Benny Hill' (1990, 245).

Indeed, forms of comedy the world over, whether social or broadcast, have insistently relied on the clash between the physical and the intellectual for their potency (Bakhtin, 1984), and it is merely Hill's particular articulation of that which has rendered his work offensive. In this way, Porter finds little to distinguish between the content of *The Benny Hill Show* and all comedy, which is inherently masculine and relies on male fears of the power of women for its meaning and effects (1998, 91). Gray notes that the limited portrayals offered to Carol Cleveland in **Monty Python's Flying Circus** (BBC, 1969–74), as well as those in other programmes 'better known for their experimental approach to humour' (1994, 22), reduce women to mere sex objects too, even though they've never been criticised quite so voraciously for it. For Novick, this is a class concern, for Hill's genius will never be accepted as he was 'a working-class oik making working-class shows for the working-class' (2000, 27). Certainly, the ways in which *The Benny Hill Show* consistently – and unashamedly – lays bare its music-hall roots, in terms of content and performance style, renders it a popular and popularist phenomenon whose prejudices are unlikely to be excused away through either ironic postmodernism or satirical intellectualism.

QUESTIONS TO CONSIDER

- What depictions of men and women can be seen in *The Benny Hill Show*? How are the relationships between the genders portrayed?
- Is the depiction of women in *The Benny Hill Show* significantly different from that in contemporary and modern comedy? Why might it be that this series has been so heavily criticised in comparison to others? Is such criticism justified?
- Is *The Benny Hill Show* offensive? Look not only at portrayals of gender, but also of race and nation. Is offensiveness in comedy ever justified?
- Is *The Benny Hill Show* representative of British comedy? How can we define British comedy? How is it different to that in other countries?
- Why do you think *The Benny Hill Show* became so globally successful? What does it say about the possibilities of international humour and the ways in which other cultures understand Britishness?

RECOMMENDED READING

Lewisohn, Mark (2002), *Funny, Peculiar: The True Story of Benny Hill*, London: Sidgwick and Jackson.

Novick, Jeremey (2000), *Benny Hill: King Leer*, London: Carlton Books.

Ross, Robert (1999), *Benny Hill: Merry Master of Mirth*, London: BT Batsford.

Chapter Four
Big Brother

Jane Roscoe

Production Details

(Endemol, 1999–)

Developed by: Jon De Mol

Big Brother is an international format that has, at the time of press, been broadcast in 17 territories around the world.

Developed by Jon De Mol of Endemol Entertainment, the first series was broadcast in Holland in 1999. Several countries are now producing their third and fourth series, as well as spin-off series, such as *Celebrity Big Brother*, and variations such as *The Battle* (in Holland) and *The Loft* (in France). In almost every country the concept has proved to be a ratings winner, and even in countries where it has proved to be less successful (the USA, Sweden) it has still outperformed other popular factual entertainment shows. It is to date one of the most popular formats traded internationally and has had a significant impact on the development of popular factual entertainment.

The format of *Big Brother* brings together elements of soap opera, game shows and observational documentary, as well as drawing on the codes and conventions of variety shows and 'live' television such as sportscasts and election coverage. The basic format brings together a group of strangers, usually between 10 and 14, and places them in 'isolation' for up to three months. The majority of the housemates are in their early to late twenties and are drawn from a range of backgrounds and locations. Each week housemates are required to nominate each other for eviction, with those with the most votes put up for eviction by the public. Audiences vote online or by phone each week, with the live evictions usually happening at the weekend. The last remaining housemate wins the cash prize, in the UK, £70,000, in the USA, $500,000, in Australia, $250,000 and so on.

Big Brother has also led the way in 'event television', utilising technological developments and making the most of the media convergent environment (Scannell, 2002). The format delivers content across television and the Internet, as well as making use of telephony, radio and print media. In some contexts interactive and digital services have allowed a further extension of the *Big Brother* format, with audiences able to choose to follow particular housemates during the day, watch material from particular cameras, and so on. Giving the audience such an active role, in terms of driving the narrative through the voting and also by authoring narratives through technological opportunities, has clearly contributed to the success of the format. It talks to media-savvy audiences who are conversant with media convergence and are active in their participation. In most countries audiences can also participate in the live evictions, providing another forum in which to be a 'fan' (Cauldry, 2002).

However, while it is an international format with a structure and style that is repeated across the territories it would be wrong to assume all *Big Brother*'s look alike. While the formula is the same, there is still room for national variations. For example, they may be cut differently – some more closely follow the structure of soap operas, while others have adopted a more 'observational documentary' look. Many of the examples also show a distinct indigenisation (Hill and Palmer, 2002). For example, the Australian *Big Brother* clearly draws on and reinforces certain concepts of Australian national and cultural identity. In the actual design of the house there was care to make it 'Aussie' through the addition of an outdoor pool and a barbecue. It was also more spacious than most overseas houses, conforming to the notion that the large house and quarter-acre block is central to the Australian experience. Commentators have also noted the ways in which the show seemed to reflect certain characteristics we associate with dominant versions of Australian national identity, in particular 'mateship' and certain versions of masculinity. This environment has also allowed producers in different territories to build innovative and integrated advertising strategies. Groups of advertisers have been linked exclusively with the *Big Brother* brand and various styles of advertising (including product placing) are frequently integrated within the programme.

The casting of the show has itself become part of the *Big Brother* phenomenon. With a team of producers, network executives, drama consultants, psychologists, lawyers and medics, the process is thorough and time consuming. Many countries receive applications in excess of 30,000, and the process of finding the final dozen is as fascinating to audiences as the show itself. Like many of the reality game shows, the auditions eventually become part of the text (see ***Popstars*** [Screentime, 2001–]). Casting the right set of housemates is certainly a central component of the process. If the audience are not interested, they won't watch. To maintain an audience for approximately thirteen weeks, the cast have to be interesting enough and sufficiently like the viewers to keep them engaged. In some countries producers have explicitly cast for conflict, most obviously in the US. While this may have provided moments of exciting, 'naturally occurring drama' it also poses serious questions for producers. Too much of the wrong sort of tension has resulted in actual physical conflict that then poses real problems for producers who have a duty of care to all the housemates. Second, while conflict can liven up a flagging narrative arc, it is unlikely to be watchable for three months. Watching people argue every day for weeks does not necessarily make good television.

In most countries, participants in the first series were genuinely surprised at how popular the show was and their sudden assent to celebrity status. When watching *BB1* in the UK or the first Australian series, participants seemed to be aware of the cameras, yet seemed able to convince us of their 'authenticity' and 'ordinariness'. This sense of 'authenticity' is central to the popularity and fascination of the format. Audiences are fully aware that *Big Brother* is a highly constructed and mediated context; this is not 'real life', but these are 'real people' and so there are certain expectations and assumptions concerning the performance of the housemates. On the one hand we expect some playing up for the camera, yet on the other we do not expect housemates to be able to maintain this performance for the full period of the series. It is this gap, between what we assume is a performance and what we think is the 'authentic' that perhaps engages us.

In this way, we might think of viewers playing a game in which the objective is to spot the moment when the 'performance' breaks down and the 'real' person is exposed. This may only be a fleeting glance, no more than a 'flicker'. These 'flickers of authenticity' are the prize for watching (Roscoe, 2001b). Both audiences and housemates implicitly acknowledge this game. The audience is not positioned as voyeurs, as is often claimed. This game and form of engagement relies upon the explicit acknowledgment of watching and being watched. The housemates are fully aware that they have invited viewers to look at them (Hill, 2002).

Housemates have to play a number of roles or take up what are often contradictory positions. To stay in the game, and to be in the running for the prize money, housemates have to avoid nomination by their fellow housemates and eviction by the general public. They have to satisfy the television audience by being 'real' and 'authentic', while at the same time keeping the other housemates on their side. This is akin to playing both the role of ordinary person, as in the observational documentary or docusoap, and the role of game-show contestant who has to do everything they can to win. Whereas we expect the subject of a documentary to be 'honest', we assume the game-show contestant will do anything to win, including lying, cheating and turning on their fellow contestants.

The structure and style of the show certainly encourages participants in these roles. While there are various tasks and activities that serve to allow the group to bond and develop friendships, there are other structures in place that serve to position the housemates as contestants fighting each other. The nomination process itself is the most obvious example. The fact that the process takes place in secret, reinforced by *Big Brother*'s request for reasons as to why people have been nominated, forces housemates to turn on each other. In *Survivor* (Planet 24, 2000), the processes of elimination and the political strategising between participants is an integral part of the show and its appeal, while in *Big Brother* these processes take place out of sight. Housemates are not allowed to talk to each other about nominations, which means it is left to producers to build implicit narratives around the various alliances and manoeuvres.

For example, in the first Australian series producers noted that a certain housemate, Johnny, hugged the people he was nominating immediately after he came out of the diary room. A narrative started to develop which positioned Johnny as two-faced. The press picked up on this and dubbed him 'Johnny Rotten'. Producers claimed that they had merely pointed out a pattern of behaviour, as they did with other housemates, and in response did attempt to show an alternative side to Johnny over the next week. In spite of this the nickname stuck, and as soon as he was up for eviction he was voted out. Of course, this could also have been because Johnny was the only gay housemate, and his eviction therefore reflected a broader social anti-gay tendency rather than the producers' construction (Roscoe, 2002).

But, all publicity is good publicity when it comes to the housemates. While the first batch of housemates may have been surprised at their sudden rise to celebrity status, the second series batch went into the house expecting it. It is no surprise that in most countries the second series presented a very different experience. Housemates generally seemed to be more media savvy and more aware of how to play the game. Many of them expressed interest in media-related careers and saw participation in *Big Brother* as a step into that world. In just about every country there is a story about a housemate getting a TV or media job after the show, and so this actually became an expectation of some of those applying. Whereas in series one, housemates may have talked about the possibility of being recognised in the street, or their dreams of being invited to movie premieres and exclusive parties, by series two participants talked about how they would handle the expected fame. It would seem that a real danger in participating in a show like *Big Brother* is a bruised ego when housemates realise that their fifteen minutes of fame are over.

QUESTIONS TO CONSIDER

- How do you think the editing of the events within the *Big Brother* house can influence an audience's reaction to certain individuals? Can you think of examples where contestants may have been unfairly treated by television and the press?

- Annette Hill (2002) argues that *Big Brother* is more than simply 'voyeuristic'. What does she mean by this and what other elements of the programme can you identify that have made it such an international television success?

- Why do you think the *Big Brother* format tends to rely on the participation of individuals in their late twenties? What might this tell us about its makers' primary aims and objectives?

- Can you think of ways in which *Big Brother* reflects the culture, preoccupations and national concerns of a particular country? What aspects of its format allow each country to create its own indigenous experience?

- How has the *Big Brother* format influenced other television programmes? Do you think its has helped to produce a sub-genre of 'cruel TV'?

RECOMMENDED READING

Dovey, Jon (2000), *Freakshow: First Person Media and Factual Television*, London: Pluto.

Hill, Annette and Palmer, Gareth (eds.) (2002), 'Special Issue: Big Brother', *Television & New Media*, Vol. 3, No. 3, August.

Jones, Janet and Mathijs, Ernest (eds.) (forthcoming 2004), *Big Brother International: Format, Critics, Publics*, London and New York: Walflower Press.

Chapter Five

Boys from the Blackstuff

Robin Nelson

Production Details

(BBC English Regions Drama, 1982)

Writer: Alan Bleasdale
Director: Philip Saville
Producer: Michael Wearing

Cast includes:

Yosser Hughes (Bernard Hill)
Chrissie Todd (Michael Angelis)
Angie Todd (Julie Walters)
Dixie Dean (Tom Georgeson)
George Malone (Peter Kerrigan)
Loggo Logmond (Alan Igbon)
Kevin Dean (Gary Bleasdale)
Miss Sutcliffe (Jean Boht)
Wino (James Ellis)

Boys from the Blackstuff foregrounds the stories of five British unemployed 'boys' from Liverpool who shared a previous experience of moonlighting (working unofficially whilst registered unemployed) laying tarmac (the 'blackstuff'). First seen as a single play by writer Alan Bleasdale simply called *The Black Stuff* (BBC, 1980), the subject seemed to offer plenty of material for a series or miniseries. However, a substantial drama about unemployed 'losers' in Liverpool did not initially capture the imaginations of London-based channel commissioners. The difficulty of raising a budget for such a project – ultimately five 50-minute episodes but pitched initially as seven 40-minute episodes – led producer Michael Wearing to make Bleasdale's *The Muscle Market* (BBC, 1981) as well, another one-off play to keep the miniseries idea alive.

Of course, eventually the five-part series *Boys from the Blackstuff* was made, finally produced under unusual conditions by BBC's Pebble Mill Studios in Birmingham. A policy in the early 1980s to devolve drama production away from London to the UK

21

series, young Snowy Malone, shouts 'bastard' at a policeman from the transit van in which 'the boys' are traveling. Unfortunately for him, the van gets halted at traffic lights, allowing the policeman to catch up and seek out the offender. Having identified the culprit and hailed him from the van, the six-foot plus policeman towers over the diminutive Snowy. Where, in consonance with the representation above, physical violence might be expected, the policeman merely tousles Snowy's hair as if he were a child and remarks, 'Midget'.

Indeed, humour, a typifying feature of Liverpudlian folk culture manifest in all Bleasdale's writing, is another important aspect of the series' style. Some of the darkest experiences portrayed are leavened or counterpointed with a joke or gag. Bleasdale appears to reject, however, the archetypal Liverpudlian solution of a ready humour in the face of adversity when, in the bedroom row between Chrissie and Angie Todd, Angie exclaims, 'It's not friggin' funny – I've had enough of that – you've got to laugh or else you'll cry – I've heard it for years – this stupid soddin' city's full of it'. In fact, the humour turns to black comedy at the end of the final episode, 'George's Last Ride', when a redundancy party in the Green Man pub is presented in almost surreal madness. Ronnie Reynald shrilly whistles 'If I were a blackbird…' against the hubbub of the proceedings, and the giant 'Shakehands' reduces many celebrants to the floor by squeezing their hand in an apparent gesture of friendship until they drop.

Notwithstanding its basis in social realism, then, *Boys from the Blackstuff* deploys overall a range of styles. With the freedom of movement afforded by a film as opposed to a TV camera with trailing cables, 'Yosser's Story' opens with a surreal dream sequence. Otherwise, the white patina in Yosser's facial make-up set against his dark coat evokes the imagery of German Expressionist cinema. The experienced film and television director Philip Saville deserves credit for his contribution in realising Bleasdale's scripts with a range of cinematic approaches that both establish and go beyond an authenticating realism. The range of styles affords sharp contrasts between the tragic and the intensely funny. Indeed, some of the strategies deployed might function as a Brechtian 'interruptus' to jolt those readers – who are perhaps being drawn too deeply into the 'reality' of the boys' predicament – into a broader awareness of the causes of their plight.

One particular contribution of Philip Saville illustrates the collaborative industrial process of TV drama production in which, unlike film, the writer is typically privileged. Saville thought the draft of episode three was not equal in standard to the others. Bleasdale acknowledges that Saville's rejection of the script and observation that, 'There are no women in this. You must have a woman's point of view' (cited in Millington and Nelson, 1986, 60), led to a much improved episode and the developed character of Angie. An irony of the series, however, is that masculinity is thrown into crisis by its context of unemployment. Millington has observed that, '[m]ale behaviour is characteristically represented in terms of physical action and the successful performance of tasks – in the workplace, on the battlefield, at sport etc.' (in Brandt [ed.] 1993, 128).

Deprived of the workplace, 'the boys' are progressively emasculated. *Boys from the Blackstuff* thus serves as a document of the impact on working-class communities of the industrial decline in the UK with the emergence of a service economy. As a result, it afforded a broad audience access to a challenging social drama that offered to interpret for a class its experience at a moment of significant historical change. In hindsight, that is the real achievement of *Boys from the Blackstuff*.

QUESTIONS TO CONSIDER

- Would a series like *Boys from the Blackstuff* with its political connotations be made under today's production conditions?
- What aesthetic differences are discernible between episode four, shot on film, and the other four episodes, shot on video?
- To what extent might the success of *Boys from the Blackstuff* be ascribed to the historical moment of its first showing? Do you think the intrinsic dramatic values of the stories and characters stand the test of time?
- How firmly is the drama located in British television drama's tradition of northern or social realism?
- To what extent does the drama foreground the 'masculine' values of an industrial age at the expense of 'feminine' perspectives of post-industrial, post-feminist times?

RECOMMENDED READING

Millington, Bob (1993), '*Boys from the Blackstuff* (Alan Bleasdale)' in Brandt, George W. (ed.) (1993), *British Television Drama in the 1980s*, Cambridge University Press.

Millington, Bob and Nelson, Robin (1986), '*Boys from the Blackstuff*': *The Making of TV Drama*, London: Comedia.

Paterson, Richard (1984), BFI Dossier 20: '*Boys from the Blackstuff*', London: British Film Institute.

Chapter Six

Brass Eye

Brett Mills

Production Details

(Channel Four [Talkback Productions], 1997, 2001)

Writer: Chris Morris
Script Associate: Peter Baynham
Additional Material: Graham Linehan, Arthur Mathews, Jane Bussman, David Quantick, and others
Director: Michael Cumming
Executive Producer: Peter Fincham
Producers: Chris Morris, Caroline Leddy

Cast includes:

Chris Morris
Peter Baynham
Doon Mackichan
Kevin Eldon
Mark Heap
Gina McKee

On July 26, 2001, Channel Four broadcast the most complained-about television programme in British broadcasting history. It was a one-off special of *Brass Eye*, a series that had first run in 1997. The programme, like all episodes of *Brass Eye*, was a parody of contemporary current-affairs programming. However, it was the subject matter of this special which led to outrage, complaints, tabloid front pages – 'The Sickest TV Show Ever' (cited by Ferguson, 2001b, 13) – and ministerial interjections: paedophilia. This intermingling of one of society's most emotional subjects with *Brass Eye*'s scathing comedy resulted in a programme that shocked many. Yet the programme has also been defended as a sophisticated interrogation of the assumptions surrounding the role and methods of news media, particularly in response to increased media competition and the development in infotainment (Sparks, 2000, 21–4). However, the programme is likely to remain significant within television history, for rarely have so many – broadcasters, politicians, journalists and members of the public – debated in such depth the acceptable limits of comedy and the information function of the media.

The original six-part *Brass Eye* series took as its starting point this dissatisfaction with the conventions of television, questioning the role of broadcasting and those who make a living off it in the process. The series focused on a different topical issue each week, with programmes centred around drugs, sex, science, crime and so on. While clearly a sophisticated and knowing parody of current-affairs programmes, it presents a much more extreme wealth of absurdities, with bizarre camera angles, colour filters and soft focuses, along with tortuously complex and nonsensical language delivered in an authoritative manner. In this way, *Brass Eye* made it clear to the audience that parody was employed in order to achieve one of its primary goals of fooling someone else: the celebrities, politicians and other talking heads who make a living and maintain their positions of authority through their repeated appearance on television – espousing facts about issues and urging society to conform to accepted social norms. It is this conjunction of television's authority and the authority of those who appear on and use it, which the series particularly set out to highlight and undermine.

To this end, *Brass Eye* used a notable, notorious and contentious technique – the fake campaign; concocting absurd and utterly fictitious causes and then convincing public figures to endorse them. One of the most famous of *Brass Eye*'s hoaxes capitalised on the fear of youngsters' consumption of drugs. To this end it assembled a number of the great and good to warn youngsters of the fictional 'Cake', supposedly flooding Britain from the 'boon raves' in Prague. British television presenter Noel Edmonds warned that the drug altered time perception by affecting the part of the brain called 'Shatner's bassoon'; Australian celebrity Rolf Harris cautioned that the drug could lead to 'Czech neck', where the body retains so much water the neck swells, making it impossible to breathe; and the English comedian Bernard Manning noted that Cake could make you so sick that 'one girl puked up her own pelvis bone'. Taking the deception to its logical extreme, Martin Amess, the British Member of Parliament, was enlisted to the campaign, not only providing a number of pieces to camera but also raising a question about the drug in the Houses of Parliament, asking what the government was planning to do about the impending threat of Cake.

While funny in its pure absurdity, the technique also appeared to have a serious intention, that is, to show how both television and celebrity can be used to create and maintain media-induced 'moral panics' (Cohen, 1980). As the journalist John Dugdale has succinctly put it, the series was clearly 'undermining *any* talking head on TV, by showing them talking bollocks with apparent authority' (Dugdale, 1994, 16). In this way, then, *Brass Eye* seemed to reflect and respond to many of the contemporary concerns about news reporting, particularly the ability of television news and documentary to actually *construct* rather than simply *reflect* the way we see the world. As the media critic Michael Gurevitch puts it (1991, 185):

> *The enhancement of the roles, and the powers, of television can be traced to its emergence, in an era of instant global communication, as an active participant in the events it purportedly 'covers'. Television can no longer be regarded (if it ever was) as a mere observer and reporter of events. It is inextricably locked into these events, and has become an integral part of the reality it reports.*

Such concerns represented the logical outcome of the career of the man behind the programme, a career that has consistently provoked complaints and outrage, while simultaneously producing perhaps the most important comic interventions in British culture of the past decade. That man is Chris Morris: 'the most loathed man on TV' (Ferguson, 2001a, 23). Morris is one of a number of contemporary comedians working in British television who are continually exploring the role of broadcast comedy as well as using humour to take unexpected satirical swipes at government, politics and society. He came to national notice on Radio 4's *On the Hour* (1991–2) and its television version, *The Day Today* (BBC, 1994), an astoundingly sophisticated and astutely hilarious parody of BBC news programming. Most significantly, the other major creative role on *The Day Today* and *On the Hour* was the writer-producer Armando Iannucci, who has followed a similar satirical path. It is from this comedy hotbed that Morris arose, and it is *Brass Eye* that most obviously represents its creative, anarchic and political apotheosis.

Considering the amount of publicity resulting from *Brass Eye*, it was surprising that, four years later, it managed to find a whole raft of public figures willing to make idiots of themselves again for the paedophilia special. By 2001, child abuse and the fear of 'stranger danger' was very palpable in British society, with paedophiles demonised as monsters and some members of the public 'becoming increasingly frustrated at the way children, and the idea of childhood, had become defiled' (Ferguson, 2001b, 13). For many critics, the media's simplistic analyses of social problems – in which the complex nature of crime and criminals are overlooked for the sake of snappy stories and easily recognisable villains – has helped foster a fearful and misinformed public concerned about 'the death of morality'. Such criticisms were at the core of *Brass Eye*'s venom, and thus it parodied the media's tendency to create moral panics as much as it poured scorn on the public's simplistic, instinctive and frequently vengeful understanding of it.

This particular episode of *Brass Eye* was controversial even before it was shown, and was eventually suspended for three weeks until its final broadcast. The resulting debates in the press and between broadcasters, government and regulators dwarf any other programming controversy, leading to *The Guardian* newspaper setting up a separate section of its online edition dedicated to the row, with links to all the relevant articles, debates and reports. After its broadcast, the Independent Television Commission, responsible for issuing broadcasting licences in Britain, received around 1,000 complaints (and

750 messages of support) and published a special finding on the programme in which it criticised not the programme itself but the announcements before it that 'failed adequately to prepare viewers for what was to follow' (ITC, 2001). It demanded that Channel Four broadcast an apology, which it did, immediately before it aired a repeat of the episode.

This offending episode began with surprisingly jolly and animated news presenters urging all parents to bring their children along to one of Britain's sports stadia, where they were being rounded up to ensure paedophiles couldn't reach them. In this way, it latched on to the media's willingness to promote unhelpful solutions to complex problems, as well as noting parents' eagerness to undermine a whole range of children's rights and freedoms in the name of good parenting and child protection. In doing so, it seems to make comic use of the informal, friendly manner in which the presenters talk to their audience at home, mirroring contemporary news media developments which have led to accusations of 'dumbing down' (Sparks, 2000, 8). The programme also made extensive use of reconstructions, recreating fictional stories about paedophiles with over-the-top rock music, special effects and grotesque make-up. As such, the programme's comedy rested partly on its aim to expose the power of the news to actively construct a viewer's perception of an event or news story. Clearly, though, there are aspects to stories which push them up the news agenda (Harrison, 2001, 115); *Brass Eye* merely exaggerated these aspects in an attempt to highlight their existence and to demonstrate the ways in which certain forms of behaviour can be either normalised or demonised at will.

Also tapping into melodramatic and ignorant worries about the dangers of the Internet, the programme-makers convinced a number of public figures to rail against an online game starring a dog called 'Pantou'. British newsreader Nick Owen warned about a man who had 'plugged his groin into his computer to get sexual pleasure from the actions of a child playing with Pantou'. MP Barbara Follett described how the game encouraged children to put their faces against the computer's screen, whereby 'online paedophiles use special gloves to feel and pulpate the child's face'. Comedian/presenter Richard Blackwood outlined how 'online paedophiles can actually make your keyboard release toxic vapours that actually make you more suggestible', and then asked, 'Does your child smell of hammers?' The duped MPs Barbara Follet and Syd Rapson, along with Nick Owen, complained to the Broadcasting Standards Council about the hoax, with Rapson also complaining that his privacy had been infringed. However, the Broadcasting Standards Commission rejected all the complaints as 'the show revealed how public figures were willing to speak "with apparent authority about matters they do not understand"' (Hodgson, 2002, 5).

Debates constantly rage about the possible offensive nature of comedy, and it is clear that humour occupies a social role which allows it to often say the unsayable (for examples, see Freud, 1960, 141–6 and Palmer, 1994, 161–75). Indeed, regulations in Britain admit that comedy has a special freedom, and decisions made by regulatory

programmes, it attracted a sufficiently large share of the highly sought-after youth demographic to make it lucrative. About to go into syndication after 100 episodes and embroiled in difficult contract negotiations, *Buffy* moved in Autumn 2002 to rival UPN. At the time of writing, *Buffy* has already spun off *Angel* (WB, 2000–) and there is the possibility of a British spin-off (*Ripper*). Meanwhile an American TV cartoon version is currently on hold.

Buffy can clearly be read on a number of levels, but its metaphoric depiction of the horrors of high school, its subversion of the traditional family and creation of substitute family units, its 'self-conscious and playful inversion of the conventions of the horror genre' (Johnson, 2001, 42), its highly 'postmodern' intertextuality and self-referentiality (Pender, 2002), its high pop culture IQ, its energetic fan base (Zweerink and Gatson, 2002), its religious themes (Erickson, 2002 and Playden, 2002), its depiction of lesbianism, Otherness and minorities (Edwards, 2002), its status as a (post-) feminist text (Vint, 2002), and its witty, pun-filled use of language ('Any Slayer can brandish a weapon', Overbey and Preston-Matto observe, 'but for Buffy the Vampire Slayer, the tongue is as pointed as the stake' [2002, 84]), certainly makes it an unavoidable text for any discerning media critic or student alike.

Indeed, many critics argue that *Buffy* has real and discernible aesthetic (as well as moral) values. Wilcox and Lavery (2002, xx–xxv) argue that it can lay claim to all the defining characteristics of 'quality television' as catalogued by Thompson (1996): a quality pedigree, a large ensemble cast, a series memory, creation of a new genre through recombination of older ones, self-consciousness and pronounced tendencies towards the controversial and the realistic. It certainly tried to create something different to the archetypal action series that seldom reached any overall narrative conclusion in its frequently self-contained episodes (Turner, 2001, 6). Having clearly learned lessons about the liabilities of multiple-season story arcs from the forever incomplete **Twin Peaks** (ABC, 1990–1) and the ever frustrating **The X-Files** (Fox, 1993–2002), *Buffy* has sought closure in each year's narrative line. In the first five seasons, in addition to a variety of individual menaces in stand-alone 'monster-of-the week' narratives, Buffy and the Scoobies battled against a single multiple-episode 'big bad' nemesis, defeating it in a non-cliff-hanging season finale.

Buffy has certainly become a television phenomenon that has evoked passionate viewer involvement. All major and some minor characters have acquired devoted fans in the US and abroad, inspiring adoring websites and generating prolific fan fiction (Zweerink and Gatson, 2002). Indeed, so attentive has *Buffy* been to its fans that devotion to the bad guy, Spike (a once vicious, bleach-blond, punk vampire), resulted in his elevation to major character status. Neutered by a computer chip in his brain in season four ('I'm saying that Spike had a little trip to the vet and now he doesn't chase the other puppies anymore'), Spike was painstakingly 'morphed' into a hero, until, at the end of season six, like Angel, he reacquired his soul. The series has also generated a multitude of ancillary texts. Official tie-in books, scores of novels, comic books and the scripts of the first two seasons are available, as well as a great deal of critical attention. At the time of writing, two book-length collections of essays have been published (Lavery, 2002 and Kaveney, 2002) and at least three more are on the way. Like *Xena: Warrior Princess* (Syndicated, 1995–2002) before it, it has also inspired an Internet scholarly journal: *Slayage: The Online International Journal of Buffy Studies* (http://www.slayage.tv).

Buffy the Vampire Slayer tells the story of Buffy Anne Summers, a southern California 'post-feminist' (Johnson, 2001) girl, a 'Gidget for the *fin de siècle*' (Siemann, 2002), living in Sunnydale, a town built over a 'Hellmouth' – a centre of demonic energy. In the show's Lovecraftian mythology, demons were the original inhabitants of the earth and vampires are demon/human hybrids. As the series begins, Buffy has already discovered (in the movie) her chosen role as the 'one girl in all the world with the strength and skill to fight the vampires'. Having moved from Los Angeles to Sunnydale to escape her past, she would prefer to be a normal teenager, but her new home town, plagued by vampires, demons and other evils will not permit her to ignore her calling. With the ongoing help of her 'Scooby Gang' friends, Buffy continues to battle not only the forces of darkness but also her own inner demons. Beginning with season four, Buffy and the Scoobies head off to college (at the University of California, Sunnydale), but with no let-up in the enemies they must confront.

Buffy's creator, Joss Whedon, a third-generation television writer, authored the screenplay for the original 1992 camp film. Partly as a result of its critical and commercial failure, he went on to write for other television programmes such as *Roseanne* (ABC, 1988–97) and subsequently gained a reputation as a script doctor – he helped rewrite such films as *Speed* (De Bont, 1994) and *Toy Story* (Lasseter, 1995). However, *Buffy*'s success as a cult hit elevated 'Joss' to rock-star status among fans of the show. Though long tempted by a career move to the movies, some critics now argue that Whedon has demonstrated a 'true genius' for the medium of television (Lavery, 2002, 251–6). Indeed, many of the truly memorable and innovative individual episodes of *Buffy* Whedon both wrote and directed, including 'Hush' (in which The Gentlemen, fairy-tale monsters, steal the voices of the residents of Sunnydale and at least half the show transpires without a word of dialogue); 'Restless' (comprising four astonishing dream sequences in which the spirit of the First Slayer tries to kill the Scoobies after they have defeated Adam); 'The Body' (minutely detailing the emotional aftermath of the sudden death of Buffy's mother); and 'Once More with Feeling' (a long anticipated musical episode in which a visiting demon causes the Scoobies and all of Sunnydale to behave as if trapped in a Broadway musical). In an interview with *The Onion*, Whedon (2002b) admits that:

> I designed Buffy *to be an icon, to be an emotional experience, to be loved in a way that other shows can't be loved. Because it's about adolescence, which is the most important thing people go through in their development, becoming an adult. And it mythologizes it in such a way, such a romantic way – it basically says, 'Everybody who made it through adolescence is a hero'. And I think that's very personal, that people get something from that that's very real. And I don't think I could be more pompous. But I mean every word of it. I wanted her*

to be a cultural phenomenon. I wanted there to be dolls, Barbie with kung-fu grip. I wanted people to embrace it in a way that exists beyond, 'Oh, that was a wonderful show about lawyers, let's have dinner'. I wanted people to internalize it, and make up fantasies where they were in the story, to take it home with them, for it to exist beyond the TV show. And we've done exactly that.

Yet despite such lofty intentions, it is clear that *Buffy* has not pleased all sections of American society. Its actors have been consistently snubbed by the prestigious Emmy Awards (individual episodes ['Hush' and 'The Body'] were nominated but failed to win, although it did receive the 'Founders Award' from Viewers for Quality Television in 2000). The series has also received criticism from the political right with the conservative 'Parents Television Council' famously ranking it as the single worst series (i.e. containing the most 'objectionable' content) on television. Interestingly, critics on the political left have also criticised the show, questioning its 'radical' credentials and its claims to be 'feminist' or 'post-feminist'. In particular, they have focused on the sometimes sexually provocative appearance of Sarah Michelle Gellar, especially in her many extra-diegetic appearances as a model (Dougherty, 2002, Helford, 2002, Pender, 2002, Vint, 2002). Others have also been troubled by its failure to include significant minority characters (Edwards, 2002). To the ever recurring critical question, 'Is *Buffy the Vampire Slayer* a ground-breaking, empowering and transgressive text or is its political potential compromised, commodity-driven and contained?' Pender offers the following tentative response (2002, 35):

Buffy *is a television series that delights in deliberately and self-consciously baffling the binary; the juxtaposition of mundane reality and surreal fantasy in the lives of the Slayer and her friends evokes a world in which the sententious morality of black and white distinctions is itself demonized as an unnatural threat from an ancient past.*

However you interpret the show, it is clear that *Buffy* means a great deal to its huge fan base around the world. With great wit, emotional realism, apocalyptic excitement and the best special effects a small television series budget can buy, *Buffy the Vampire Slayer* stands as the perfect example of what Sarah Vowell (2002) calls a 'long haul' series, capable of perpetual self-renewal and never settling for simple solutions, easy motivations or stereotypical characters. For that reason, at least, it remains a key television text for a generation increasingly defined by political, moral and personal uncertainties.

QUESTIONS TO CONSIDER

- *Buffy* is sometimes described as a 'post-feminist' text. What is meant by this term and how far do you think it is an appropriate way of understanding the drama?
- Critics like Larbelestier (2002) and Zweerink and Gatson (2002) have shown how *Buffy* has responded to its fan base. In what ways does *Buffy* exhibit an awareness of

its audience and can you pinpoint specific scenes that demonstrate its self-consciousness as a television text?

- *Buffy* is highly dependent upon cultural and pop-cultural references in establishing its humour and its meanings. Can you give some examples and why do you think it is obsessed with such references?

- Some critics have been perplexed by *Buffy*'s mixture of drama and humour. Do they work well together and how do the creators of the series succeed or fail at mixing such diverse elements?

RECOMMENDED READING

Kaveney, Roz (ed.) (2002), *Reading the Vampire Slayer: An Unofficial Critical Companion to Buffy and Angel*, London: Tauris.

Wilcox, Rhonda, V and Lavery, David (eds.) (2002), *Fighting the Forces: What's at Stake in Buffy the Vampire Slayer*, Lanham, MD: Rowman and Littlefield.

Wilcox, Rhonda V (1999), 'There Will Never Be a "Very Special" *Buffy: Buffy* and the Monsters of Teen Life', *Journal of Popular Film and Television* 27 (2), 16–23. Republished in *Slayage: The Online International Journal of Buffy Studies*, No. 2 (March 2001): http://www. slayage. tv/essays/ slayage2/wilcox.htm

Chapter Eight
Cagney and Lacey

Ros Jennings

Production Details

(CBS/Orion, 1981–8)

Creators: Barbara Avendon, Barbara Corday, Barney Rosenzweig
Executive Producer: Barney Rosenzweig
Producers include: Terry Louise Fisher, Steve Brown, Peter Lefcourt
Directors include: Georg Stanford Brown, Bill Dukes, Arthur Karen
Writers include: Terry Louise Fisher, Ronie Wenker-Konner
Theme Music: Mace Neufeld, Barney Rosenzweig

Cast includes:

Det. Mary Beth Lacey (Tyne Daly)
Christine Cagney (Meg Foster/Sharon Gless)
Harvey Lacey (John Karlen)
Lt. Samuels (Al Waxman)
Det. Petrie (Carl Lumbly)
Det. Isbecki (Martin Cove)

The appearance of the police drama *Cagney and Lacey* in the 1980s marked one of the most important genre transformations in the police/cop series. By placing two female protagonists at the centre of its narrative, *Cagney and Lacey* readjusted the parameters of the genre by producing a credible police series with specific appeal for women. As a prime-time quality drama, it won a string of Emmys (including Outstanding Drama Series [1984–5, 1985–6]) during the six years it was on air and was responsible for many 'firsts' in terms of television and the representation of women and women's issues.

It is well documented (Fiske, 1987; Gamman, 1988) that Molly Haskell's book *From Reverence to Rape: The Treatment of Women in the Movies* (1973) was the spark that led to the realisation of the female buddy formula that was to form the basis of *Cagney and Lacey*. Together, the team of producer Barney Rosenzweig and the writing partnership of Barbara Avendon and Barbara Corday devised a series that had its roots firmly in second-wave feminism and the women's movement. In the context of the 1980s, *Cagney and Lacey* was most definitely 'progressive' because it articulated contemporary discourses of feminism 'in a constant tension with those of the dominant ideology of patriarchy'

(Fiske, 1987, 47). As such, it made a significant intervention in television history by not only carving out new territory for women within the well-established masculine conventions of the police/detective genre, but also attracting an unprecedented and wide-based, loyal female audience for this genre form.

Rosenzweig, Avendon and Corday initially developed their concept as a comedy film that focused on a crime-fighting partnership between two women cops. Originally entitled *Newman and Redford* (after the acting partnership at the heart of one of the most famous fictional buddy partnerships, *Butch Cassidy and the Sundance Kid* [George Rot Hill, 1969]), the idea wasn't received with much enthusiasm. The creators were therefore forced to repackage their idea as a serious crime drama. Calling it *Cagney and Lacey*, they finally got the green light for production from CBS to produce a made-for-TV movie. In the original movie, CBS insisted on the casting of *M*A*S*H* (CBS, 1972–83) star, Loretta Swit, as one of the crime-fighting duo. Her co-star was Tyne Daly, who had already caused something of a stir as the tough cop sidekick of Clint Eastwood in the film *The Enforcer* (Fargo, 1976). The unexpected success of the pilot movie *Cagney and Lacey* (1981) persuaded CBS to commission a six-episode television series the following year. However, because of other commitments, Swit was unable to take part and was replaced by Meg Foster. Although the show gained respectable ratings from the outset, it was regularly threatened with cancellation. With its overt feminist agenda, it was always an object of suspicion for the networks. They lived in constant fear of losing their advertising revenue and the production team worked with a perpetual sword of Damocles suspended over their heads. As Julie D'Acci (1993) explained in her excellent study of the production context of *Cagney and Lacey*, as far as the networks were concerned, closely linked to worries about feminism were particular worries about accusations of lesbianism.

At first, certainly as far as CBS was concerned, not only was the feminism in the series too controversial but Meg Foster was deemed to look (and also to be characterised as being) too 'butch', thus reinforcing CBS's two great anxieties about the series. Additionally, as Fiske also outlines (1987, 113), the scheduling package devised for *Cagney and Lacey* by CBS for broadcast in the US did not get it the audience share it deserved (originally it ran straight after *Magnum P.I.* [CBS, 1980–8], a traditional police/detective drama package). Overseas (particularly in the UK) the series was doing very well and a strong UK fan base and grass-roots activity from women viewers in the US (including articulate support from the figurehead of the American Women's Movement, Gloria Steinem) helped to put pressure on the networks to keep the series in production. In effect, the combination of CBS interference and grass-roots campaigns from women viewers transformed *Cagney and Lacey* from cop show to women's programme.

In the US, *Cagney and Lacey* was moved to Monday nights and placed as part of a 'women's night' (Fiske, 1987, 113). Both characters were 'feminised' and Foster was replaced with the more glamorous Sharon Gless (in addition, her character, Cagney, was re-presented with an 'improved' class background and more stylish wardrobe). In

Chapter Nine

Cathy Come Home

Catrin Prys

Production Details

(BBC, 1966)

Producer: Tony Garnett
Writer: Jeremy Sandford
Director: Ken Loach

Cast includes:

Cathy Ward (Carol White)
Reg Ward (Ray Brooks)
Mrs Ward (Winnifred Dennis)

Cathy Come Home is probably one of the most famous and controversial dramas to be broadcast on British television. Originally transmitted on the December 16, 1966 as part of *The Wednesday Play* (BBC, 1964–70) – a celebrated anthology series of single dramas – it was seen as instrumental in bringing the problem of homelessness to the attention of the British public. Although the housing charity Shelter was in the process of being established when it was first broadcast, the programme certainly helped it to gain both national attention and desperately needed funds. Written by Jeremy Sandford (*Edna, the Inebriate Woman* [BBC, 1971], *Don't Let Them Kill me on Wednesday* [Granada, 1980]), produced by Tony Garnett (*Between the Lines* [BBC, 1992–4], *Cardiac Arrest* [BBC, 1994–6], *This Life* [BBC, 1996–8]) and directed by Ken Loach (*Up the Junction* [BBC, 1965], *Kes* [1969], *Raining Stones* [1993]), *Cathy Come Home* is often seen to be emblematic of the so-called 'Golden Age' of British television, a time when committed, socially confrontational and politically motivated drama consistently found its way onto the small screen. Whatever one thinks of the notion of the 'Golden Age' (and clearly nostalgia inevitably plays an important part in its conception), this programme has certainly become an important symbol of the power of 'event television', seemingly confronting and helping to form and even change public opinion.

Cathy Come Home tells the story of Cathy, a young northern girl, who travels to London, marries a local van driver (Reg), has three children and subsequently finds herself homeless. After Reg's accident at work (for which he receives no compensation) and his fruitless struggle for employment, they steadily descend into a life of increasing poverty and despair. After losing their home they move into Reg's mother's flat in a tenement block, but are forced to move into a terraced house when relations become difficult within their cramped conditions. However, when the landlady of their terraced house dies they are evicted by its new owners and forced to move again, this time to a small caravan on a dangerous and derelict site. Then, after their caravan is set on fire by vandals they are forced to move to a 'squat' and then to a tent. Finally, Cathy is taken into emergency hostel accommodation, a place where only she and her children are allowed. Inevitably, Reg and Cathy become distanced and when he stops paying for her rent in the hostel she is eventually thrown onto the streets and her children (in a notoriously harrowing scene set in a train station) are cruelly taken from her and put into care (for a more detailed narrative breakdown see Corner, 1996, 92–3).

Like **Culloden** (BBC, 1964) before it, *Cathy Come Home* provoked a great deal of debate not only about its content, but also about its controversial mixture of dramatic and documentary techniques. Originally, its writer Jeremy Sandford had made a radio documentary called *Homeless Families*, but was disappointed by the apparent lack of response to the problem that it generated. As a result, he used his large amount of newspaper clippings, audiotape transcripts and notes and developed it into a screenplay (Sandford, 1973, extract in Goodwin et al., 1983, 18). Consequently, the script of *Cathy Come Home* has an 'authentic' and 'improvisational' feel to it that reflects real conversations and actual events. For example, rather than adhering to straightforward dramatic dialogue, much of the narrative relies on snatches of conversations, voice-overs (sometimes from anonymous sources set over a montage of actual places and people) and the reading of statistics over pertinent points in Cathy's story. In this way, Sandford hoped that the particular problems faced by Cathy could somehow become emblematic of a wider social problem, that the way in which he incorporated his earlier research would mean that the voices and lives originally recorded in his documentary could become part of Cathy's story, producing what Jacob Leigh refers to as a form of 'fictional journalism' (2002, 39).

This sense of actuality is clearly heightened by the unerring sense of realism achieved by Loach's influential style of direction. Indeed, *Cathy Come Home* can be seen as part of a wider tradition of 'social realism', a British realist film aesthetic that was focused on contemporary, working-class life and the representation of the marginalised and 'voiceless' members of society (Jordan, 1981, 27; see also **Coronation Street** [ITV, 1960–] and **Boys from the Blackstuff** [BBC, 1982]). However, Loach went further than most social realist directors of the 1960s by actually applying many documentary techniques into an otherwise dramatic form. With *Cathy Come Home*'s producer, Tony Garnett, Loach had made *Up the Junction*, an earlier *Wednesday Play* that tackled the social issue of back-street abortion. In an attempt to create an authentic context around which the debate could take place, they had incorporated 'quasi-documentary' techniques into the drama (for example, direct address to camera and voice-overs from doctors and figures of authority) and also made use of new lightweight (16 mm) film cameras that could be taken on location. As John Caughie has put it, 'it does indeed exploit the objectivity of the documentary camera; it breaks up natural time' and 'it replaces a drama of conversation with a drama which is composed of dialogue and monologue fragments…' (2000, 118).

These techniques were not only incorporated but actually foregrounded in *Cathy Come Home* so that the whole drama takes on a sense of documentary authenticity. Consequently, the programme is actually shot more in the style of documentary than drama; as an example, John Corner refers to the scene when Cathy and Reg are thrown out of their house by bailiffs (Corner, 1996, 99):

> *the sequence is shot with some of the stylistic markers of action-led camera. That is to say, stability of frame and composure of mise-en-scène give way to a visualisation appearing to have caught a real incident and filmed it within the limitations of composition, the following of action, a soundtrack containing 'incidental' sounds, and so on. Together with the intensity of the event itself, reinforced by the gathering of neighbours jeering the bailiffs as they force their way into the house and remove the couple and their possessions, such filmic 'limitations' draw on the language of factual reportage.*

As such, *Cathy Come Home* can be best categorised as a hybrid form that merges together elements of both drama and documentary sometimes known as 'drama-documentary' or 'documentary-drama'. Although often and incorrectly used as interchangeable, the distinction between these two terms is relevant. According to Derek Paget, while drama-documentary tends to use 'the names and identities of real historical individuals', documentary-drama tends to use 'fictional constructs such as an invented plot and characters composited from several real-life originals' (1998, 114). Seen in this light, *Cathy Come Home* is clearly a documentary-drama, not portraying actual people or events, but instead using real events to compose a fictitious story with invented characters.

Indeed, it was the programme's employment of the documentary-drama form that created a large part of the controversy that surrounded it. Critics of the programme complained that despite setting itself up as a set of *real* events (through its overt use of a recognisable documentary *mise-en-scène*), it was simply a creative fabrication that should never have been generalised into having actual social realities or political implications. Some critics noticed how viewers had been emotionally manipulated by dramatic elements and choices made by the programme-makers. For example, many felt that sympathy was clearly weighted unfairly towards Cathy, not least by giving her part to such a pretty, young-looking actress. This emotional manipulation was further enforced by the unfair representation of those in authority (particularly the social workers and hostel workers) who were frequently presented as callous, uncaring and downright cruel. Added to this, the statistics and general comments cited by voice-over were almost never referenced properly in the way that a documentary or television newsreel would have done. In fact, on its second showing, most of the background comments and statistics were taken off the film because of doubt surrounding their accuracy (Shubik, 1975, 126). As a result, it was argued that the programme lacked any real objectivity and played on viewers' (who were often confused where the line between 'fact' and 'fiction' was actually drawn) emotional involvement with the story.

However, such accusations have been defended by many, not least John Corner, who argues that despite its flaws, *Cathy Come Home* actually grew out of Sandford's earlier radio documentary and was based on a good amount of actual research. Furthermore, the fragmented style of film-making that Sandford, Loach and Garnett produce constructs a 'documentary space' around which the story of Cathy is only a part. As Corner puts it, '[w]hilst the imaginative freedom of the dramatist could be claimed for the general social knowledge generated by its narrative-in-context, it use of voiced-over data inevitably carried it into the more narrowly contentious arena of controversial current-affairs broadcasting' (1996, 106).

The way in which *Cathy Come Home* is remembered is also difficult to measure. For many it is still a benchmark of British broadcasting that symbolises all that was good about television within its years as a 'public-service' provider. But for others it epitomises the power of television to reduce public debate to entertainment, turn social problems into personal drama and political rhetoric into little more than melodrama or soap opera (Postman, 1987). Even the effect it had on the social climate of the time is contested, with some critics now pointing out that between 1966, when it was first shown, and 1969, the problem of housing in Britain actually grew worse (Banham, 1981, 211). Whatever your view of the programme, it is clearly a 'key' television text, not simply because of the way so many people responded to its subject matter at the time of its first broadcast, but for the very complexity of discussion that both its form and content have given to the debate about the merging of documentary and dramatic techniques.

QUESTIONS TO CONSIDER

- What are the major differences between the documentary-drama and the drama-documentary? What do you think the problems and limitations of such generic mutations are?

- In what ways does *Cathy Come Home* try to manipulate viewer emotion? Do you think this makes its investigation into homelessness any less credible?

- How typical do you think Cathy and Reg's circumstances are? Is their string of bad luck an unrealistic distortion of what could happen to couples in the 1960s?

- What does John Corner (1996) mean when he talks about the 'documentary spaces' opened up by *Cathy Come Home*? How might these create a legitimate piece of current-affairs broadcasting?

- How important do you think the structures of television in Britain (primarily its three terrestrial channels) helped *Cathy Come Home* became such an important example of 'event' television? Do you think such a programme would have the same sort of impact today?

RECOMMENDED READING

Banham, Martin (1981), 'Jeremy Sanford' in George W Brandt (ed.), *British Television Drama*, Cambridge and New York: Cambridge University Press.

Corner, John (1996), 'Cathy Come Home' in *The Art of Record: A Critical Introduction to Documentary*, Manchester and New York: Manchester University Press.

Leigh, Jacob (2002), 'Cathy Come Home: Fictional Journalism' in *The Cinema of Ken Loach: Art in the Service of the People*, London and New York: Walflower Press.

Chapter Ten

Charlie's Angels

Jason Jacobs

Production Details

(ABC/Spelling-Goldberg Productions, 1976–1981)

Production company: Spelling-Goldberg Productions for ABC
Executive producers: Aaron Spelling, Leonard Goldberg

Cast (and seasons they were in) includes:
Sabrina Duncan (Kate Jackson) [1–3]
Jill Munroe (Farrah Fawcett) [1]
Kelly Garrett (Jaclyn Smith) [1–5]
John Bosley (David Doyle) [1–5]
Kris Munroe (Cheryl Ladd) [2–5]
Tiffany Welles (Shelley Hack) [4]
Julie Rogers (Tanya Roberts) [5]
Charles Townsend (voice) (John Forsythe) [1–5]

Charlie's Angels was one of the most popular US television shows of the 1970s and
has subsequently acquired a kitsch notoriety and a dedicated fan base, as well as two
Hollywood translations, *Charlie's Angels* (McG, 2000) and *Charlie's Angels: Full Throttle*
(McG, 2003). It has also attracted criticism for its formulaic shallowness and its objecti-
fication of women. Conceived by producer-mogul Aaron Spelling, the show combined
the detective drama with glamorous fantasy. According to Chris Mann (1997, 343):

> Not only were [the] Angels beautiful and sexy, they were smart and powerful heroines who
> used provocative attraction (and feminine, often feigned, vulnerability) to lure and capture
> unsuspecting male criminals. Though Charlie's Angels *was among TV's first dramas to
> instil female characters with typically male 'powers' via a dominant subject position, the
> show's critics, including infuriated feminists, countered that* Charlie's Angels *was little
> more than patriarchal production that sexually objectified its characters.*

Charlie's Angels is about three women who work as private detectives for the rich and
powerful Charles Townsend, whose face we never see – instead we hear his disembodied voice coming from a speakerphone. Charlie provides the Angels with regular
assignments – investigating various crimes such as murder, extortion, abduction, etc.

Character differentiation was organised around basic types: Sabrina was the smart leader, Jill the athletic one and Kelly a 'former showgirl', while the only male – the unglamorous and comic John Bosley – assists them. The narrative structure of each show was simple: we see an event – a murder, a robbery, an abduction, etc. – that sets up an enigma; then we meet the Angels who are given their assignment by Charlie. After formulating a plan that usually involves adopting various guises, they gradually manage to unravel the mystery. A brief, sometimes violent action sequence follows, the villains are apprehended and the episode typically ends on a comic note. These capers are framed with an address that stresses the sexual appeal of the Angels, even though they never in fact engage in any sexual activity. As Ellen Seiter notes, 'Charlie's assignments frequently sent the women to hotels, casinos, spas or night clubs in search of crime and corruption. While the women were presented as competent detectives, the threat of sexual violence against them was the primary narrative source of the show's suspense' (1985, 138).

Charlie's Angels was created by Aaron Spelling in partnership with Leonard Goldberg for the ABC network in the US. Spelling is one of the best-known US television producers, a self-made mogul from a humble background who became a major producer in the 1970s with shows such as *The Mod Squad* (ABC, 1968–73) and *Starsky and Hutch* (ABC, 1975–9) before moving into super-soaps such as *Dynasty* (ABC, 1981–9) and *Beverly Hills 90210* (Fox, 1990–2000). Typically his shows incorporate contemporary fashion (clothing, gestures, phrases) with a strong element of fantasy, all rendered in bright primary colours. Plots are simple and dialogue is clear and explanatory. According to Jostein Gripsrud, 'Spelling [is] known to prefer "tennis match dialogue", simple lines and counterlines from characters A and B shot over the other's shoulder; and he is supposed to insist on a "show and tell" technique in which something is first shown and then in the next scene talked about by the characters' (1995, 30). However, this was not Spelling's style alone but part of a wider trend that John Caldwell has described as 'zero-degree television' – shows with 'uniform settings, lighting, looks, and cutting', where 'the only thing that changed from week to week were stories, plots, and guest stars. Locations, on the other hand, were all recognizably southern Californian *and redundant*' (emphasis in the original, 1995, 57–8). *Charlie's Angels* was clearly part of this trend where visual style was more about the content than the organisation of the frame (ibid., 58):

> *In the homogenous, studio-bound style of the 1970s dramatic telefilm, 'stunning visuals' frequently meant placing loaded objects and libidinous bodies in front of the disinterested 35 mm camera. Stylistic excess during this period had more to do with softcore fashion posing and automotive product photography than it did with painterly or expressionistic control over the image.*

In 1974, Spelling and Goldberg developed a programme concept called *The Alley Cats* about three crime-busting women. When they took the idea to ABC the network was sceptical about the credibility of women in action roles. However, by 1975 the new head of network programming, Fred Silverman, expressed interest. During a meeting with the network, Spelling and Goldberg (in an effort to explain what the show was about) invented the framing device of three women working for a man. It was Kate Jackson, noticing a painting of three angels in Spelling's office, who suggested one half of the title. (Originally called *Harry's Angels*, it was changed because the network was already running *Harry-O* [ABC, 1974–5]). A 90-minute pilot was released in 1975 and rated extraordinarily well; Silverman loved it and the show was born.

The first season was one of the highest ever rated and in 1976 ABC's advertising rate for it was reportedly $100,000 per minute. The show's success led to various merchandising spin-offs – lunchboxes, dolls, games, etc., magazine covers such as *Time* and *People* and an Emmy nomination. With several other shows it helped the ABC network rise to a position of dominance for the first time in its history. Along with her famous swimsuit poster and hair, the show also contributed to Farrah Fawcett's rise to superstardom. Fawcett, disillusioned with the low pay of the show (her husband, Lee Majors, was reportedly paid ten times more than his wife for *The Six Million Dollar Man* [ABC, 1973–8]) and interested in developing a big-screen career, left the show after the first season. She was replaced in season two by Cheryl Ladd, who played Jill Munroe's younger sister, Kris, and the ratings for that season were even higher than for the first.

Charlie's Angels is clearly important in terms of its efforts to figure women in action roles, but much of the criticism of the show picked up on its sexism. One network executive claimed, 'A series like *Charlie's Angels* performs a very important and valuable public service. Not only does it show women how to look beautiful and lead very exciting lives, but they still take their orders from a man' (cited by Gitlin, 1983, 73). In contrast, many believed that the programme represented an advance in having three women in leading roles in a prime-time television show. Women had been cast in leading roles before, notably Teresa Graves in *Get Christie Love* (ABC, 1974–5) and Angie Dickinson as 'Pepper' Anderson in *Police Woman* (NBC, 1974–8), but *Charlie's Angels* seemed to respond to these efforts by multiplying the leading roles and explicitly taking the women out of the public law enforcement sphere. The title sequence, narrated by Charlie, makes this explicit: 'Once upon a time there were three little girls who went to the police academy... And they were each assigned very hazardous duties. But I took them away from all that. And now they work for me. My name is Charlie.'

Several critics have commented on the astonishing address of this framing narration, which clearly figures the Angels in a childlike relation to Charlie (Seiter, 1985). While it may not be *King Lear*, it does signal some rather strange family relations: here is a fairy-tale story of a man who rescues three women from dull jobs (the line 'hazardous duties' is delivered over images of individual Angels coping with mundane jobs such as traffic control, working the telephone exchange, etc.) and brings them into the world of leisure, glamour and danger. John Forsythe's gravelly voice has a strong parental authority, which combines power and experience with a hint of schmaltz. The fact that Charlie remains unseen but is adored by the Angels (in a way that is playfully exaggerated in the Hollywood versions) codes this parental figure as sexually attractive. Virginia Wright Wexman argues that '...the freedom offered by the program's formula is that of a libidinous male domination under which the prohibitions of traditional family structures need not apply' (1984, 9).

Other networks and critics attacked the show for beginning a period of 'T & A' ('Tits and Ass') TV, while feminist scholars lambasted it as an example of the 'commercialisation of the female image' (Schwichtenberg, 1981, 16). Certainly the spectacle of three beautiful women was the product of considerable investment and labour: the clothes alone cost over $100,000 per season and the actresses had to be in at 5 a.m. each day for make-up and hairstyling. One can also see the patriarchal web extending beyond the frame – from Charlie, Spelling-Goldberg, to the network. For example, once Farrah Fawcett quit, the network slapped on a $13 million lawsuit, which effectively prevented her working in the mainstream movie business. (The settlement required Fawcett to guest star on the show six times over three years.) Nevertheless, popular interest in the show waned after the third season and it dropped out of the top 10; the lead Angel, Kate Jackson, quit and the network began to move the show around the schedules. Changes in the cast clearly did not help the ratings and in 1981 the show was axed.

By the 1990s and 2000s *Charlie's Angels* experienced something of a revival. The Hollywood versions and various television retrospectives are evidence of this trend, but the fact that many more feminised action figures were on television at this time is also important. The mainstream figuring of women in leading action roles in shows such as **Cagney and Lacey** (CBS, 1981–8) and **Buffy the Vampire Slayer** (Fox, 1997–2003) means that *Charlie's Angels* seems less like an historical curiosity and more like the primitive beginning of an important trend. However, one crucial difference between *Charlie's Angels* and these other shows is the absence of significant character development. For example, in **Buffy**, our knowledge of the characters deepens as the show develops over its episodes; and its delineation of the feminine subjective is often rich and complex. In contrast, the Angels remain the same throughout. Yet the fascination with women in action roles continues, most recently in Quentin Tarantino's *Kill Bill* (2003) about an elite group of women assassins working for an enigmatic man. With all its attention to trend-conscious, empowered women, karate-chopping and shooting their way out of trouble, it seems that *Charlie's Angels* has now, surprisingly, become fashionable for the second time.

QUESTIONS TO CONSIDER

- Do you think *Charlie's Angels* objectifies women? In what ways do you think the programme actually portrays women in a positive/active light?
- Do you think *Charlie's Angels* fits into Caldwell's (1995) notion of 'zero-degree television'? Do you think it's fair to say that its visual style was clearly more important than its content?

- What role do you think the disembodied voice of Charlie plays in the narrative? What difference do you think his presence makes to some critics' attempt to transform the programme into a 'feminist' text?

- In what ways do you think *Charlie's Angels* may have influenced and affected later female-orientated shows like **Cagney and Lacey** and **Buffy the Vampire Slayer**? Do you think the programme's legacy has generally been a negative or positive one?

RECOMMENDED READING

Mann, Chris (1997), '*Charlie's Angels*' in Horace Newcomb (ed.), *The Encyclopedia of Television*, London and Chicago: Fitzroy Dearborn.
Schwichtenberg, Cathy (1981), 'A Patriarchal Voice in Heaven', *Jump Cut*, No. 24/25.
Seiter, Ellen (1985), 'The Hegemony of Leisure: Aaron Spelling Presents *Hotel*' in Phillip Drummond and Richard Paterson, *Television in Transition: Papers from the First International Television Studies Conference*, London: British Film Institute.

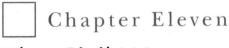

Chapter Eleven
The Civil War

Gary R Edgerton

Production Details

(Public Broadcasting Service, 1990)

Director: Ken Burns
Producers: Ken Burns, Ric Burns
Writers: Geoffrey C Ward, Ric Burns with Ken Burns
Editors: Paul Barnes, Bruce Shaw, Tricia Reidy
Cinematographers: Ken Burns, Allen Moore, Buddy Squires
Narrator: David McCullough

It's been more than a dozen years since *The Civil War* premiered over five consecutive evenings (September 23–27, 1990) on prime-time TV in the US, amassing the largest audience for any series in public television history. Ken Burns' documentary version of the war acted as a kind of lightning rod for a new generation, attracting a great deal of attention and praise, as subsequent research indicated that nearly half the viewers would not have been watching TV at all if it had not been for *The Civil War*. In the US, 38.9 million Americans tuned in to at least one episode of the five-night telecast, averaging 12 million viewers at any given moment (Statistical Research Incorporated, 1990, 2.1–2.8). Film and television critics from across America were equally attentive and admiring. *Newsweek* reported 'a documentary masterpiece' (Walters, 1990, 68); *Time* 'eloquen[t] ... a pensive epic' (Zoglin, 1990c, 73), and *US News & World Report* 'the best Civil War film ever made' (Lewis, 1990, 74). Political pundit, George Will, wrote: 'Our *Iliad* has found its Homer ... if better use has ever been made of television, I have not seen it' (Will, 1990, 23). The miniseries (renamed *The American Civil War*) for foreign distribution, also became a surprise success in international syndication as well.

Between 1990 and 1992, accolades for Ken Burns and the series took on institutional proportions. He won 'Producer of the Year' from the Producers Guild of America; two Emmys (for 'Outstanding Information Series' and 'Outstanding Writing Achievement'); Best Foreign Television Award from the British Academy of Film and Television Arts; a Peabody; a duPont-Columbia Award; a Golden Globe; a DW Griffith Award; two Grammys; a People's Choice Award for 'Best Television MiniSeries'; and eight honorary doctorates from various American colleges and universities in 1991 alone. *The Civil War* also became a phenomenon of popular culture. The series was mentioned on episodes of **Twin Peaks** (ABC 1990–1), *Thirtysomething* (ABC, 1987–91) and *Saturday Night Live* (ABC, 1975–) during the 1990–1 television season. Ken Burns appeared on *The Tonight Show* (NBC, 1954–) and he was selected by the editors of *People* magazine as one of their '25 most intriguing people of 1990'. The series, moreover, developed into a marketing sensation: the companion volume by Knopf, *The Civil War: An Illustrated History*, became a runaway best-seller, as did the accompanying Warner soundtrack, featuring the bitter-sweet anthem 'Ashokan Farewell' by Jay Ungar, and the nine-episode videotaped version from Time-Life reached sales of one million in less than two years.

Several interlocking factors evidently contributed to the extraordinary level of interest surrounding *The Civil War*, including the overall technical and dramatic quality of the miniseries itself, its accompanying promotional campaign, the momentum of scheduling Sunday through Thursday, the synergetic merchandising of all its ancillary products and a TV industry strike earlier in the year which disrupted the fall season and caused the network competition to briefly delay its season premieres. Most significantly, though, a new generation of historians had already begun addressing the war from the so-called 'bottom-up' perspective, underscoring the role of African-Americans, women, immigrants, workers, farmers and common soldiers in the conflict. This fresh emphasis on social and cultural history had revitalised the American Civil War as a subject, adding a more inclusive and human dimension to the traditional preoccupations with 'great men', transcendent ideals and battle strategies and statistics.

Burns employed 24 consultants on this project, including many prominent historians, but, understandably, not all of these scholars and film-making specialists agreed with everything in the final series. With so many experts, and with a subject the size and scope of the American Civil War as the historical terrain, a certain amount of controversy was unavoidable. One historian even concluded his analysis of *The Civil War* by calling the series 'a flawed masterpiece' (Koeniger, 1991, 233), thus evoking the customary judgement of DW Griffith's *Birth of a Nation* (1915). This analogy only goes so far, however, making more sense on the grounds of shared cinematic brilliance than because of any similarities in outlook and sensibility. Indeed, one of Burns' stated intentions was to amend the 'pernicious myths about the Civil War from *Birth of a Nation* to *Gone with the Wind*', especially in regard to racial stereotyping and the many other bigoted distortions in plot and imagery (Milius, 1990, 1, 43).

Much of the success of Ken Burns' *The Civil War* must be equated in kind to the extent with which his account makes this nineteenth-century conflict immediate and comprehensible for its audience in the 1990s. The great questions of race and continuing discrimination, of the changing roles of women and men in society, of big government versus local control and of the individual struggle for meaning and conviction in modern life, all form essential parts of Burns' version of the war. *The Civil War* attracted a record-setting viewership to public television because, in his own words, 'I realized the power that the war still exerted over us … surely [the story of the Civil War] ought to be retold for every generation' (Ken Burns, telephone interview with author, February 18, 1993).

Certainly part of the pervading sensibility of this series is rooted in the common experience of many Americans at the time who had seen numerous images of graphic violence and suffering during the country's first full-scale television war in Vietnam (1962–75). Burns, in many ways, is the ideal television producer for this period of transition between generations, bridging the beliefs and ideals of the people who came of age during World War II with his own frame of reference as a baby boomer. The debut telecast of *The Civil War*, moreover, occurred in the midst of the Persian Gulf conflict. Iraq had just invaded Kuwait, on August 2, 1990. An imminent escalation of hostilities was continually on the minds of most television viewers as they watched the miniseries.

Overall, Ken Burns articulates a version of the country's past that conveys his own outlook as a producer-director, intermingling many widely held assumptions about the character of America and its liberal pluralist aspirations. Like other documentarists of his generation, he addresses matters of race, gender, class and regional division, but unlike many of his contemporaries, he presents an image of the US eventually pulling together, despite its many chronic differences, rather than a society coming apart at the seams. Exploring the past is Burns' way of reassembling an imagined future from a fragmented present. *The Civil War*, in particular, reaffirmed for the members of its principal audience (which skewed white, male, 35–49 and upscale in the ratings) the relevance of their past in an era of unprecedented multicultural redefinition (Statistical Research Incorporated, 1990, 2.1–2.8). For Burns, producing and directing documentaries is a way of re-evaluating the country's historical legacy and reconfirming it from a wholly new generational perspective.

Ken Burns is a hands-on and versatile producer who was personally involved in researching, fund-raising, co-writing, shooting, directing, editing, scoring and even promoting *The Civil War*. The series, a production of Ken Burns' Florentine Films in association with WETA-TV in Washington, DC, featured many of the film-maker's usual collaborators, including his brother and co-producer, Ric Burns, writer Geoffrey C Ward, editor Paul Barnes, cinematographer Buddy Squires and narrator David McCullough. Writer, historian and master raconteur, Shelby Foote, also emerged as the on-screen star, peppering the series with entertaining anecdotes throughout. All told, *The Civil War* took an estimated five years to complete and cost $3.2 million, garnered from support by the National Endowment for the Humanities ($1.3 million), General Motors ($1 million), the Corporation for Public Broadcasting and WETA-TV ($350,000), the Arthur Vining Davis Foundation ($350,000), and the MacArthur Foundation ($200,000).

The originality of Ken Burns' well-recognisable and distinctive style has now become normative for an entire generation of historical documentarists on TV. All of his narrative stylistics came together on a grand scale in this 11-hour miniseries, blending narration with what he calls his 'chorus of voices', with readings from personal papers, diaries and letters from such distinguished performers as Sam Waterston, Jason Robards, Julie Harris and Morgan Freeman, among others; interpretive commentaries from on-screen experts, usually scholars, critics and witnesses; his rephotographing technique, which closely examines old photographs, paintings, drawings and other artefacts with his movie camera; all backed up by sound effects and a musical track that favours period compositions and folk music. The effect of this collage of techniques is to create the illusion that the viewer is being transported back in time, finding an emotional connection with the people and events of America's past.

So much about Ken Burns' career defies the usual expectations. He became one of public television's busiest and most celebrated producers during the 1980s, a decade when the historical documentary held little interest for most American TV viewers. He operates his own independent company, Florentine Films, in a small New England village (Walpole, New Hampshire), more than four hours north of New York City, hardly a crossroads in the highly competitive and often insular world of corporately funded, PBS-sponsored productions. His 16 major specials so far – *Brooklyn Bridge* (PBS, 1982), *The Shakers: Hands to Work, Hearts to God* (PBS, 1985), *The Statue of Liberty* (PBS, 1985), *Huey Long* (PBS, 1986), *Thomas Hart Benton* (PBS, 1989), *The Congress* (PBS, 1989), *The Civil War* (PBS, 1990), *Empire of the Air: The Men Who Made Radio* (PBS, 1992), *Baseball* (PBS, 1994), *The West* (PBS, 1996), *Thomas Jefferson* (PBS, 1997), *Lewis and Clark: The Journey of the Corps of Discovery* (PBS, 1997), *Frank Lloyd Wright* (PBS, 1998), *Not For Ourselves Alone: The Story of Elizabeth Cady Stanton and Susan B Anthony* (PBS, 1999), *Jazz* (PBS, 2001) and *Mark Twain* (PBS, 2002) – are also strikingly out of step with the special effects and frenetic pacing of most non-fiction television, relying mainly on filmic techniques that were introduced literally decades ago.

Most remarkably, however, 70 million Americans have now seen *The Civil War*; 50 million have watched *Baseball*; 30 million *Jazz*; and audiences in the tens of millions have viewed his television productions internationally. The cumulative popularity of Burns' biographical or quasi-biographical histories is striking by virtually any measure, and they have over time redefined the place of documentaries on primetime TV in the US. *The Civil War*, specifically, asserted in one fell swoop that history is no longer the principal domain of specialists, but is now relevant and compelling for everyone – only this time on television.

QUESTIONS TO CONSIDER

- What specific characteristics make *The Civil War* a documentary? In what ways does it compare and contrast with a fictional TV miniseries?

- How do made-for-TV histories such as *The Civil War* differ from written histories on the same subject? How is the language of television evident in Burns' film-making style?
- Is Ken Burns more of a storyteller or an historian? What are his strengths and weaknesses in each regard?
- Biography is an essential part of Ken Burns' historical approach. How then does Burns' depiction of two common soldiers – Elisha Hunt Rhodes, a Yankee from Rhode Island, and Sam Watkins, a Confederate from Tennessee – function in comparison to his characterisations of 'great men' such as Abraham Lincoln and Robert E Lee?
- How is race handled in *The Civil War*? In particular, how are slaves and black soldiers represented and to what effect?
- Historian Barbara Fields reminds us in the final episode that 'the Civil War is in the present as well as the past'. Consequently, what themes and issues in *The Civil War* are still relevant to people today?
- Do you think either the Vietnam experience or the Gulf War affected the reception of *The Civil War*? Explain why or why not.

RECOMMENDED READING

Edgerton, Gary R (2001), *Ken Burns's America*, New York: Palgrave for St. Martin's Press.
Toplin, Robert Brent (ed.) (1996), *Ken Burns's The Civil War: Historians Respond*, New York: Oxford University Press.
Ward, Geoffrey C, with Ric Burns and Ken Burns (1990), *The Civil War: An Illustrated History*, New York: Knopf.

Chapter Twelve

Coronation Street

Ros Jennings

Production Details

(ITV, Granada Television, 1960–)

Creator: Tony Warren
Directors have included: Quentin Lawrence, Lawrence Moody,
June Wyndham-Davies, Richard Argent
Writers have included: Tony Warren, HV Kershaw, Vince Powell, Harry Driver,
Jack Rosenthal, John Finch, Adele Rose, Geoffrey Lancashire, Kay Mellor
Theme Music: Eric Spear

Cast has included:

Ena Sharples (Violet Carson)
Annie Walker (Doris Speed)
Elsie Tanner (Pat Phoenix)
Hilda Ogden (Jean Alexander)
Albert Tatlock (Jack Howarth)
Ken Barlow (William Roache)
Rita Sullivan/Fairclough (Barbara Knox)
Mike Baldwin (Johnny Briggs)
Jack Duckworth (William Tarmey)
Vera Duckworth (Elizabeth Dawn)
Sally Webster (Sally Whitaker)
Gail Tilsley/Platt/Hillman (Helen Worth)
Richard Hillman (Brian Caprone)

The British soap opera *Coronation Street* was broadcast for the first time in the UK in December 1960 and has run continually since (initially twice a week and now three or sometimes five times weekly). It has also been sold consistently overseas to countries such as New Zealand, Canada and Australia, primarily for British expatriate audiences. Its longevity has certainly contributed to its status as a British institution. Known affectionately for some time now in Britain as '*Corrie*', the serial's durability and continuing popularity is remarkable, consequently holding a significant place in British television history as a whole (Little, 1995).

One of *Coronation Street*'s early functions was the way it helped to establish a pivotal place for commercial television in the British nightly viewing schedules. As Richard Paterson has suggested, the key function for commercial television schedules is to ensure 'anchorage of the audience into a regular slot' (1981, 61). Indeed, the familiar and haunting signature tune by Eric Spear has become a beacon of the post-evening meal/pre-watershed family-viewing slot, acting as a 'call to viewing' for generations of British audiences. In the course of its long life, it has also been a prominent nursery for British writing and acting talent. Over the years, it has introduced the British public to the writing talents of the likes of Tony Warren, Jack Rosenthal, John Finch and Harry Kershaw and the acting talents of Joanna Lumley, Prunella Scales, Michael Elphick and Ben Kingsley, to name but a few.

However, discussing such a long-running serial has its difficulties. As Robert C Allen suggests, 'Even if we wished to view the entire text of [...] *Coronation Street* to this point in its history, we would be unable to do so; a soap opera is like a novel whose chapters we rip up immediately after reading them' (Allen, 1992, 109). Yet it does have elements of continuity, both in the televisual imaginary of its viewers who have grown up and grown old with the serial and in its own formal devices. Even if the only character to remain in the street from the first episode is Ken Barlow (played for over 40 years by William Roache), earlier characters are frequently mentioned to re-enforce the street's communal memories. On occasion, certain characters even return to provoke new plot spins and, quite frequently, to help viewing figures. In the genre where there is no end to the narrative, the only real points of closure occur with the death of a character.

Originally created by Tony Warren, the initial conceptualisation of *Coronation Street* (originally to be titled 'Florizel Street', but legend has it that a tea lady at Granada said it sounded too much like a lavatory cleaner) also coincided with the contemporary realisation of a new dominant mode in British fiction and cinema, that of social realism (see also **Boys from the Blackstuff** [BBC, 1981]). Consequently, although moulded within the conventions typical of the soap opera form, *Coronation Street* also sought to explore the 'social problems of the working class in terms which were recognisable to members of that class' (Jordan, 1981, 27). It represented the everyday lives and experiences of a small fictional community in an almost self-consciously generic northern setting (loosely associated with Manchester). Its purpose, in its earliest incarnations, at least, was certainly not ideologically neutral. On the cusp of the 1960s, *Coronation Street*, like its contemporary British cinematic counterparts such as *Saturday Night and Sunday Morning* (Reisz, 1960), reflected constructions of working-class identities in transition – from more traditional concepts connected to work and occupations to more contemporary understandings of a 'new' working class defined less by work than by 'leisure, patterns of consumption and recreational pursuits' (Hill, 1986, 154).

Although unequivocally exploring working-class northern identities, this did not limit the appeal of *Coronation Street* to a national audience. In fact, it quickly established itself at the top of the television ratings and by the end of its first year on air it was the most popular television programme in Britain (Corner, 1991, 128). This may be explained partly by the serial's familiar *mise-en-scène* that typified a commonly held mental picture of a working-class community in the industrial North. In the early days of its broadcast this was conveyed all the more clearly within a black and white aesthetic, now closely associated with realism. The everyday dramas that were lived out in this fictional terraced street took place in the typically restricted set of all soap operas. Located in the fictional town of Weatherfield, it presented, or so one might argue, a series of private spaces as public. The back rooms and kitchens of the key characters were the locus of everyday domestic life, as befitting the working-class socio-geographic location where the community was situated (in such communities, the front room was still primarily reserved for 'best'). As this suggests, the structure of the serial was entwined around a set of substructures based in ideas of family and community. The strong and overlapping ties of family and community therefore permitted wide access to these often quite private domestic spaces, whilst the more public community life and interaction was mobilised around meetings in the local pub (the *Rovers Return*), church hall, corner shop, etc. As Christine Geraghty suggests, *Coronation Street* is 'presenting the viewer with a community in which difference from outsiders is asserted not by money or ambition or power but by qualities which can be shared by virtue of living in the same place' (2000, 180).

More so than the *mise-en-scène*, however, the 'authenticity' of the working-class North was communicated in the voices of the characters. Their accents and inflections were distinct from the west side of the Pennines and, as Geraghty also suggests, 'the north invokes, partly of course because of *Coronation Street* itself, an ethos of down-to-earth good humour and a stoical acceptance of disappointment and tragedy' (2000, 180). This 'imagined community' may have inhabited an environment coded in various ways as regionally specific, but even to an affluent middle England, its realist mode and more particularly its everyday concerns were universally intelligible.

In academic writing, the soap opera has long been considered to be a 'feminine' genre because of its narrative focus on relationships, kinship and community. Consequently, in a rather over-determined way, its address has been seen as being aimed primarily at a female audience. The ideological 'glue' of soap opera life has certainly been the continued valuing of the so-called 'feminine' repertoires of nurturing and empathy, and in the context of this northern soap opera, a good deal of 'down-to-earth common sense' and hardiness can be added to this mix. One of the great strengths of *Coronation Street* is that its particular combination of soap convention and social realism has crafted a range of women characters who span (and have always done so during its long incarnation) the continuum of constructions of hegemonic femininity (from 'sluttish' to 'saintly'). The core values and expectations of the fictional community are articulated and sutured by way of what Richard Dyer calls *Coronation Street*'s 'plethora of splendid mums' (1981, 185). The matriarch and also, especially in relation to *Coronation Street*, the grandmother figure (both real and/or 'honorary' in terms of status to the community and established over the years by characters such as Ena Sharples and Minnie Caldwell) are the lynchpins of the serial.

After 40 years, *Coronation Street* has developed its own dynamic and, as such, can be said to have grown almost organically. However, like all societies, the community in *Coronation Street* is always in formation and cannot be conceived of as being inherently stable. Yet a form of enduring stability is created under the guidance of its core values, which are hegemonic 'female-centred'. And, although never displaced, this core ideology does come under challenge. It has been argued that because 'strong women' character types dominate the genre, it has been hard to establish potent male characters. One type of male character that has challenged the feminine status quo, however, has been the 'bastard figure' typified by a character such as Mike Baldwin. According to Geraghty, this figure constitutes a complex presence of masculine power in his dealings with women and his workforce of female employees (Geraghty, 2000).

Although crafted in the cradle of realism, *Coronation Street* now also perhaps acknowledges the 'knowing' and self-parodying expressions of postmodernism. Over the years the characters have become more complex and less one-dimensional, but the visibly working-class narratives established in the early years of the serial still shape the concerns of today's episodes. However, since the arrival of *EastEnders* (a BBC soap opera that finally and successfully challenged the hegemony of *Coronation Street* when it arrived in 1985) it has been decidedly more daring in some of its subject matter. Recently, for example, in a drive to boost flagging ratings, its rather cosy image has been jolted by presenting the British public with the first television soap serial killer, Richard Hillman. Even so, the resulting narratives are still concerned with personal events such as the effect on family and friends and the way that these personal tragedies interface with the life of the community as a whole.

Yet, in some ways, *Coronation Street* remains an old-fashioned serial; as Buckingham indicates, 'In a sense, *Coronation Street* had grown old with its audience' (2000, 153). For instance, although the serial's community has become more diverse in recent years, it has still (at least at the time of writing) not introduced any gay and lesbian characters like the more recent British soaps, and although they have now been firmly established, it has taken a long time for black and Asian characters to appear. Yet because of both its long life and the organic process of its development, *Coronation Street* has its own logic and its own pace of development which, at this stage in time, is not really externally generated but internal and self-referential. This formula has made *Coronation Street* Britain's longest running television soap opera, with a special place in the heart of the British soap and television viewing public. Although in terms of ratings, it can no longer be said to be the 'Queen' of the British soaps, the daily life of this fictional street has woven itself into British popular culture and allowed it to evolve and take on a new mantle as the 'Queen Mother'.

QUESTIONS TO CONSIDER

- Identify the aesthetic characteristics of British 'social realism' (Jordan, 1981) that *Coronation Street* originally reflected and employed.

- *Coronation Street* was originally viewed as a strongly 'matriarchal community'. Do you think this is still true and how has it helped shape and determine the type of male characters it tends to create?

- What generic characteristics have made *Coronation Street* so enduringly popular? How do you think it manages to continually change and develop without losing its original appeal?

- It has often been said that *Coronation Street* is 'character-based' while a soap opera like *EastEnders* is more 'plot' or 'issue' led. What do you think is meant by such a distinction and do you think it is helpful in explaining the differences between these two soap operas?

- Some critics have suggested that *Coronation Street* today simply presents its viewers with a 'cosy' and 'nostalgic' view of northern, working-class life in Britain. Do you think this assessment is justified and can you identify ways in which the programme has tried to become more contemporary in recent years?

RECOMMENDED READING

Bazalgette, C et al (1983), *Teaching Coronation Street*, London: British Film Institute.
Dyer, Richard, Christine Geraghty, Marion Jordan, Terry Lovell, Richard Paterson, John Stewart et al (eds.) (1981), *Coronation Street*, London: British Film Institute.
Little, Daran (1995), *The Coronation Street Story*, London: Andre Deutsch Ltd.

Chapter Thirteen

The Cosby Show

Justin Lewis

Production Details

(NBC television, 1984–92)

Creators: Bill Cosby, Ed Weinberger, Michael Leeson
Producer: Bill Cosby

Cast includes:

Dr Heathcliff (Cliff) Huxtable (Bill Cosby)
Clair Huxtable (Phylicia Ayres-Allen/Rashad)
Denise Huxtable Kendall (Lisa Bonet)
Theodore Huxtable (Malcolm-Jamal Warner)
Vanessa Huxtable (Tempestt Bledsoe)
Ruddy Huxtable (Keshia Knight Pulliam)
Sondra Huxtable/Tibideaux (Sabrina Le BSeauf)

The Cosby Show takes its place in US television history as one of the most successful TV programmes of the 1980s. Its portrayal of the upper-middle-class Huxtable family regularly topped the ratings during the second half of the decade, attracting both critical acclaim and widespread public affection. It made its star, Bill Cosby – already well known as a stand-up comedian and for his co-starring role in the 1960s *I Spy* (NBC, 1956–68) TV series – one of the most respected, wealthy and popular entertainers in the US. But *The Cosby Show* was more than just another successful American sitcom. What made it significant was the way its gentle, everyday humour was employed in a self-conscious mission to change the way in which African-Americans were represented on television. Cosby and the show's adviser (Harvard psychiatrist Alvin Poussaint) were mindful of the history of negative, demeaning images of black people on television and in film: what Poussaint called the 'jivin, jammin, streetwise style stuff' of earlier shows like *The Jeffersons* (CBS, 1975–85), *Sanford and Son* (NBC, 1972–8) and *Good Times* (CBS, 1974–9) – shows which also featured predominantly black casts but which often degenerated into 'the worst kind of stereotyping' (quoted in Hartsough, 1989).

While well-intentioned liberalism was not new to prime time, the conventional wisdom among television executives was that the broad mass of middle-class white

America – so beloved by advertisers – would feel uncomfortable welcoming a black family into their homes. Indeed, the fact that the ABC network turned the series proposal down was, perhaps, less surprising than NBC's decision to air it. *The Cosby Show*'s success was, in this sense, ground-breaking. Its cast asked its viewers to laugh *with* them, not *at* them, to identify and empathise with black characters rather than view from a distance. And in so doing it provided a compelling demonstration that television did not need to resort to tokenism or racial stereotyping to be popular with white audiences.

For most black Americans, used to decades of demeaning or negative images of themselves, *The Cosby Show* came, as black actor and producer Tim Reid put it, as 'a breath of fresh air' (cited by Jhally and Lewis, 1992, 2), with none of the depressing list of black stock characters so remorselessly parodied by Robert Taylor's *Hollywood Shuffle* (1996). When jazz singer Lena Horne publicly thanked Cosby 'for giving us back ourselves', she spoke for millions of black Americans (ibid., 48–50), tired of watching an image system controlled by white people largely for the benefit of white audiences, failing to do them justice.

Bill Cosby's track record, not least his ability to sell mainstream American products on TV commercials, was clearly instrumental in persuading NBC to take on the series. The network was, nonetheless, sensitive to the supposed anxieties of its white audience, and their commitment to Cosby and Poussaint's vision was rather less than wholehearted. If the shows' references to African-American culture were invariably subtle or incidental, NBC were undoubtedly nervous about anything that might alienate white viewers. During the second series, the network tried to have an anti-apartheid sign (on the bedroom door of son Theo) removed from the set. They failed, not only because Cosby and others wanted to keep it there, but also because the show's success in the ratings meant they fought from a position of considerable strength.

The anti-apartheid sign on Theo Huxtable's door was symptomatic of *The Cosby Show*'s approach, part of what John Downing referred to as the 'abundance of black culture presented in the series, expressed without fanfare, but with constant dignity' (Downing, 1988, 61). These cultural and – occasionally – political signs were there for all to see, but, crucially, they were not obtrusive enough to be threatening. Theo's sign played no part in the show's storyline; it simply hung there, its significance in the eye of the beholder. Just as high street shops tend to be more noticeable if their contents concern us, a black viewer would be likely to notice such things – and to value their presence – while white viewers could have their consciousness undisturbed or even remain entirely oblivious to these cultural references (Jhally and Lewis, 1992).

If we compare *The Cosby Show* with another 1980s show, *Frank's Place* (CBS, 1987–8), we can appreciate the difficulty of this balancing act in a ratings-driven system. Like *The Cosby Show*, *Frank's Place* was a critically acclaimed sitcom with a predominantly black cast that consciously avoided stereotyping. But *Frank's Place* was a little more serious and, while not ostentatious, was more overtly expressive of African-American culture and politics. And if *The Cosby Show* was emboldened by its ratings success, the makers of *Frank's Place* were weakened by their failure to pull in large white audiences. The show's producer and star, Tim Reid, described how they 'caught constant flak [from the network]. They didn't want us to do it. They kept wanting us to be funny... They really want you to be colourless. They want you not to bring your race with you' (Riggs, 1991). According to Henry Louis Gates, '*Frank's Place* showed a broader range of types than any other black television show' (Riggs, 1991), but in doing so it made itself more marginal to the upscale environs of American television.

The Cosby Show, on the other hand, was better designed to fit the norms of mainstream American television. Although it was innovative in its comic style and its rejection of racial stereotype, it was perfectly attuned to the class conventions of much of the programming that surrounded it. The Huxtable family, headed by a doctor father and a lawyer mother and living in a comfortable New York brownstone, blended effortlessly into the upper-middle-class world of prime-time in the US – a place in which the legal and medical professions are particularly well represented and where a self-consciously working-class family like the Connors in *Roseanne* (ABC, 1988–97) looked conspicuous (and deliberately so). Ironically, it was partly its upscale setting that allowed *The Cosby Show* to be celebrated for its ordinary, everyday humour and the Huxtable family for their typicality (Riggs, 1991; Jhally and Lewis, 1992). In TV terms, they were indeed ordinary.

The Cosby Show was thus something of a compromise, and cultural critics like Henry Louis Gates (1989), Michael Dyson (1989) and Herman Gray (1995) were mindful that television images of black success were in stark contrast to the declining fortunes of many African-Americans during the 'trickle-up' economics of the Reagan era. As Dyson put it, 'It is perhaps this lack of acknowledgement of the underside of the American dream that is the most unfortunate feature of the Huxtable opulence' (1989, 7). Perhaps the most damning comment, in this context, came from Shelby Steele. For him, 'the success of this handsome, affluent black family points to the fair-mindedness of whites who, out of their essential goodness, changed society so that black families like the Huxtables could succeed. Whites could watch *The Cosby Show* and feel complimented on a job well done... On Thursday nights, Cosby, like a priest, absolves his white viewers, forgives and forgets the sins of the past' (1990, 11).

For Gates, the problem was not so much the show itself, but the fact that '*Cosby*'s success ... led to a flow of TV sitcoms that feature the black middle class, each of which takes its lead from *The Cosby Show*' (1989, 1). And it was not just sitcoms – the lesson US network executives appeared to learn from *The Cosby Show* was that white audiences were happy to watch black characters play leading roles as long as they were well-heeled professionals. This idea sat well with the fashionable but class-bound notion of 'positive images' and the importance of 'role models', in which it was assumed that to be dignified, admirable or worthy of respect necessarily involved a well-paid job. If *The Cosby Show* broke the racial mould of US television – thereby freeing black actors from the confines of the 'Hollywood Shuffle' – it simultaneously reinforced class conventions and expectations.

Needless to say, one can scarcely hold *The Cosby Show* culpable for this: it could be reasonably argued that the show simply did what it had to do, did it with style and that US television culture is all the richer for it. But it is also plausible that the networks – in creating a post-*Cosby* world replete with black professionals but parsimonious in its treatment of the black working class – were pursuing well-intentioned liberal instincts with insufficient heed to the symbolic logic of such representations. As Gates suggested, it was possible that 'The social vision of *Cosby* ... reflecting the miniscule integration of blacks into the upper middle class, reassuringly throws the blame for black poverty back onto the impoverished' (1989, 40). In other words, if television was abundant with stories of black people effortlessly living the American Dream, white Americans might be encouraged to regard racial inequity as an historical rather than contemporary problem. If so, the disproportionate number of African-Americans on low incomes, with few qualifications or behind bars could not, therefore, be seen as a function of discrimination or structural inequities.

The use of this symbolic logic is certainly all too apparent in Jhally and Lewis's audience study, encapsulated in the widespread rejection of affirmative action by the show's white viewers. The abundance of black upward mobility sanctioned by *The Cosby Show* made it much easier to argue that, as one viewer put it: 'there really is room in the United States for minorities to get ahead, without affirmative action'. Affirmative action has, of course, always been a bitterly contested policy, but what was striking about the reaction of white respondents was the notion that discrimination and racial inequity, once rife, was now a thing of the past. And by the early 1990s, for all the setbacks suffered during the Reagan/Bush years (Hacker, 1992), television provided viewers with a succession of images that made the whole idea of affirmative action anachronistic. In this symbolic climate, to say that 'when the whole idea was first discussed, it was a very good idea ... In recent years, I don't think it's necessarily getting anybody anywhere', was an entirely reasonable response (Jhally and Lewis, 1992, 88–90). Since then, affirmative action has become a hot issue in contemporary US politics, and, as the tide has gradually turned against it, many states and universities have succumbed to pressure to abandon the policy.

Whether self-consciously or not, Bill Cosby's next sitcom venture, titled simply *Cosby* (CBS, 1996), amounted to a modest move against the tide of black upward mobility. Whatever its merits, it did not garner the kind of ratings success of its predecessor. The different reaction to the two shows may be symptomatic of white America's acceptance of equal rights, combined with a deep difficulty or discomfort about dwelling too long on the intersections of class and race that lie behind the persistence of racial inequality in the US (Wilson, 1987). Unlike *The Cosby Show*, *Cosby* refused to flatter to deceive.

QUESTIONS TO CONSIDER

- How do you think *The Cosby Show* challenged conventional stereotypes of black people in America during the 1980s?
- Do you think *The Cosby Show* could have been just as successful if the family were white? What aspects of the family strike you as culturally specific to black people?
- How do you think *The Cosby Show* may have been 'customised' for a white audience? Do you think these changes could ever be justified?
- By being a 'handsome, affluent, black family' do you think *The Cosby Show* necessarily failed to question wider issues about racial inequality in America?
- Think of one or two programmes that may have learnt from *The Cosby Show*'s portrayal of black or Asian people. How have they attempted to avoid some of the 'mistakes' that the show may have made during the 1980s?

RECOMMENDED READING

Downing, J (1988), '*The Cosby Show* and American Racial Discourse' in Smitherman-Donaldson, G and van Dijk, T (eds.), *Discourse and Discrimination*, Michigan: Wayne State University Press.

Jhally, S and Lewis, J (1992), *Enlightened Racism: The Cosby Show, Audiences, and the Myth of the American Dream*, Boulder: Westview.

Steele, S (1990), *The Content of Our Character*, New York: Harper Perennial.

Chapter Fourteen

Culloden

Jamie Sexton

Production Details

(BBC, 1964)

Producer: Peter Watkins
Director: Peter Watkins
Writer: Peter Watkins, based on the book *Culloden* by John Prebble
Historical Advisor: John Prebble
Cinematography: Dick Bush
Editing: Michael Bradsell
Production Design: Anne Davey, Colin MacLeod, Brendon Woods
Sound: John Gatland, Lou Hanks
Make-up Artist: Ann Brodie

Cast includes: 'The men, women and children of Inverness'

First transmitted on BBC2 on December 15, 1964, *Culloden* was a widespread critical success, marking its director and producer, Peter Watkins, as a significant television *auteur* (a short-lived reputation due partly to the subsequent banning of his next programme, *The War Game* [BBC, 1965], which led to his departure from the British television industry). Watkins had made a name for himself in the field of amateur film-making, directing films such as *Diary of an Unmarried Soldier* (1959) and *The Forgotten Faces* (1960), which were also documentary reconstructions. These films garnered awards and led to Watkins being employed by the BBC's Documentary Films Department, where he worked as an assistant to Stephen Hearst before eventually being commissioned to make *Culloden* by Huw Wheldon.

The main source material for *Culloden* was the book of the same name by John Prebble, which inspired this televisual reconstruction of the 1746 battle. This last land battle in Britain saw 9,000 Redcoats (loyal to the Protestant King George II and led by William Augustus, the Duke of Cumberland) slaughter around 1,000 Highlander troops (fighting for the Catholic Prince Charles Edward Stuart, 'Bonnie Prince Charlie'). At the time of its transmission, *Culloden* was hailed as a new, important step in the field of documentary film-making, but the manner in which it blurred distinctions between documentary and drama led to some confusion regarding its actual status. Whilst drawing many of the facts and details from the book into his film, Watkins incorporated them in a non-conventional manner, reconstructing events in the manner of a contemporary current-affairs programme, as though documenting scenes which were happening in the 'here and now'. The film therefore conflates two fictional spaces: the eighteenth-century battlefield and twentieth-century television reporting.

Watkins has argued that the choice of reconstructing history in this manner was intended to 'rescue' the 'exotic' image of Bonnie Prince Charlie and to draw a parallel between the Battle of Culloden and the Vietnam War (Watkins, 2002). For example, in one scene there is a moment when the camera follows soldiers into a shelter for injured men; a man then turns towards the camera and puts his hand in front of it, asking for it to be turned off. This mimics the volatility of 'real-life' interactions between camera crew and filmed subjects. Added to this, *Culloden* is narrated throughout by a 'reporter' who reels out facts in a rather dry, dispassionate manner, telling us details leading up to the battle, facts about the battle itself and information on individual protagonists. At one point, an historian and biographer from the day even talks directly to the camera (complete with map), mimicking newsreel reports of the time and documentary programmes like *World in Action* (Granada, 1963–5). *Culloden* thus enacts a dialectic between those represented and those enacting the representation (although, of course, the latter were fictionalised). It attempts to go beyond the neat and unified diegesis of a conventional dramatic representation by encoding representational devices.

At the time Watkins made *Culloden*, many figures within television documentary production were becoming influenced by *cinéma-vérité* or, more correctly, direct cinema, particularly films made by American proponents of the style such as Richard Leacock and Don Pennebaker. Direct cinema was a mode of film-making that, with the benefits of lightweight cameras and synchronised sound equipment, could closely observe everyday events as they happened, attempting to present 'direct' access to the material as it unfolded before the cameras (see *An American Family* [PBS, 1973]). Because direct cinema was concerned with capturing as much material as possible, it was marked by an absence of elaborate lighting and careful framing, as these were mediating devices thought to intrude between camera and subject. In the same way, *Culloden* is filmed on rather grainy film stock and features shaky camera movements, as well as out-of-focus shots, in order to mimic the signifiers of direct cinema. Gomez has argued, though, that because *Culloden* employs these techniques in a self-consciously stylistic manner, it is of a qualitatively different order than direct cinema films: whereas direct cinema attempts to break down the barriers between camera and subject, Watkins is more concerned to break the barriers separating film and audience (1979, 37). That is, Watkins uses these filmic codes in a stylistic manner in order to create a dialogue with the audience in terms of what is signified and how it is represented.

On a different tack, SMJ Arrowsmith (1981) has argued that *Culloden* should be related to the rise of new attitudes in the theatre, which attacked old conventions and attempted to represent new areas of life, particularly the working classes. He stresses that these gradually entered television through ITV's drama slot *Armchair Theatre* (ITV, 1956–74), which in turn provided a backdrop for the emergence of films such as *Culloden*. It may well be that some *Armchair Theatre* episodes – for instance, *Lena, O My Lena* (1960) and *Where I Live* (1960) – did provide precedents to some extent in that, whilst not being shot on location, they did construct 'realistic' milieu through set design, a greater sense of camera movement (which opened up fictional space) and a commitment to a more contemporary, gritty atmosphere, which explored class and social mobility. However, it should not be forgotten that the Documentary Films Department of the BBC actually commissioned *Culloden*, and it is as a 'documentary' (albeit a fictionalised one) that it clearly attempts to present itself.

The actual battle scenes in *Culloden* take up a small amount of screen time. In one sense this was down to a small budget, which prevented the number of actors and the amount of special effects work required for 'epic' battle scenes. Instead, the film focuses upon the internal tensions within the Highland resistance army, in tandem with documenting the statistics of the battle. Not until a third of the way through the film do we witness reconstructed battle scenes; before this, we get to understand what has been happening through voice-over reportage and interviews. The film particularly focuses upon the decision of Prince Charles to fight against British battalions on a wide, open moor, a decision that Lord George Murphy calls 'suicidal' due to the way it favours the superior canon-fire of the British army. In contrast to Lord George's comments, the Prince backs up his decision by claiming that 'God is on our side'.

The detailed mockery of the Prince's commands feeds into the battle scenes when they finally occur, imbuing them with inevitability. The battle scenes themselves are carefully constructed, often in close-up or of wider compositions obscured by the dust of various explosions (presumably in order to dissimulate the limited resources the film-makers had to work with). During scenes of battle the camera moves around in a mobile and often shaky manner, sometimes jerking in a frenetic and almost abstract style. These reconstructions give the film an 'authenticity', creating a hard and gritty vision of a past war, bolstered by the amateur cast, who do not bring with them the extra-textual connotations of known actors. The careful compositions are also used in a more symbolic manner: thus, the British army is often shot from a distance, marching in a controlled manner. This sense of control is contrasted with the chaos and confusion of the Highlanders, whose bodies are strewn across the screen in a haphazard manner (sometimes in the foreground, whilst the ordered Redcoats march behind them in the background).

The film then focuses on the suffering of the victims, witnessing Highlanders being shot down like flies, lingering over dying bodies, interviewing wives of victims. The Prince, throughout, makes no alternative plans, but neither will he sanction a retreat. After the Redcoats' victory, some of the victors are interviewed, displaying a lack of care over the sufferings caused. The film finally shows how the maltreatment of the

Highlanders continues after the battle has been won, through Cumberland's order to 'pacify' the rebels. In contrast, Prince Charles escapes to France, whilst the rebellious Lord George is exiled.

The way, then, in which Watkins merged fictional and factual codes in a self-conscious manner can be read in two opposing ways. In one sense, such techniques can be seen as a kind of 'Brechtian' distancing ploy in which the codes of documentary film-making are foregrounded in order to expose any structural 'transparency' (this is argued by Cubit, 1997, 1807). On the other hand, the film-making techniques can be read as providing a greater sense of viewer absorption, taking us into the events as if they were happening live. These two modes of viewer decipherment do not, of course, exhaust strategies by which to read *Culloden*, but they do represent two opposing poles that were employed by contemporary critics at the time of its transmission and point to the ambiguity of the technical strategies employed within the programme.

In fact, Terry Lajtha (1981) has argued that *Culloden* provides a strange hybrid of 'alienation' devices and empathetic strategies. He contends that it employs a number of Brechtian techniques, which include the lack of a central identifying figure, the use of leitmotifs that build up a 'step-by-step' revelation in favour of a conventional dramatic climax, as well employing occasional jarring edits and sounds. On the other hand, the improvisation of the amateur actors, as well as the intimate manner in which they are framed, invites empathetic involvement. Lajtha proposes that this hybridised aesthetic is successful, because 'too much alienation or lack of empathy can distance us to the point where we dismiss or lose sight of the essential issues' (1981, 10).

Analyses of *Culloden* that interpret it as a drama should therefore be related to the subsequent development of drama and documentary forms. Without knowledge that the documentary department produced the programme, it is understandable that it has been perceived as a drama because the nature of departmental categorisation has shifted over the years. Since the programme was transmitted, more dramas have been produced that incorporate documentary elements into a dramatic programme (and this can be traced back partly to Loach's **Cathy Come Home** [BBC, 1964]). But like other programmes that merge fact and fiction together, *Culloden* can also be criticised for its 'reinvention' of real events. For while it clearly borrows the codes of contemporary current affairs, it importantly goes against such codes in one important area – *impartiality*.

During the 1960s, British current affairs and news had to adhere to strict notions of fairness as laid down in broadcasting statutes; balance was supposed to be achieved and bias avoided. In reality, series such as **World in Action** (Granada, 1963–5, 1967–98) often attempted to buck this trend, yet the fact that Watkins was not covering a contemporary event meant that he could totally avoid such balance. Thus, whilst at times the narration does seem dry and dispassionate, it nevertheless pillories some of the figures, most notably Prince Charles Edward Stuart, who is openly described in derogatory terms. While clearly original and innovative for its time, it is this lack of impartiality (the slippage and confusion that occurs when the 'factual' and the 'dramatic' meet) that *Culloden* will also be remembered for.

QUESTIONS TO CONSIDER

- How does *Culloden* merge drama with documentary? What problems of historical truth do you think can occur in such a hybrid genre?
- How are the different leaders of the battle portrayed? What elements in the narration and the way they are represented suggest that their treatment by the film is anything less than impartial?
- How are the battle scenes shot? From whose perspective do we witness and perceive the conflict and what difference does this make to our overall understanding of the history?
- Do you think history can ever be truthfully 'reconstructed' by drama? What elements might a film-maker introduce in the drama to make it appear less biased?
- Do you think *Culloden* stands the test of time? Giving reasons for your answer, do you think it would cause as much controversy today as it did when it was first shown?

RECOMMENDED READING

Arrowsmith, SMJ (1981), 'Peter Watkins' in George Brandt (ed.), *British Television Drama*, Cambridge: Cambridge University Press, 217–30.
Gomez, Joseph A (1979), *Peter Watkins*, Boston: Twayne.
Lajtha, Terry (1981), 'Brechtian Devices in Non-Brechtian Cinema: *Culloden*', *Literature/Film Quarterly*, Vol. 9, No. 1, 9–14.

Chapter Fifteen
Dallas

Ros Jennings

Production Details

(CBS, 1978–91)

Creator: David Jacobs
Producer: Leonard Katzman
Executive Producer: Philip Caprice
Directors include: Larry Hagman, Patrick Duffy, Leonard Katzman, Corey Alen,
Linda Gray
Writers include: David Jacobs, DC Fontana, Richard Fontana
Theme music: Jerrold Imel

Cast includes:

John Ross (JR) Ewing (Larry Hagman)
Miss Ellie (Barbara Bel Geddes/Donna Reed)
John Ross (Jock) Ewing (Jim Davis)
Bobby Ewing (Patrick Duffy)
Pamela Barnes Ewing (Victoria Principal)
Lucy Ewing Cooper (Charlene Tilton)
Sue Ellen Ewing (Linda Gray)
Cliff Barnes (Ken Kercheval)

When the dramatic (or more accurately, melodramatic) serial *Dallas* appeared in America in the late 1970s, it became the first successful night-time American soap opera since *Peyton Place* (ABC, 1964–9). Originally conceived as a limited series with a run of five programmes, *Dallas* eventually ran to 356 episodes, which were aired once a week during its main run over a period, in total, of 13 years. However, *Dallas* was not just a domestic success but became an international phenomenon. It was popular in over 90 countries and, to date, has inspired more academic reception/qualitative studies internationally (e.g. Katz and Liebes, 1986 [Israel]; Ang, 1985 [Holland]) than perhaps any other single television programme. The series centred on the lives of the Ewing family, wealthy Texan oil barons who lived at the luxurious Southfork Ranch, Braddock County, near Dallas, Texas. All around the world, viewers tuned in avidly to a saga of power, rivalry, lust and greed. This formula was further complimented with the additional narrative layer consisting of a long-running feud between the Ewing and the Barnes families. This vendetta was dramatised in such a way as to be on a par with Shakespeare's Capulets and Montagues, leading to the development of a new and dynamic serial form that captured the global imagination. At its peak, 'the moment of *Dallas*' (Ang, 1985, 1) was hard to ignore.

Dallas played with the generic conventions of the soap opera in such a way as to bring about a change in prime-time conceptions about narrative. As Robert Thompson suggests, one of the most important effects of *Dallas* was that: 'It gave memory to an entire medium. Soon many dramatic shows – even those that weren't exactly soaps – began employing ongoing storylines' (1996, 34). In *Dallas* the ongoing events were established in relation to a substantial fictional heritage related to a set of events that took place some 40 years earlier. These events provided a framing mechanism for all subsequent narratives in the series. Thus, all narratives in *Dallas* stemmed from the entanglements and rivalries initiated by two partners in the wildcat oil-prospecting business, the young Jock Ewing and the young Digger Barnes. It subsequently unfolds during the series that four decades before the drama is set, Jock not only took most of the profits from their venture, but also stole Barnes' true love, Ellie Southworth, heir to Southfork Ranch. The Ewing/Barnes rivalry continued to simmer throughout the narrative of the series with the marriage of one of Jock's sons, Bobby, to Digger's daughter, Pamela, used as an important plot device to weave together a legacy of injustices and misunderstandings between the two families into a melodrama on a grand scale. In *Dallas*, family values and loyalties are constantly appealed to but ultimately always undermined.

Unusually for a melodrama self-consciously moulded around soap-opera conventions, *Dallas* revolved around the ties of patriarchy rather than the more usual matriarchal values so dominant in the soap genre (see **Coronation Street** [Granada, 1960–]). This new departure contributed forcefully to its unprecedented success in peak viewing slots, extending its appeal beyond that of the traditional female audience. Although its focus was still on the family, *Dallas* was much more preoccupied with the story of fathers and sons, the ownership of land and of oil businesses, than the usual female-centred relationships of kith and kin characteristic of the soap genre. Indeed, the father/son dynamic provided a deep-rooted motif in *Dallas*'s complex structure. At the hub of the series was JR Ewing, the eldest of Jock's legitimate sons and the fulcrum around which all plot and storylines were developed. Jock's two other legitimate sons (Gary and Bobby), along with his illegitimate son (Ray Krebbs), functioned as foils to (and targets of) JR's insecurities and scheming. They also acted as witnesses to his Oedipal struggles for power in relation to his father. In addition to his three brothers, JR's main adversary in both love and business was Digger Barnes' son Cliff, continuing the father/son motif by neatly extending the rivalries of their fathers to another generation.

In addition to their struggles for power and ownership in the spheres of power and commerce, the men in *Dallas* also struggled to control their women. This is quite clearly illustrated in the construction of one of the central partnerships in the drama, the marriage between JR Ewing and Sue Ellen, where their whole relationship is conducted on a 'war footing' (Ang, 1985, 7). *Dallas* certainly included a bevy of feisty women but, with the notable exception of Miss Ellie (the Southfork matriarch) and Pamela Barnes-Ewing, they were constructed for the most part as murderers, drunkards and scheming sluts. The women of *Dallas* did, however, provide points of glamorous connection for their female audiences at a time dominated by company downsizing, rising unemployment and a marked cultural turn towards individualism in both Reagan's America and Thatcher's Britain.

Dallas had a large core cast in a style characteristic of soaps, but personal relations were particularly complicated because of the quick circulation of secondary characters and the multiple plots that were employed. The multi-layered complexity of *Dallas* was also mirrored in the series' formal strategies of representation (for instance, in the tactic of repeatedly framing JR within a shot with his father's portrait placed behind him in such a way that it looked as if Jock were constantly looking over his shoulder). *Dallas* adapted soap-opera form in such a way as to heighten its melodramatic effect. Working within the confines of a limited set of locations and a typical format of 20 to 30 scenes, *Dallas* pushed the envelope in terms of visual and narrative excess. The *mise-en-scène* of *Dallas* was so lavish and dense that it stood out from other prime-time programmes of the time and provided a style and standard for later programmes such as *Dynasty* (ABC, 1981–9) to take further. Despite the privileging of male characters and concerns, *Dallas* was dominated by conversation and emotional confrontations rather than action (as befits a reworking of soap-opera format). As Jane Feuer has argued, 'The hyperintensity of each confrontation [was] accentuated by a use of underscoring not found in any other TV genre and by conventions of exchanged glances, shot duration, and the zoom lenses' (1995, 120). The iconography of fast cars, cowboy hats and ranch activities did give a strong nod towards the more traditionally masculine elements than was usual in a soap-based series but, as Hjorth's research reveals, the key to *Dallas*'s success was in the fact that 'it so directly appeal[ed] to the ambivalent (and unconscious) emotional and psychic conflicts in viewers, and because it provid[ed] an aesthetic bombardment of the senses' (Hjorth cited in Gripsrud, 1995, 103).

Added to this, Ien Ang has argued in her ground-breaking study that *Dallas* still provided its audience with a form of 'emotional realism' that transcended its apparently stylistic surface, both articulating and granting its viewers insight into difficult personal problems such as divorce, alcoholism and domestic abuse (Ang, 1985). As Anna McCarthy has recently put it, 'viewers derived a sense of realism from the show's apparently true-to-life depiction of psychological situations' which did not 'require verisimilitude on the level of plot, character or setting' (2001, 50).

Dallas certainly had a huge influence on both contemporary and current television. In the late 1970s/early 1980s it not only sparked a spin-off series, *Knots Landing* (CBS, 1979–93) (focusing on Gary Ewing), it also provided the inspiration for a flurry of other family melodramas focused on the rich and the powerful (e.g. *Falconcrest* [CBS, 1981–90], *Dynasty* [ABC, 1981–9] and *The Colbys* [ABC, 1985–7]). As Stuart Hall has argued, '[a]t a certain moment the programme achieved the kind of popularity other than merely in terms of numbers of viewers. It had repercussions on the whole culture, the involvement of the viewers became of a different order' (Hall cited in Ang, 1985, 5). This was especially true of the 'Who shot JR?' storyline, which made a huge popular cultural intervention. With such a distasteful character (JR Ewing was played by Larry Hagman, who had a ball playing against the character type that he had established in his previous most successful role in *I Dream of Jeannie* [NBC, 1965–9]) and with such a large cast of possible suspects, 'Who shot JR?' became a hot topic of public conversation, accompanied by 'a national craze, with the proverbial empty streets and a dramatic drop in water consumption' (Ang, 1985, 1), until the mystery was solved.

The success of *Dallas* clearly spurred its writers and producers to take self-conscious risks with this prime-time vehicle; for instance, throughout its existence, *Dallas* was an artful exponent of the end-of-season cliffhanger. The series was also particularly audacious in its use of plot devices, its most daring being a ruse to cover for the absence of actor Patrick Duffy while he underwent protracted contract negotiations. During the negotiations, Duffy's character Bobby was killed off, only to emerge from the shower at the end of the season (once Duffy's contract had been secured) to reveal that the narrative for the entire season had been a dream. Eventually, however, the audience for the programme started to dwindle, partly due to the over-exploitation of such plot devices. The final episode, as might be expected, ended on a cliffhanger. By means of a reworking of Frank Capra's film *It's a Wonderful Life* (1946), JR is taken through a review of his life, but rather than being seen to turn the corner from his despair about his shameful life he pulls out a gun, only for the camera to cut to a shot of his brother Bobby just as he hears the sound of a shot.

QUESTIONS TO CONSIDER

- What sort of genre do you think *Dallas* is? Can you think of ways in which it might transcend the traditional boundaries of soap opera?
- How are women portrayed in *Dallas*? What difference do you think foregrounding the men in the story made to the reception and image of the programme as a whole?
- Do you think *Dallas* ever offered anything more than prime-time melodrama? How does the 'emotional realism' (Ang, 1985) of the show manage (if at all) to transcend its stylistic surface?
- How important do you think the style of *Dallas* was to its success? Can you see other shows that have been inspired by its lavish *mise-en-scène*?
- How did *Dallas* change prime-time conceptions about ongoing storylines? Do you think the influence of its narrative structure is still detectable today?

RECOMMENDED READING

Ang, Ien (1985), *Watching 'Dallas': Soap Opera and the Melodramatic Imagination*, London: Routledge.

Feuer, Jane (1995), *Seeing Through the Eighties: Television and Reaganism*, London: British Film Institute.

Swanson, Gillian (1981), '*Dallas*, part 1', *Framework*, No. 14, spring, 62.

Chapter Sixteen

Doctor Who

Matt Hills

Production Details

(BBC, 1963–89 and BBC Worldwide/Universal Television co-production, 1996)

Creator: Sydney Newman
First producer: Verity Lambert
Longest-serving producer: John Nathan-Turner
Executive producer of 1996 TV movie: Philip David Segal
Other producers have included: Philip Hinchcliffe, Barry Letts, Graham Williams
Writers working on the series have included: Douglas Adams, Christopher
Bidmead, Chris Boucher, Terrance Dicks, Stephen Gallagher, Robert Holmes,
Barry Letts, Terry Nation, Dennis Spooner
Directors have included: Christopher Barry, Douglas Camfield, Chris Clough,
Graeme Harper, Matthew Robinson

The Doctors:

William Hartnell (1963–6)
Patrick Troughton (1966–9)
Jon Pertwee (1969–74)
Tom Baker (1974–81)
Peter Davison (1982–4)
Colin Baker (1984–6)
Sylvester McCoy (1987–92)
Paul McGann (1996)

Doctor Who has frequently been promoted, interpreted and valued by fans and academics through its 'longest-running TV SF series' tag (Brosnan and Nicholls, 1979, 180;
Lewis and Stempel, 1993, 18; and Hockley, 2001, 28). If *Doctor Who* is a key TV text, then
in large part this status is due to the show's durability and reinvention across 26 years
and 26 seasons on BBC TV, its appearance as two 1960s movies and its continued vitality
in non-televised forms (BBC novels and licensed audio adventures) fully forty years
after its inception. The programme has had its own Appreciation Society (DWAS) since
1976 (see http://dwas.drwho.org/) and has sustained a commercially published

75

magazine, now known simply as *Doctor Who Magazine*, since 1979. Part of the show's ability to run for such a long time stems from its narrative explanation for changing lead actors: the Doctor, as a Time Lord, could regenerate his bodily appearance. This gave a diegetic plausibility to the show's periodic recasting of the lead role (see production details) and became a vital part of the show's mythology.

Produced by the BBC, *Doctor Who* was initially linked in 1963 to the ethos of public service broadcasting; as a science-fiction programme aimed at children and adults (hence its early Saturday evening scheduling), it was intended to entertain and educate, relying on historical settings for its time-travel narratives rather than featuring 'bug-eyed monsters'. *Doctor Who*'s connection with British public service ideals, its eccentric lead character and its sometimes less-than-glossy production values have all caused it to be thought of as a very British programme. With so many discursive links made between the programme's format and 'Britishness', it is perhaps unsurprising that when the show was moved from its Saturday evening time-slot, this became the subject of a 1982 editorial in the UK broadsheet newspaper *The Guardian* (quoted in Tulloch and Alvarado, 1983, 14):

> *All those who have grown up or grown old with* Doctor Who *(for some who watched it in the early days … are now men of destiny and captains of what industry this country still has left) know it to be as essential a part of a winter Saturday as coming in cold from heath, forest, or football, warm crumpets … before the fire …*

After its cancellation in 1989 as a result of falling ratings, a lack of sympathy for the show within the BBC and an institutional shift away from in-house production (*Doctor Who*'s producer, John Nathan-Turner, was the last BBC staff producer at the time of the show's cancellation), the programme refused to die. It was eventually brought back as a US/UK co-production, a move that had to be carefully managed so that the show's 'British' values were not threatened or undermined. The resultant 1996 TV movie features a scene in which the Doctor confronts a US policeman and moves as if he's about to draw a gun. To dissuade the cop from reacting and shooting first, the Doctor's American companion, Grace Holloway, shouts: 'No! He's, um …, he's British'. 'Yes, I suppose I am!' replies the Doctor, extracting a bag of jelly babies from his capacious pockets rather than a gun. Of course, diegetically speaking, the Doctor is nothing of the sort; he's a Time Lord from the planet of Gallifrey. However, the TV movie's reference to the Doctor's 'Britishness' is a textual attempt to acknowledge how the character has become wedded to imagined notions of British cultural identity, as well as being an in-joke for fans of the show. Rather symbolically, the BBC's seventh Doctor was killed in a hail of gangland bullets upon stepping out of the TARDIS, a victim of US gun culture.

The 1996 TV movie threatened to turn the eighth Doctor into a more 'American-style' SF hero, portraying him as a dashing, romantic figure who even kisses his female companion. It also boasted production values undreamt of in the show's BBC years, including sumptuous costumes and a vast, Jules Verne-style TARDIS interior (TARDIS stands for 'Time and Relative Dimensions in Space' – it is the Doctor's time-travel machine which resembles a British 'Police Box' on the outside). The TV movie also made intertextual references to **Star Trek** (NBC, 1966–9) (the TARDIS had a 'cloaking device' rather than the original BBC version's Chameleon Circuit) and to **The X-Files** (Fox, 1993–2002).

Doctor Who's duration means that the show can be interpreted in relation to changes in cultural context and in the media industry. Tulloch and Alvarado (1983) consider different institutional and narrative phases of the programme. They separate out the programme's early days, where the Doctor as played by William Hartnell was a mysterious anti-hero; the shift of lead actor to Patrick Troughton that established the show's ability to reinvent itself; the era of the third Doctor, Jon Pertwee, who was an establishment figure and whose stories were mainly Earth-bound; the send-up and parody of the Tom Baker years; and the move towards using many guest stars and an emphasis on press and publicity that accompanied Peter Davison's tenure within the more showbusiness-oriented production style of John Nathan-Turner. To these we could add the phase of Colin Baker's sixth Doctor, which was an attempt to revitalise the show's narrative possibilities by making the Doctor more alien and less sympathetic. And finally, the seventh Doctor, Sylvester McCoy, spearheaded another attempt to re-inject mystery into the show's format, as hints began to emerge that the Doctor was more than a Time Lord. Just as the programme was successfully reinventing its main character once more, shifting towards a darker representation of the Doctor as a manipulative anti-hero, it was cancelled.

Rather than analysing narrative and production changes, Nicholas J Cull interprets the stories of *Doctor Who* as related to their UK cultural contexts, 1963–89. Analysing *Doctor Who* as a 'text of its time' (2001, 103), Cull notes that in the area of gender representations the programme shifted from showing female companions as 'screamers' to depicting them as the Doctor's equals, even if this did pose narrative problems (who do you explain plot details to?) and was, perhaps, never entirely realised. Cull argues that the programme also took on an increasingly camp tone across the 1980s, using this camp quality to disguise but articulate challenges to the politics of the day. He suggests that Margaret Thatcher was satirised in the character of Helen A in 'The Happiness Patrol' (1988), a story in which the inhabitants of Terra Alpha were forced to be happy at all times, even upon pain of death.

Interestingly, JK Muir's American interpretation of this same *Doctor Who* story makes no mention of Thatcherism and instead reads its social commentary as being about 'the ultimate extension of the political correctness doctrine that the US sees today' (Muir, 1999, 380). This should caution us about claiming that national contexts are simply reflected 'in' key TV texts, given that audiences and critics placed in different national contexts (Cull in the UK and Muir in the US) may interpret the same *Doctor Who* story very differently as a result of their own social contexts of reading. Still, as Cull notes, whether satirising Thatcher or mocking political correctness, *Doctor Who* 'frequently included philosophically subversive ideas' (2001, 105).

But it is not only academics who have discussed *Doctor Who*'s sophistication. The show's loyal fans – who have themselves been discussed in a range of academic material (Jenkins, 1992; Tulloch, 2000; McKee, 2001 and forthcoming) – haven't only appeared as an object of academic study; they have also used media and cultural theory to explain their favourite show (Hills, 2002, 18–19). An excellent example of this is an article written by fan author Lance Parkin, exploring whether *Doctor Who* is an example of 'postmodern' TV (its first ever episode was delayed seventeen minutes due to the assassination of President Kennedy, a moment, according to some post-modern critics, when all 'certainties' were lost). Parkin's argument builds around the fact that virtually every *Doctor Who* story routinely pastiches a range of source material, while wearing 'its … source … on its sleeve' (2002, 12). Indeed, it has knowingly reworked *Frankenstein*, various myths, Sherlock Holmes, James Bond, Escher prints, Hammer horror, pulp science fiction, *Dune* (Lynch, 1984), *Metropolis* (Lang, 1926), Agatha Christie and HG Wells' *The Time Machine*, among many others. And from season 18 onwards, under John Nathan-Turner, the show showed a self-awareness of its fandom, offering stories that required detailed fan knowledge, promoting entire seasons of old foes and monsters (season 20 in 1983) and including a self-referential depiction of the show's fans in the figure of the character Whizzkid in 'The Greatest Show in the Galaxy' (1988–9).

Especially under the producership of Graham Williams, and with Douglas Adams writing or script-editing, the programme also parodied its own production limitations. In 'Destiny of the Daleks' (1979), the Doctor taunts his arch-enemies the Daleks with the line, 'If you're supposed to be the superior race of the universe, why don't you try climbing after us?' This refers to the joke that all you have to do to escape from a Dalek is climb some stairs. Eventually the programme solved this 'problem' through improved special effects, showing an on-screen Dalek floating up a flight of stairs in 'Remembrance of the Daleks' (1988).

Doctor Who's claim, then, to being a key TV text lies in its flexible format – allowing for reinvention and recasting over 26 years – its status as a British TV 'institution' worthy of broadsheet editorials, its textual sophistication (if not 'postmodernism') and its cultural endurance. The importance of the programme's 'longest-running' status as a badge of its cultural value for its fans, as well as the programme's importance as a marker of 'Britishness', have both recently been attested to in a letter in *Doctor Who Magazine* (Bates, 2002, 11):

> As of four episodes into Season 3 of Enterprise, Star Trek *will be equal with* Who *for longest-running science fiction series – an episode later, and the Trekkies will be able to lord it over us poor Whovians! We will have to change* Doctor Who *'s appellation to 'longest-running British science fiction TV series'… or maybe 'longest-running science fiction TV, audio and book series'. …Hundreds of web pages will need to be updated! Books will have to be rewritten! The very fate of British television hangs in the balance!*

QUESTIONS TO CONSIDER

- Why has *Doctor Who* been thought of as quintessential British TV science fiction?
- What aspects of *Doctor Who*'s format could have led to its devoted fan following?
- How would you explain the long-running success of *Doctor Who*? Consider contextual, media-institutional and textual factors.
- Can *Doctor Who* be thought of as 'postmodern TV' given its playful pastiches of other source material?
- Was *Doctor Who* a 'text of its time', and if so, how did it reflect British politics, culture and the ethos of public service broadcasting?
- How would you reinvent *Doctor Who* for a new audience today? Consider issues of target marketing, scheduling, format, casting, 'postmodern TV', 'Britishness', etc.

RECOMMENDED READING

Cull, Nicholas J (2001), 'Bigger on the inside...: *Doctor Who* as British cultural history' in Graham Roberts and Philip M Taylor (eds.), *The Historian, Television and Television History*, Luton: University of Luton Press, 95–111.

Tulloch, John and Alvarado, Manuel (1983), *Doctor Who: The Unfolding Text*, London: Macmillan.

Tulloch, John and Jenkins, Henry (1995), *Science Fiction Audiences: Watching Doctor Who and Star Trek*, London and New York: Routledge.

Chapter Seventeen

ER

Jason Jacobs

Production Details

(NBC, 1994–)

Production company: Constant-C/ Amblin Television/Warner Brothers Television
Executive producers: Michael Crichton, John Wells, Jack Orman
Producers: Christopher Chulack, Lydia Woodward, Carol Flint
Directors include: Mimi Leder, Thomas Schlamme, Jonathon Kaplan, Rod Holcomb, Donna Deitch, Lesli Linka Glatter, Christopher Chulack
Writers include: Lance A Gentile, Jack Orman, R Scott Gemill, Carol Flint, John Wells, Lydia Woodward, Paul Manning

Cast includes (with seasons they were in):

Dr Mark Greene (Anthony Edwards) [1–8]
Dr John Carter (Noah Wyle) [1–]
Dr Kerry Weaver (Laura Innes) [3–]
Dr Elizabeth Corday (Alex Kingston) [4–]
Dr Luka Kovac (Goran Visnjic) [6–]
Dr Doug Ross (George Clooney) [1–5]
Nurse Carol Hathaway (Julianna Margulies) [1–6]
Dr Peter Benton (Eriq La Salle) [1–8]
Dr Susan Lewis (Sherry Stringfield) [1–3, 8–]
Jeanie Boulet (Gloria Reuben) [2–6]
Abby Lockhart (Maura Tierney) [6–]

ER is the most popular medical drama of all time, consistently at or near the top of the US ratings; it has received numerous Emmy awards (including best drama); and it is widely syndicated in North America, Asia, Europe and the Pacific. The show explores the lives of a set of doctors and nurses who work in the Emergency Room (or ER) of the County General hospital in Chicago. In particular, its depiction of high-speed emergency care, combined with its sensitive handling of character development, was widely regarded as both innovative and realistic. Its title sequence alone was an astonishing aural and visual achievement that blends textures and layers of medical technology with images of the characters, as well as promoting the show's signature style and speed. Made for Warner Television by subsidiary production companies and then sold (for a reported $13 million per episode) to NBC, *ER* premiered in 1994 on the same night as *Chicago Hope* (CBS, 1994–2000), but it was the former that attracted most of the audience and most of the critical acclaim.

ER inherited many of the generic features of 1970s medical shows such as *Marcus Welby, MD* (ABC, 1969–76) and *Medical Centre* (CBS, 1971), which departed from *Dr Kildare*'s (NBC, 1961–6) figuring of reassuring paternal relationships between doctors and paid attention to disagreement and conflict (as well as tackling more taboo topics such as venereal disease and abortion). *ER* also adopted some of the features of *M*A*S*H* (CBS, 1972–83), most obviously its sense of the absurd, but also its figuring of chaotic treatment taking place in a war zone; *ER*'s inner-city setting afforded many opportunities for injuries caused by violent means. Indeed, the multiple-storyline structure of a pioneering programme like **Hill Street Blues** (ABC, 1981–7) is clearly discernible in its frequently chaotic, fragmented and convoluted narrative complexity. In addition the show adopted *St. Elsewhere*'s (NBC, 1982–7) interest in the existential crises of its doctors and in the burden of providing healthcare successfully and honestly. However, *ER* was also a significant departure from these shows. Its primary generic innovation was to blend scenes of emergency care with character development and set them at a very fast pace. The spectacles of Hollywood action cinema were transposed to interior settings focused around saving the ruined body, typically rendered with fast cutting, snaking camera movements and the technobabble of medical instructions.

Many of these innovative features were to be found in the original script for the show. Created by Michael Crichton (who originally trained as a doctor), *ER* was initially intended it to be a feature based on his 1974 script, but Hollywood did not pick it up, apparently baffled by its fragmented structure and unresolved storylines (Jacobs, 2003, 22). However, nearly twenty years later Crichton was working with Steven Spielberg on the film adaptation of Jurassic Park (1993). When Spielberg expressed an interest in the script it was made as a TV pilot, using Crichton's Constant-C production company and Spielberg's Amblin Television. It also recruited quality television veterans, notably John Wells, who had been executive producer on the critically acclaimed *China Beach* (ABC, 1988–91) and later *The West Wing* (NBC, 1999–). Once the script was adapted as a pilot and series format, shooting proceeded on location in East Los Angeles. The director of the pilot, Rod Holcomb, described the script as depicting 'controlled panic'. According to Crichton (cited by Jacobs, 2003, 22):

> *I wanted to write something that was based in reality... Something that would have a fast pace and treat medicine in a realistic way. The screenplay was very unusual. It was very focused on the doctors, not the patients – the patients came and went. People yelled paragraphs of drug dosages at each other. It was very technical, almost a quasi-documentary. But what interested me was breaking standard dramatic structure. I understood that's what the screenplay did, but I always felt like it was compulsively watchable.*

The pilot and the first season certainly did lay claim to realism and they were also very stylised. Most obvious was the speedy camera movement and the rapid alternation of scenes, with narrative and character development constantly disturbed by incoming patients. According to John Caldwell, 'An unheard of 75% of the scenes in *ER* ... were shot using the Steadicam. Many of these were included in the spectacular and complicated ... sequences that defined the show, complicated flowing action shots in one take with multiple moves and no cutaways' (1997, 1580–1).

This is not simply a style for style's sake: such long takes enable a smooth blending of dialogue-based scenes with action-oriented ones and have specific dramatic impact. For example, in the first episode of the first season ('Day One'), we see Dr Susan Lewis treating an infant who has stopped breathing. The camera circles the treatment bed and, as it does so, the image achieves an evolving variation in what it shows. No one character is favoured in this shot, so it has the effect of showing a group activity in action with the circling movement underlining a feeling of tense urgency. It is also an efficient way to reveal an economy of looks between the medical staff and the parents – looks that are variously concerned, diagnostic, compassionate and anxious. In terms of production these mobile scenes require a considerable amount of time (sometimes up to two hours) to construct. But camera mobility does not necessarily overrule editing as a stylistic choice: later in the sequence we return to a process of decoupage – shots of the worried parents; a close shot of Lewis looking into the throat of the child with a light; and a broader shot of her to contextualise that look in relation to her hands (using tweezers to remove the blockage – an ear ring – from the baby's airway).

The characters' commitment to one another is evident in the various relationships the doctors and nurses share. *ER* is set in a teaching hospital, and as viewers we see the rigours of medical training enacted in teaching–learning relationships between the central characters. In the early seasons this relationship was exemplified by the training of John Carter by *ER* surgeon Peter Benton, but as with many of the relationships we see in the show, this was often characterised by conflict, suspicion and evident hardship for Carter. The focus is not only on junior doctors, but more senior figures such as Susan Lewis and Mark Greene and their conflicts with immediate superiors. The sense of working in a war zone (County General serves an inner-city area where many of the patients are products – or perpetrators – of crime, domestic abuse, drug use, etc.), with beleaguered doctors treating waves of patients, is compounded by internal conflicts, particularly those between hospital management and the doctors on the ground (Schatz, 1997, 1873).

Another set of relationships explored in the show are those between patients and their healers. Commonly, a patient is brought in not only with an injury or disease but also moral or domestic problems that have become acute as well. This is a device that promotes character development, since it often functions as a stimulus for doctors who have parallel problems to reflect on themselves, and in this sense patients act as 'reflectors' for those who treat them. For example, in 'Of Past Regret and Future Fear' a chemical burn victim is brought into the *ER*. At first sight his condition seems superficial. However, he has come into contact with deadly poison and is informed that he will die in less than a day. As the nurse, Carol Hathaway, sits at his side, he reveals he has a wife and daughter who he is separated from and has not seen in six years. This makes Carol think about her own life and she reveals to him – and us – that her father killed himself when she was a child. *ER* frequently uses reflectors of this sort, where the main characters are often provoked into introspection or a change of mind by the actions, thoughts and feelings of their patients.

Similarly, romantic relationships in the show are conducted always in tension with the demands of the job, and this frequently causes their breakdown. Benton's affair with Jeanie Boulet disintegrates when she refuses to leave her husband, causing considerable acrimony between them when they are required to treat patients. Doug Ross and Carol's relationship is only really resolved when the two characters leave the series. Kerry Weaver, the authoritarian chief resident, is involved in a lesbian relationship that seems equally bereft of joy. Most of all, Mark Greene is shown to suffer from a series of relationships that are doomed to collapse. The first season details the breakdown of his marriage, and subsequently he is involved in a near-miss relationship with Susan Lewis (who leaves the show, only to return in the later seasons) and a number of disastrous affairs, until eventually he marries the English *ER* surgeon, Elizabeth Corday. However, this marriage also falls apart, with their reconciliation taking place only shortly before Greene's death.

These rather sad plot developments and dramas underline the show's overall 'apocalyptic' feel, its robust sense of impending failure and its disillusionment with the ability of medical care to make any difference. As the seasons developed there was an increasing interest in ethical and moral issues (in fact, episodes of *ER* are used in medical ethics training courses), particularly around the doctors' responsibilities in relation to DNR (Do Not Resuscitate) patients and other issues that imply 'playing God'.

As the show went into its seventh season there were indications that its direction and dramatic potency were becoming hostages to dramatic opportunism. Set-piece emergencies – quarantines in the *ER*, massive car accidents, the murder of doctors, etc. – and a more explicit depiction of injury and wounds suggested a desperate attempt to regain the sense of shock and innovation that characterised the earlier seasons. By season nine most of the original cast had left the show, leaving John Carter to take up the mantel left by Mark Greene, who died from brain cancer. Nevertheless there are still outstanding moments: Wyle's superb performances provide the dramatic centre of many of the episodes, and the sensitive delineation of Carter's rocky and uncertain romantic relationship with Abby Lockhart demonstrates that *ER* can still achieve excellence in its drama.

QUESTIONS TO CONSIDER

- Assess how important the 'quasi-documentary' style of *ER* is to its overall sense of realism.
- Examine the relationship between the camerawork and the setting in the show. How is the sense of urgency in the emergency room generated by the show's overall style?
- Examine to what extent *ER* is indebted to earlier instances of the hospital drama genre. In what ways does it differ from other television portrayals of hospital life?
- How do you think the emotional relationships in *ER* both reflect and are affected by the pressures of the job?
- To what extent is the spectacle of injury and medical intervention related to the narrative patterns in the show?

RECOMMENDED READING

Bailey, Steve (2001), '"Professional Television": Three (Super) Texts and a (Super) Genre', *The Velvet Light Trap*, No. 47.

Jacobs, Jason (2003), *Body Trauma TV: The New Hospital Dramas*, London: British Film Institute.

San Martin, Nancy (2003), 'Must See TV: Programming Identity on NBC Thursdays' in Mark Jancovich and James Lyons (eds.), *Quality Popular Television: Cult TV, Industry and Fans*, London: British Film Institute.

Chapter Eighteen

The FIFA World Cup

Rod Brookes

Production Details

(Various national broadcasters)

Organisers: The Federation of International Football Associations, est. 1904

The football (or soccer) World Cup's organisers FIFA claimed that an unprecedented 1.1 billion people watched the 2002 final between Brazil and Germany. This may be a lower figure than that claimed for **The Olympic Games**, but as a television event the FIFA World Cup (which, like the Olympics, takes place every four years) can be said to be equally significant as an international television phenomenon. Television channels certainly pay a great deal of money to secure the rights to broadcast the tournament. In Britain, for example, the BBC and ITV made a successful joint £160m bid for the rights to the 2002 and 2006 FIFA World Cups. Although broadcasters would probably have to bid considerably more to win the rights if national 'listed events' restrictions hadn't precluded pay-TV broadcasters like Sky from bidding, this is still a significant investment and the need to recoup it through attracting large audiences is essential. Although in 2002 the BBC and ITV decided between them which matches were to be shown by which broadcaster (despite going 'head-to-head' on the prestige matches involving England and the final itself), they both competed with each other to build audiences generally. As such, both broadcasters were prepared to invest heavily in salaries for their star presenters and in assembling an attractive team of pundits, as well as taking great care with opening sequences and set design.

Watching the FIFA World Cup is certainly a collective experience, bringing together the 'imagined community' of the nation – reflected in the increasing proportion of the television audience worldwide watching the 2002 tournament on public screens in places such as bars, cafés and even places of work like offices. As such, national broadcasters are clearly keen to obtain the rights for the tournament, either as a means of fulfilling their public service broadcasting obligations (in its role as a 'forger of national identity' [Whannel, 1992, 20]) or as a means of selling huge audiences to advertisers. Pay-TV broadcasters would love to secure the FIFA World Cup rights as a means of selling subscription television, but presently are discouraged by FIFA's own preferences and those of national governments to protect the tournament on a free-to-air basis. Multinational corporations are also keen to exploit this huge global popularity through sponsorship – a keenness that FIFA has been able to exploit through its marketing programme. National governments certainly recognise the value of the tournament in terms of nation-building internally and in terms of projecting a vision of national identity externally.

Hence the FIFA World Cup is hugely significant as a television event for audiences, broadcasters, advertisers/sponsors and national governments. But how does it work as a text? As television, the event is similar to the Olympics but different from most of the other entries in this book in a number of aspects. Firstly, it is impossible to identify a single broadcasting organisation as responsible for the production of the event. Instead the host nation's national broadcaster is responsible for producing a 'clean feed' which national broadcasters all over the world use as the basis for their own presentation, featuring their own nationally recognisable anchors, panellists, commentators, etc., subject to the level of resources available. Even the style of 'clean feed' is predictable, following the type of coverage viewers have come to expect for most sporting events. A set of conventions has emerged during the historical development of the television presentation of field sports events which broadly follow the rules of the 180 degree system. Cameras tend to be positioned on one side of an imaginary line running from one end of the playing area to the other. While there have been significant presentational changes over the years – faster editing, the use of a more adventurous range of camera positions, including aerial ones, for example – this basic principle still holds (Brookes, 2001, 87).

However, unlike **The Olympic Games**, where visuals and natural sound from the universal feed and the national broadcaster's own cameras are seamlessly edited together, in coverage of the FIFA World Cup the distinction between the two is clearer. National broadcasters may also set up a studio and camera crew to provide supplementary footage before, at half-time and after the game, but the host nation's feed will provide the basis for all the action during the game itself, customised by national broadcasters only by commentators and summarisers. The centrality of the universal feed to worldwide coverage of the tournament therefore tends to lead to conservatism in terms of technological innovation. The reason for this conservatism is that an internationally recognisable form of televisual presentation has had to be developed that client broadcasters and audiences all over the world find equally acceptable. However, while there is now international agreement about the type of 'clean feed' available to broadcasters, this was not always the case. In the 1978 FIFA World Cup in Argentina, representatives from the European Broadcasting Union (EBU) were not happy with the coverage of the event and decided to intervene. As Bill Ward, the head of EBU's 1978 World Cup operations group, put it (Whannel, 1992, 166):

> We didn't want to upset the hosts, but the standard of coverage was just not up to European expectations. So we took extracts from British and European coverage, held seminars for the Argentine cameramen, directors and producers, and pointed out all the faults in our own work. On this basis they accepted the system we adopt.

Yet if World Cup matches themselves have come to be presented using a set of universally accepted televisual conventions, this has not impeded national broadcasters from customising this coverage to encourage identification with the nation. Commentary is one obvious means, often through the unthinking stereotyping of the styles of play or temperament of the players of other nations or regions of the world. But it is the assumptions built into the overall presentation which is most important in structuring sports events in terms of national identity. Tending to ignore or play down issues of national fragmentation and multiculturalism, the BBC has generally tended to portray the 'English' nation as completely united in its obsession with football, constructing the sport as a straightforward and unproblematic expression of patriotism. For example, for England's game against Argentina in 2002 (broadcast in the early afternoon in the UK when many people would have taken extended lunch hours from work), cameras were set up to record the various reactions of the fans watching the match on public screens in Newcastle and Manchester city centres, Epsom racecourse and the Royal Cornwall show. Whereas suggestions of partisanship may be frowned upon in news coverage or documentaries, national allegiances (including racial/national stereotypes) are frequently employed and encouraged in this type of international sport coverage. As Garry Whannel puts it (1992, 29):

> Football [soccer] commentaries have several identifiable modes of address: in club matches, neutrality prevails; in England internationals against foreign sides, partisanship prevails; in England playing Wales, Scotland or Northern Ireland, there is an uneasy combination of the two; and in Scotland internationals against foreign teams, the level of surrogate partisanship – committed yet distanced – often depends on how well Scotland is doing.

It has also become a convention of major international sports events coverage that the television presentation of broadcasts also evokes a sense of the 'national character' of the host nations. In the 2002 World Cup finals (jointly hosted by Japan and Korea) both the BBC and ITV represented the hosts of the tournament in terms of the 'exotic' or 'oriental'. ITV drew on a predictable stock of *traditional* images of Japan – geishas, the rising sun, a Kodo drummer – and for the music used an adapted version of 'Un bel di vedrema' from Puccini's opera *Madame Butterfly*. By contrast, the BBC adopted a more contemporary or 'techno-orientalist' (Morley and Robins, 1995) approach to the host nations. A frequently aired extended animated trailer depicted the likely stars of the tournament and the BBC's own presenters and pundits in a style that was half *Manga* comic, half video game. While the opening sequences featured bullet trains and neon lights, the set design also alluded to a vague sense of 'Japaneseness' through the use of calligraphy (Kawakami, 2002).

However, what was missing from both the BBC's and ITV's trailers and opening sequences were any really distinctive references to Korea – except the occasional use of the flag. The Korean Embassy in London even wrote to ITV asking them to replace 'Un bel di vedrema' with a more neutral piece on the basis that the opera was set in Japan, although arguably *Madame Butterfly* has much more to do with the late nineteenth-century European fascination with Japonism than anything to do with Japan.

This televisual construction of national identity also seems to be reflected in the way fans from different countries are portrayed. In 2002 Japanese fans tended to be represented as 'postmodern' consumers of international football, promiscuous in their support of whichever national team took their fancy (particularly pronounced in their apparent adulation for England's David Beckham), while Korean fans were represented as authentic and totally committed in their support for their own national team. Footage of stadia full of Korean fans all wearing the bright red shirts and proclaiming to 'be the reds', along with huge banners declaring love for their team and its manager, provided confirmation of the ultimate example of the totally fanatical, passionate supporter.

Indeed, the 2002 FIFA World Cup can be taken as an indicator of future developments – after a particularly acrimonious bidding process for the 2006 World Cup, the privilege of hosting future tournaments is likely to be rotated between each continent. While Europe used to be able to count on hosting one in every two World Cups, it can now look forward to hosting only one in every five. Similarly, the allocation of African and Asian nations represented at the World Cup finals has increased from one shared place between them up to 1978, to five African and four Asian teams in 2002. How this will effect the sort of television coverage of future World Cups is hard to tell, but clearly it will remain one of the most prestigious and crucial dates in the global television calendar. Despite this, television presentation of many other sporting events are perhaps more innovative in terms of their use of computer graphics, interactivity, commentary, etc. However, its importance as a television event does not lie simply in its claims to be distinctive *as television*. While there have been hugely significant and memorable examples of its television coverage (for example, Geoff Hurst's final goal for England in the 1966 World Cup Final, immortalised by the legendary commentary of Kenneth Wolstenholme: ' … there are people on the pitch, they think it's all over … it is now!'), this resonance lies as much in the event itself as the way that it is televised.

QUESTIONS TO CONSIDER

- In what ways do you think the FIFA World Cup is used by national television channels to tap into and create a sense of national identity among its viewers? Do you think its coverage can ever adequately reflect the subtleties and complexities of contemporary nationality?
- Do you think the FIFA World Cup should remain in the hands of non-pay-TV broadcasters like the BBC and ITV? List as many characteristics as you can that could make coverage of the tournament part of a general philosophy of 'public service broadcasting'?

- Do you think stereotyping plays an important role in the coverage and construction of the different countries that compete and host the event? How and why do you think different national teams and fans are portrayed in distinctive ways?
- In more recent years the viewing of the FIFA World Cup has increasingly become a communal event. How do you think these changes in viewing habits may have affected the style and content of its coverage as a whole?

RECOMMENDED READING

Horne J and Manzenreiter W (eds.) (2002), *Japan, Korea and the 2002 World Cup*, London: Routledge.

Miller, Toby, Lawrence, Geoffrey A, McKay, Jim, Rowe, David (eds.) (2001), *Globalization and Sport: Playing the World*, London: Sage.

Sugden J and Tomlinson A (1998), *FIFA and the Contest for World Football*, Cambridge: Polity Press.

Chapter Nineteen

Grange Hill

Brett Mills

Production Details

(BBC, 1978–)
Creator: Phil Redmond
Producers have included: Albert Barber, Colin Cant, Anna Home, Susi Hush, David Leonard, Kenny McBain, Ben Rea, Ronald Smedley
Directors have included: Angela De Chastelai Smith, Graeme Harper, Dez McCarthy, Nic Phillips
Writers have included: Tara Byrne, John Godber, Tanika Gupta, Anthony Minghella, Phil Redmond, Si Spencer
Original theme music: Alan Hawkshaw

Cast includes:

'Arnie' Arnold (Aidan J Davids)
Justin Bennett (Robert Craig-Morgan)
Roland Browning (Erkan Mustafa)
Luke 'Gonch' Gardener (John Holmes)
Ziggy Greaves (George Christopher)
Benny Green (Terry Sue Patt)
Alan Humphries (George Armstrong)
Peter 'Tucker' Jenkins (Todd Carty)
Danny Kendall (Jonathan Lambeth)
Fay Lucas (Alison Bettles)
Samuel 'Zammo' McGuire (Lee MacDonald)
'Bullet' Baxter (Michael Cronin)
Maurice 'Bronco' Bronson (Michael Sheard)
Mr Griffiths (George Cooper)
Mr Hankin (Lee Cornes)
'Hoppy' Hopwood (Brian Capron)
Bridget 'The Midget' McCluskey (Gwyneth Powell)

Recently celebrating its 25th anniversary, *Grange Hill* is now firmly established as a part of British children's television culture, its longevity pointing towards the success of the programme. In essence, the format is simple: make a drama for children about a school, detailing everyday problems (bullying, loss of homework, failure at sport, unrequited crushes) as well as more dramatic storylines (deaths of schoolchildren, parents and teachers). The fact that *Grange Hill* burst onto children's television like nothing before it, and has remained a staple of children's broadcasting since, demonstrates the lamentable and outdated position children's drama was in before its inception. Buckingham et al. (1999) outline the development of the Children's Department at the BBC throughout the Corporation's history. They show how, determined to move away from imported drama series, Anna Home, the head of the Children's Department, wanted to produce more home-grown drama, which would not only reflect the lives of British audiences, but also attempt to move away from the BBC's perceived position as 'too bloody middle class' (ibid., 35). In came Phil Redmond, a Liverpool-based comedy writer, with a clear intention to make a working-class programme. *Grange Hill* arose, then, from the BBC's desire to better fulfil its public service broadcasting duties, colliding with a writer and production team intent on shifting children's television towards more contemporary realism.

Grange Hill was radical in three central ways. First, it included storylines about children's issues not seen anywhere on British television previously. Characters' discussions about training bras and periods accurately reflected playground talk up and down the country, yet this was the first time they had been seen to be coming out of teenage actors' mouths. Yet the programme also reflected concerns about the nature of education in Britain as whole. Rather than setting the programme in a well-funded – or even private – school, Grange Hill was a comprehensive, with mixed ability students from a variety of backgrounds. As such, *Grange Hill* attempted to demonstrate how this led to an interesting cultural mix of students and staff, while inevitably failing those with the highest and lowest abilities. The programme is, then, not only about school, but also about schooling.

Second, *Grange Hill* introduced viewers to a range of characters – both pupils and teachers – never before seen on children's television. From the first series, pupils such as the underprivileged, black Benny Green, the stroppy, whining Trisha Yates and, most famously, the cheeky, good-at-heart Tucker Jenkins, seemed exactly like the kind of people populating schools up and down the country. Indeed, Tucker was so popular that, on leaving school, he got his own series, *Tucker's Luck* (BBC, 1984), in which he attempted to work out what to do with his life in times of increasing unemployment and urban decay. Similarly, teachers such as the liberal 'Scruffy' McGuffy, the sadistic PE teacher, Mr Hicks, the long-running headmistress, Bridgit 'the midget' McLusky and the fearsome Mr Bronson represented the conflicting and confusing approaches to teaching and the role of education encountered by many students and resulting from the comprehensive system.

The third way in which *Grange Hill* was radical was in its style. By showing characters living and playing on run-down housing estates, it attempted to latch into forms of realism conventionally associated with much popular adult drama, but which were then unknown for children. The (initial) school itself was an old, brown, brick monstrosity, which gained its resonance by being similar to that which many of the programme's viewers would be attending. Perhaps more importantly, the producers attempted to present events literally from the viewpoint of a child; cameras are positioned at the height of a child's eyes, so that buildings, teachers and, most worryingly, older pupils, look large and looming. For many viewers these techniques accurately reflected the experience of going to a comprehensive: for younger viewers about to go to a comprehensive (myself included) they painted a scary picture of an educational future.

Unsurprisingly, this resulted in *Grange Hill* being 'the most controversial product of the Children's Department in the 1970s' (Buckingham et al., 1999, 37). Parents complained because it dealt with topics they had assumed had not yet entered their children's minds. Teachers complained because the programme depicted their profession as flawed, working under strict budgetary constraints, and credited schoolchildren which much more intelligence and power than had previously been thought. Members of Parliament complained because the education system was shown to be failing many and, on a broader scale, the diegesis of *Grange Hill* was one of a multi-ethnic, class-ridden Britain in which, most tellingly, children were the best equipped to deal with such contradictions. And *Grange Hill* has continued being controversial, dealing with, in its most recent series, date rape and asylum seekers.

It is significant, however, that such complaints were rarely raised by children themselves, and it is this that has kept *Grange Hill* on the air. It can certainly be seen as a watershed in children's programming in Britain generally, in which the focus moved away from family viewing, where the parent is in control, towards series aimed specifically at children, and only truly intelligible by children. It is no accident that the BBC's initial children's programming zone was called *Watch with Mother* (1950–80), just as it is no accident now that children's television has its own presenters, its own sets, its own logo and its own times (and, in a multichannel environment, its own channels) to distinguish itself from that intended for adults. Buckingham et al. (1999) argue that there is a way in which children feel an ownership towards programming intended for them, one which manifests itself in children writing in and entering competitions. This requirement for children's television to reflect and respond to children's issues and lives, and children's active response towards such narratives, arises from the shift away from family viewing of which *Grange Hill* was a part. The ownership children feel towards such programming is noted by Davies, who quotes a 14-year-old girl who wrote to the BBC in response to adults, complaints about Grange Hill: 'I'm not saying that adults are not allowed to watch our programmes, but it was written for us, the children, the pupils at schools like Grange Hill, who really understand what they're like' (1989, 57).

Grange Hill's most famous – and perhaps most controversial – storyline concerned one pupil's drug addiction. Told over two years (1986–7), the story showed 'Zammo' McGuire's descent into drug addiction and eventual recovery. The fact that, prior to this story, Zammo had been one of the most popular regular characters in the series, meant that audiences had already built up much empathy and identification with him and his relationship with his girlfriend. Of course, it also suggested that drugs were something that could happen to anyone, which frightened many parents. Worries about the storyline centred on its length, which required supposedly fickle children viewers to remain committed to a programme over two series, which they did. Many adults also raised concern over a children's drama mentioning drugs at all, missing the whole point of the narrative. To demonstrate the way in which children's drama could be socially committed, the producers set up helplines and information packs, and the cast of *Grange Hill* released a pop single about drug addiction and the problems of peer pressure – 'Just Say No' – which reached the top of the UK charts. They also travelled to the States where they met Nancy Reagan as part of her war on drugs in America. For viewers like me – 14 at the time – Zammo and the 'Just Say No' campaign remain a significant part of teenage memories, in which I felt that television was speaking to me in a way in which education and society often were not.

Because of this, *Grange Hill* has been used by a number of researchers to explore children's relationship with, and understanding of, drama and realism, and fiction's connection to the real world. Gunter and McAleer (1997) show how viewers of a variety of ages responded to the 'Just Say No' storyline, both criticising and condemning it. In a manner similar to adult concerns over children, older viewers worried that Zammo's initial joy in heroin might influence younger viewers into trying drugs, even though, as more mature viewers, they felt they could understand this joy within the context of Zammo's eventual decline (1997, 164). Buckingham (1993) demonstrates teenage viewers' awareness of the requirements of fiction, in which dramatic events accumulate at an unrealistic pace. In an interview with a 10-year-old about to start at a comprehensive, the child states clearly that she knows that many of the events depicted in *Grange Hill* – children going on demonstrations, children suffocating in locked cupboards – aren't going to happen to her or at her school (1993, 229). In these ways, research into audience reception of *Grange Hill* demonstrate the sophisticated ways in which children understand and make sense of drama created for them and how they negotiate such fiction's relationship with their own reality. Indeed, the success of *Grange Hill* seriously undermines adult notions of children as passive, unintelligent consumers of television and other media, for the programme can only be understood and enjoyed by sophisticated, television-savvy viewers.

The influence of *Grange Hill* can be seen in British programmes such as *Byker Grove* (BBC, 1990–), *Children's Ward/The Ward* (ITV, 1991–), and *Press Gang* (Central, 1989–93). Canadian series such as *The Kids of Degrassi Street* (WGBH, 1982–6) and *Degrassi Junior High* (WGBH, 1986), and the Australian drama *Heartbreak High* (ABC, 1994–9) used similar formats and offered similar points of identification for teenage audiences tailored to other countries. In a broader sense, *Grange Hill* opened up the possibility for children's television to actively engage with the audience's concerns, and to treat them as a discrete group with specific needs, worries and, most importantly, intelligence. And *Grange Hill* continues to evolve and shock. The most recent series ended with the whole school being blown up, killing an unidentified number of regular characters. When the programme returns for its 26th season it will have changed production company, moved to another location (somewhere non-specific in the north of England) and include a whole new cast. After 25 years, the programme is attempting to go back to its roots, re-injecting a dose of fun into the proceedings and, by moving away from its increasingly specific London setting, hoping to return to its much more representative beginnings.

QUESTIONS TO CONSIDER

- How does *Grange Hill* depict the realities of school life? How does it attempt to convince viewers that it is 'realistic' and how does it differ to other portrayals of school life in other television series?

- How is the series shot? What visual elements does it use to give a child's view of school life?

- What does *Grange Hill* say about the relationship between pupils, teachers and government? With whom does the programme side?

- How does the series treat the issues it confronts (relationships, death, poverty, etc.)? Is it comforting for young viewers, or possibly distressing?

- Why might teachers and government ministers be worried about the things *Grange Hill* has to say about education, children's roles and rights and social issues? Is the programme balanced? Should it be?

- What distinctions should exist between television made for children, that for families and that for adults? Does *Grange Hill* conform to such distinctions?

RECOMMENDED READING

Buckingham, David, Davies, Hannah, Jones, Ken and Kelley, Peter (1999), *Children's Television in Britain*, London: British Film Institute.

Docherty, Mark J and McGown, Alistair D (2003), *The Hill and Beyond: Children's Television – An Encyclopaedia*, London: British Film Institute.

Gunter, Barrie and McAleer, Jill (1997, second edition), *Children and Television*, London and New York: Routledge.

Chapter Twenty

Heimat

Glen Creeber

Production Details

(WDR, SFB, 1984)

Creator: Edgar Reitz
Director: Edgar Reitz
Screenplay: Edger Reitz, Peter Steinbach
Music: Niko Mamangakis
Costume: Regine Bätz
Make-up: Lore Sottung

Cast includes:

Maria (Marita Breuer)
Paul (Michael Lesch, Dieter Schaad)
Pauline (Karin Kienzler, Eva Maria Bayerswalter)
Eduard (Rüediger Weigang)
Hermann (Peter Harting)
Glasisch-Karl (Kurt Wagner)
Anton (Mathias Kniesbeck)
Otto (Jörg Hube)

When this 16-hour television drama was first shown in West Germany in the autumn of 1984, no fewer than 25 million people saw at least one of its eleven episodes (Kaes, 1989, 163). It later went on to achieve widespread international acclaim, not least in Britain, where it was shown (with English subtitles) by the BBC, and in America, by Bravo and PBS. However, *Heimat* (subtitled *A Chronicle in Eleven Parts*) also attracted enormous controversy, with many critics accusing it of bias in its fictional portrayal of real historical events. Dramatising German life from the First World War to the 1980s (a second less successful series, *The Second Heimat: A New Generation* [sometimes known as *Leaving Home*] [SFB, 1992], took it further and at the time of writing *Heimat 3* is in production), its critics felt that *Heimat*'s prominently 'romantic' image of rural German life and its generally sympathetic treatment of its people blatantly downplayed the atrocities of Germany's past.

Heimat originally began life as a self-conscious reaction to the American miniseries *Holocaust* (NBC/Titus, 1978). Following quickly on the heels of the hugely successful and award-winning American miniseries *Roots* (ABC, 1977) – which dramatised the history of Negro slavery in America – this four-part television drama dealt with the Nazi atrocities of the Second World War. Like *Roots*, *Holocaust* won considerable praise and numerous awards, but its critics argued that it simply transformed one of the most horrific periods of recent world history into a sentimental soap opera (Herf, 1980, 37). But it was not just critics who responded unfavourably to the American miniseries; German film directors like Edgar Reitz also condemned the drama. In an article entitled 'Let's work on Our Memories', published in 1979, Reitz argued that 'Authors all over the world are trying to take possession of their history ... but they often find that it is torn out of their hands ... With *Holocaust*, the Americans have taken away our history' (cited by Elsaesser, 1996, 176).

It was in direct response to *Holocaust*, then, that Reitz eventually directed and co-wrote (with Peter Steinbach) *Heimat*, an attempt to make a version of German history that was not controlled by a dominantly American point of view. Indeed, this narrative mission was explicitly evoked by its original title *Made in Germany*, an epithet that can still be seen chiselled into a rock at the beginning of each episode. As this suggests, Reitz envisaged *Heimat* as a deliberate and self-conscious attempt at reclaiming German national identity from America, clearly distinguishing it from, as he put it, 'German history – made in Hollywood' (cited by Kaes, 1989, 185).

The original German title *Heimat* remained for an English-speaking audience because the word was generally believed to be untranslatable. In its crudest form 'Heimat' simply means 'home' or 'homeland'. But the word also has other important artistic and cultural connotations. In fact, 'Heimat' was originally a literary genre with its origins in the 1890s, a style of storytelling that tended to hark back to a pre-industrial, romantic conception of rural Germany – depicting its people as existing in perfect harmony with nature. However, by the 1920s the National Socialists had begun claiming the genre for themselves, imbuing it with racist and anti-Semitic connotations that embedded it in notions of race and territory. Although after the war its Nazi associations were exorcised, hugely popular 'Heimat' films still offered German audiences a nostalgic retreat into a sentimental depiction of a rural idyll – perhaps reflecting the country's own longing to return to some mythical homeland that was now seemingly lost forever. As such, the word 'Heimat' produces a whole host of complex and ambiguous connotations amongst the German people, a word that has been claimed and reclaimed by numerous ideologies but still manages to retain some of its simple and honest longing for home and identity. As Anton Kaes puts it, 'Like no other the word, Heimat encompasses at once kitsch sentiment, false consciousness, and genuine emotional needs' (ibid., 166).

It is in this context that the 11-part serial is best understood, as both a reaction against the 'Americanisation' of German history and as an attempt to reclaim the Heimat tradition from its Nazi contamination. Like Heimat films and literature before it, the story primarily centres around a nostalgic depiction of German village life, a seemingly innocent world far away from the corrupt metropolis. Set in a small fictional rural community called Schabbach (located somewhere in the Hunsrück region of Germany where Reitz himself grew up), the serial spends a great deal of time lovingly portraying provincial life in surprisingly intimate and leisurely detail.

Five years in the making, both Reitz and Steinbach spent more than a year researching oral history and writing the script on location, including many of the villagers they met as extras in the film. As in many Heimat stories, the central figure of the narrative is that of the mother, a symbol of the safety and permanence that the genre often imagines lies at Germany's heart. In Reitz and Steinbach's story it is Maria; born in 1900, she acts as the symbolic heartland around which all her friends and relatives revolve as the century unravels until her death in the 1980s. As the most potent and continuous symbol of Heimat itself, the serial primarily tells her life history, all the other stories from four generations of three large families spreading out from and finally returning to her metaphorical centre.

It was this attempt to portray the everyday life of the German people that critics like Anton Kaes refer to as the 'history of the everyday'. Rather than attempting to dramatise the large and important events of world history, the drama seems more interested in depicting the everyday reality of 'ordinary' German people. Such an approach thus reflects the aims of *Alltagsgeschichte*, a form of historical methodology that attempts to tell history from the point of view of 'the people' or 'the masses'. Using such sources as photograph albums, diaries, oral histories and home movies, this form of history is interested in interrogating the past not from 'above' but from 'below', excavating the historical remains that determine and colour everyday experience (Kaes, 1989, 172–3).

However, the serial received angry criticism for concentrating mainly on domestic affairs, seemingly ignoring the wider historical facts of Germany's past. In particular, the Nazi Holocaust is hardly ever mentioned by the serial, despite the fact that 5 of its 11 episodes (3–7) take place during the time of the Third Reich. Although at one point we see a village boy briefly come across the outside of a concentration camp, he tells no one what he has seen and it is never discussed in any detail. In fact, the gradual rise of the Nazi regime comes about so slowly and gradually that it seems barely noticeable at times, so caught up is the story in the personal and emotional dynamics of its characters' lives. As a result, critics like Timothy Garton argued that 'you inevitably find yourself asking: But what about the other side? What about Auschwitz? Where is the director's moral judgement?' (cited by ibid., 184). Similarly, the film critic Thomas Elsaesser has suggested that the serial's 'normalisation' and 'routinisation' of Fascism means that it is fundamentally 'apologetic in tendency if not in intent' (1996, 160).

Yet, in defence of the drama, some critics have argued that by presenting the rise of Nazism as a relatively 'normal' event in these characters' lives, the insidious danger of such a political system is more accurately revealed. Not attempting to offer an unrealistically 'objective' or 'omnipotent' version of German history, *Heimat* self-consciously attempts to portray how Fascism can slowly and almost unconsciously creep into the very fabric of everyday life. As such, the Holocaust is pushed to the margins of the narrative because this subjective version of the past reveals the way the German people themselves may have learnt to accept and deny the horrors taking place around them and in their name. In doing so, it gives a self-consciously contrasting view of history, particularly from versions of the Second World War that tend to cast German characters as intrinsically and unquestionably evil (Creeber, 2001, 452).

Central to this portrayal of Germany's past is Reitz's unusual use of photography. Whilst the majority of *Heimat* is shot in black and white (adding a sense of documentary authenticity to its depiction of history), brief colour sequences (sometimes only lasting a few seconds) continually threaten to disturb the serial's underlining sense of realism. Unpredictable in their arrival, these colour sequences seem to self-reflexively foreground the fact that these are not *real* events taking place, that they are being 'filtered' by something or someone that recalls some moments more intensely or warmly than others. In the first episode, for example, Paul Simon returns home from the First World War to find his father, the village blacksmith, hard at work. When Paul (in black and white) looks through the window of the workshop, so the scene of his father pounding red-hot metal at the anvil is shot entirely in colour. As the camera's point of view briefly alternates between Paul watching from outside (in black and white) and his father working (in colour) so the emotional significance of the scene to the returning soldier is underlined. In this way, the unexpected and momentary use of colour appears to alert the audience to the fact that this view of the past is not entirely objective, that the warm glow of his father's workshop somehow symbolises something safe and familiar to the homesick Paul.

As the story develops, so the personal nature of the history *Heimat* deals with seems to be further highlighted. For instance, the character Glasisch-Karl introduces every episode (apart from the first) to the audience, taking on the role of an unofficial narrator. Sitting at a table covered with old sepia photographs, this eccentric outsider briefly talks about particular characters, stories or events while leafing through the faded images before him. While these recurring sequences crucially remind us of past storylines, the sheer act of him looking at old photographs perhaps also emphasises the artificiality of the photographic/filmic image – a representation that only signifies something now past and ultimately unobtainable. As Kaes points out, with each new episode so more and more photographs fill his desk, perhaps aptly dramatising the problem we all have of ordering, selecting and representing the past (Kaes, 1989, 179). This is perhaps the real project behind *Heimat*: an attempt to capture a personal view of the past that is usually denied by the history books. Even if its view of the Second World War is best understood as implicitly subjective and inherently selective, *Heimat* arguably offers a truly oppositional reading of German history, an attempt to reintroduce some aspect of colour into a world so frequently portrayed as morally black and white.

QUESTIONS TO CONSIDER

- Some viewers apparently found the mixture of colour and black and white photography got in the way of their enjoyment of *Heimat*. What can you think would be some of the positive and negative effects of using such an unusual technique?

- Compare the use of colour and black and white photography in *Heimat* with the way the same technique is used in a film like Steven Spielberg's *Schindler's List* (1993). Do you think both directors were after similar effects?

- Do you think *Heimat* was justified in not depicting the Holocaust? What arguments for and against such a decision can you think of?

- Do you think *Heimat* was right to try and depict the 'history of the everyday'? What problems can you anticipate may arrive out of such an approach to representing real historical events?

RECOMMENDED READING

Creeber, Glen (2004), '*Heimat*' in Glen Creeber, *Next Week On …: Television Drama in the Age of Serial Fiction*, London: British Film Institute.

Elsaesser, Thomas (1996), 'Subject positions, speaking positions: from *Holocaust, Our Hitler*, and *Heimat* to *Shoh* and *Schindler's List*', in Sobchack, Vivian (ed.), *The Persistence of History: Cinema, Television and the Modern Event*, London: Routledge.

Kaes, Anton (1989), 'Germany as Memory' in *From Hitler to Heimat: The Return of History as Film*, Massachusetts and London: Harvard University Press.

Chapter Twenty One
Hill Street Blues

Robin Nelson

Production Details

(NBC, 1981–7)
Original idea: Fred Silverman, NBC network executive
Executive Chair, NBC: Grant Tinker
Production company: MTM Enterprises, Inc.
Directors have included: Robert Butler, Gregory Hoblit, Georg Stanford Brown,
Arnold Laven, Jack Starrett, Corey Allen
Writer/Producers: Steven Bochco, Michael Kozoll
Writers have also included: Michael Kozoll, Geoffrey Fischer, Robert Crais,
Robert Earll, Mark Frost, David Milch
Line Producer: Greg Hoblit
Director of Photography: Billy Cronjager
Music: Mike Post

Cast includes:
Capt. Frank Furrillo (Daniel J Travanti)
Sgt. Phil Esterhaus (Michael Conrad)
Officer Bobby Hill (Michael Warren)
Officer Andy Renko (Charles Haid)
Joyce Davenport (Veronica Hamel)
Det. Mick Belker (Bruce Weitz)
Lt. Ray Callentano (Rene Enriquez)

Hill Street Blues might be flatly introduced as a 1980s American TV drama cop series, set on the wrong side of the tracks in an unnamed Eastern metropolis (similar to Chicago) and focusing more on the professional and private lives of the cops themselves than catching the perpetrators of crime. More flamboyantly, it is the most celebrated of cop shows in the history of network American television production. *Hill Street Blues* is mythologised for breaking the mould of 60s/70s heroic, case-solving cop shows, establishing a new approach to ratings, articulating a particular cultural moment and breaking the established dominants of style, content and narrative form in American television. Whilst it is demonstrable that *Hill Street Blues* achieved all these and has had a big influence on subsequent television, it is important to recognise that, 'in network television, even the exceptions prove the rules' (Gitlin, 1994, 273).

Writer/producers Steven Bochco and Michael Kozell were given extraordinary licence with *Hill Street Blues*, even by MTM's standards (Feuer, 1984, 1–31 and Gitlin, 1994). Subsequently, the prevailing assumption in American TV drama has been that good writing given creative freedom is the basis of 'quality television'. They were supported, however, by other production personnel in an industrial process, notably the first director, Robert Butler, who is credited with the visual style of the series and Mike Poster who created the soundscape. Moreover, without the counter-intuitive support of network executive producers, *Hill Street Blues* would have been short-lived. To summarise a well-rehearsed story (Feuer, 1984 and Gitlin, 1994), the series pilot was kept on despite being, 'possibly the lowest-rated programme ever to be retained' (Hoblit cited in Feuer, 1984, 25–26). Once it had captured viewers' loyalties, however, it received 98 Emmy nominations and won 26 during its seven-year run.

The ultimate popularity of the series offers a lesson for executives who allow themselves to be instrumentally guided by the size of an audience alone. Where product is innovative, it may take time for audiences to adjust their viewing assumptions in response. In specific terms, Grant Tinker contradicted his assertion on appointment at NBC that the industry could no longer afford 'loss leaders', to sustain the strategy he brought with him from MTM to turn 'quality' into profits. The novelty of this approach, perhaps anticipated by Silverman (Feuer, 1984, 24–5), was to recognise that the purchasing power of audience segments ultimately matters more to advertisers than raw numbers. Establishing what is now a commonplace in a 'market niche' industry in the UK as well as the US (Nelson, 1997), Tinker traded in capturing the '18–49, high-income and well-educated audience that was threatening to defect to cable and pay-TV' (Feuer, 1984, 25).

That the broader audience for the pilot did not initially latch on to the joys of *Hill Street Blues* is not surprising given the density of the text and number of established conventions it flouted. To begin with narrative form, the dominant convention of 60s/70s cop shows in which a central character or duo (*Ironside* [NBC, 1964–74], *Kojak* [CBS, 1973–8] and *Starsky and Hutch* [ABC, 1975–9]) solves a key crime in the course of a single episode, was abandoned. Instead multiple storylines ran concurrently and extended across episodes. As Gitlin records, '[i]n one episode, for example, five major stories were set up in the first three minutes. In the course of that two-hour sequence, three more storylines were introduced and two others continued. By the end, at least eight major stories were still unresolved' (1994, 274).

This may be an extreme example, but viewers accustomed to one storyline, albeit with the twists of a whodunnit, resolved in a comprehensible manner by the end of the episode, were simply confounded by the narrative complexity. Executive pressure

encounters, incidents and situations' (cited in Feuer, 1984, 194). However, this by no means diminishes the achievement of the series; rather it attests to the artistry of the writer/producers in constructing a controlled but rich cross-referential text. Without some adherence to established conventions, the series would have been incomprehensible, as it threatened to be at the pilot stage.

Modern viewers may find *Hill Street Blues* unremarkable, even slow. Precisely because the series' innovations influenced much subsequent television drama, in cop series and beyond, the 'new' codes have now themselves become customary. The blurring of genre boundaries paved the way for the dominance of the series/serial hybrid and a means of building audiences comprised of different market segments (Nelson, 1997). In production terms, *Hill Street Blues* established niche markets, targeting audiences with more disposable wealth. Specifically in terms of cop/detective series, Bochco proceeded to produce a number of successful series, *L.A. Law* (NBC, 1986–4), *NYPD Blue* (ABC, 1993–) and *Murder One* (ABC, 1995) amongst them. His committed approach to production, challenging an essentially conservative industrial medium, set an example for stylistically distinctive, well-written American series up to *Homicide* and *24* (Fox, 2001–).

QUESTIONS TO CONSIDER

- How did *Hill Street Blues'* use of multiple storylines (sometimes left unresolved) affect the way the police genre had been portrayed in the past? In what ways do successful American cop shows tend to differ from British police series?
- In what ways did *Hill Street Blues* subvert the traditional portrayal of TV policemen and women?
- Does it make sense to say that *Hill Street Blues* is more 'realistic' than a police show like *Starsky and Hutch*? If so, in what way is that realism conveyed?
- Despite supposedly 'progressive' treatments of women, does *Hill Street Blues* remain predominantly 'masculine'?
- To what extent does 'the look' of TV drama depend upon directing/camera style? How important is the soundscape in establishing the feel of *Hill Street Blues*?
- Since boundaries between one type of drama and another have become blurred, does it make sense still to talk of 'the police genre'?

RECOMMENDED READING

Feuer, Jane et al. (eds.) (1984), *MTM: 'Quality Television'*, London: British Film Institute.
Gitlin, Todd (1983, revised and reprinted 1994), *Inside Prime Time*, London: Routledge.
Nelson, Robin (1997), 'Flexi-Narrative from *Hill Street* to *Holby City*' in *TV Drama in Transition: Forms, Values and Cultural Change*, Basingstoke: Macmillan.

Chapter Twenty Two

I Love Lucy

Brett Mills

Production Details

(CBS [Desilu Productions], 1951–7)

Producers: Jess Oppenheimer, Desi Arnaz

Writers: Jess Oppenheimer, Madelyn Pugh, Bob Carroll Jr., Bob Schiller and others

Directors: William Asher, James V Kern, Marc Daniels

Cast includes:

Lucy Ricardo (Lucille Ball)
Ricky Ricardo (Desi Arnaz)
Ethel Mertz (Vivian Vance)
Fred Mertz (William Frawley)
Betty Ramsey (Mary Jane Croft)
Ralph Ramsey (Frank Nelson)
Little Ricky Ricardo (Richard Keith)

Lucy and Ricky Ricardo are a married couple living in New York. Ethel and Fred Mertz are their next-door neighbours and good friends. *I Love Lucy* is a sitcom documenting their comic adventures. Every week Lucy and Ricky fall out over some minor problem, the whole explodes into comic excess and by the end of the episode all is as it was at the beginning. Narratives often revolve around work, social roles and, more commonly, the battle of the sexes. Put that way, *I Love Lucy* sounds like pretty much every sitcom produced in the last 50 years, whether in Britain or America. So why the big fuss? The reason why *I Love Lucy* sounds derivative, formulaic and predictable to a contemporary audience is because it invented what we now know to be the sitcom; all sitcoms are like *I Love Lucy* because it inaugurated the format, shooting style, social location, performance style, narrative structure and prevailing ideology of American sitcom, becoming a huge hit in the process. If *I Love Lucy* looks old and safe now, it is only because every sitcom that followed it has tried to recreate its formula and success. Without *I Love Lucy* television entertainment would be nothing like we know it today: 'It almost single-handedly defined the genre' (Lewisohn, 1998, 57).

Lucille Ball was a recurring character actor in a string of film comedies in the 1930s and 1940s, playing with such stars as the Marx Brothers, Bob Hope and Laurel and Hardy. While encapsulating the good looks required of female actresses, her 'deep, guttural voice that has no softness or romanticism' (Horowitz, 1997, 23) had prevented her from making the leap to leading lady. With her husband, the Cuban bandleader Desi Arnaz, she had toured America in sketches and stage shows, solidifying a comic double act that was to inform their whole working relationship. After the success of her appearances in a radio sitcom – *My Favorite Husband* (CBS Radio, 1948–51) – Ball was approached by CBS TV to turn the programme into a television series. Determined to star opposite her real-life husband, Ball and Arnaz were knocked back and told that American audiences would never believe that they were married (Jones, 1992, 64). Deciding to take the production process into their own hands, Ball and Arnaz commissioned their own scripts and put together a self-produced pilot. After discovering other networks were interested, CBS eventually caved in and commissioned the series, with Arnaz as the leading man.

Ball and Arnaz continued their fights with the network. Determined that the programme be broadcast from Los Angeles, where they lived, and taped for New York, the networks insisted on it being recorded on film rather than video to maintain picture quality. The prohibitive costs of film were met by the stars accepting pay cuts, on condition that they received full ownership of the programme. Such control continued throughout the series, with Ball and Arnaz eventually buying Ball's former employer RKO, resulting in their ownership of 'the biggest production facility on earth' (Higham quoted in Mellencamp, 1992, 326).

More significant was *I Love Lucy*'s shooting style. Ball wanted to capture the immediacy of working before a real studio audience without ending up with a programme that looked like recorded theatre. Employing the respected cinematographer Karl Freund, they developed the shooting style evident in virtually all sitcom: the 'three-headed monster' (Jones, 1992, 66). Here, any exchange between two characters was simultaneously recorded by three cameras, two capturing close-ups of each performer and one a mid-shot of the two. This 'freed television situation comedy from its stiff stage restraints' (Putterman, 1995, 15) and allowed one vital aspect of Ball's performance to be captured in all its glory: her reactions. Realising that the response to a joke was as vital as the joke itself – particularly considering Ball's trademark set of laughter-inducing reactions (Horowitz, 1997, 32) – Ball, Arnaz and Freund unlocked the essence of comic performance while simultaneously establishing the visual style still found in the majority of television sitcom.

Because of this, *I Love Lucy* – and Lucille Ball herself – have often been explored in terms of performance. Plots for individual episodes are constructed to allow Ball to excel at what she does best – physical comedy. Her talent for mimicry, facial expression, mime and dance resulted in a programme whose visuality was vital to its comedy, and that visuality was centred within Ball's manic performance. Famous scenes from the series have become the stuff of television legend: Lucy training to do ballet, which she inadvertently turns into a Charleston; Lucy stomping grapes to audition for a role as a peasant in a film; and, most memorably, Lucy dancing the tango with Desi with dozens of eggs stuffed down her shirt until the two finally come together, face to face, with the expected splat! The last – a perfect piece of delaying the comic moment until the audience can no longer bear it – still holds the record for the longest recorded laugh in American television history (Mellencamp, 1992, 325).

I Love Lucy exploited performance further by being about performance. Plots repeatedly revolved around Lucy's desire to escape her domestic prison and become, like her husband, a star of the stage. In doing so, she symbolised the plight of many American women everywhere. In the 1950s America was finally escaping from the shadow of the Great Depression and the Second World War, into a future which promised prosperity, consumption and leisure. As a result, women were promised a contradictory future in which each should adopt the domestic role and support their husband's efforts to work, while simultaneously living in homes with a plethora of domestic machinery that made their work redundant. Similarly, women were required to stay at home just as they were being told that opportunities were everywhere: television, radio and the telephone brought the world into their homes, just as housewives were retreating from interaction with that world. *I Love Lucy*, then, demonstrated a world in which life wasn't difficult, just stultifyingly dull; 'she is a comic demon called forth from the boredom and frustration of an entire generation of housewives' (Jones, 1992, 68).

Because of this, *I Love Lucy* has repeatedly been examined for its possible feminist critique of a consumerist, patriarchal society. Certainly it offers points of identification for disgruntled housewives, even if there is a distressing irony to television offering the salve to the consumerist structures it relies on for its existence. Press (1991) finds, however, that identification with Lucy's situation is predicated along lines of class, with working-class women finding Lucy merely zany and unappealing. Middle-class women, on the other hand, responded to Ball's performance in the role, separating it from its meaning in relation to social structures. In these readings, *I Love Lucy* is either merely comedy with no other meaning or it presents a housewife whom those whose lives are most bound up in domesticity find too distressing. If there is a radical, feminist interpretation to the programme, then, it's not being actively read as such by many audiences.

Indeed, many critics have argued that, because each episode ends with Lucy resigned to her domestic role, it offers nothing other than limited resistance. Worse than this, it may even punish Lucy for her attempts to be something other than wider society finds acceptable. Jones argues that '*I Love Lucy* simultaneously legitimized the yearnings of women for fuller lives and assured them that they would be better off keeping their dreams in their heads' (1992, 71). So, while Lucy wants a better life for herself, she's unwilling to give up many of the shackles which imprison her within her role. Scenes showing her enjoyment of shopping with Ethel, using new domestic gadgets and, most significantly, her love and respect for her husband, mean that the programme foregrounds the pleasures of being a housewife over the difficulties, even if it does find comedy within the gap that often appears between the two. While centring on a female star, *I Love Lucy*, then, offers 'a male point of view' (Mellencamp, 1992, 81), meaning that the audience 'laughs at Lucy Ricardo, not with her' (Marc, 1989, 93).

However, critics have suggested that the programme offers some resistance in the very notion of a female performer. That is, in a society in which women's bodies exist to take up as little space as possible and any physical pleasure that can be gained from them should be that which men enjoy, Lucy's sheer physical exuberance and ability to reduce an audience to tears through her physicality represents a depiction of the female form which is highly threatening to patriarchy (Horowitz, 1997, 28–32). In this way, Rowe (1990, 1995) compares Lucy with a much later female comedian – Roseanne – finding that the latter's excesses continue the development of female comic anarchy kick-started by Lucy. Yet not only is the notion that a woman may take, and give, through her body enjoyment and pleasure a significant feminist stance, but it also undermines the notion that comic physical performance is best left to the men. Lucy's unassailable popularity with the American – and worldwide – public, 'demonstrates her mastery of physical comedy, burlesque, and vaudeville, historically a male domain' (Mellencamp, 1992, 330).

Such contradictory readings of the programme – feminist pioneer or constrained housewife? – certainly demonstrate the ongoing difficulties in examining representations within comedy and, more importantly, the wide range of readings it is possible for audiences to construct. However, what is certain is that *I Love Lucy* continues to be popular, remaining in syndication around the world. While such continuing popularity rests predominantly on the sheer excellence of the production as a whole, clearly the programme must remain intelligible – and its humour funny – within a range of societies for whom life generally and gender roles specifically have changed to at least some degree since the 1950s. That is, social relationships still predominantly remain centred around those cultural structures on which the programme's comedy centres: the family and gender differences. Thus, 'The more gender power relations have changed, the more Lucy seems pioneering and relevant' (Wells, 1998a, 189), suggesting the programme will remain popular for some time to come. With the television industry acknowledging the debt they owe to the programme and academics continuing to explore the legacy and radicalism of the programme, both *I Love Lucy* and Lucille Ball herself are likely to remain 'the queen of television comedy' (Putterman, 1995, 156).

QUESTIONS TO CONSIDER

- Look at the ways in which *I Love Lucy* represents women and compare it to its portrayal of men. Does the programme make clear distinctions along gender differences in terms of the roles of men and women and the power relationships between them?
- Does the programme offer hope that Lucy can finally break out from her 'prison' of housewifery?

- Is there a difference between physical comedy performed by women and by men? Is Lucy's celebration of her physicality a radical feminist portrayal or merely a continuation of the tradition of women out of control?

- How is the relationship between Lucy and Ricky portrayed? Who do we laugh at and who do we laugh with? Is there a 'subtle racism' in the portrayal of Ricky?

- How is *I Love Lucy* different to contemporary comedies in its portrayal of the genders? What differences in readings of the programme might there be between contemporary and modern audiences?

- What sort of legacy has *I Love Lucy* left? Do you see similarities between it and programmes like *Roseanne* (ABC, 1988–97) and *Absolutely Fabulous* (BBC, 1989–96)?

RECOMMENDED READING

Horowitz, Susan (1997), *Queens of Comedy: Lucille Ball, Phyllis Diller, Carol Burnett, Joan Rivers, and the New Generation of Funny Women*, Amsterdam: Gordon and Breach.

Mellencamp, Patricia (1992), *High Anxiety: Catastrophe, Scandal, Age, and Comedy*, Bloomington and Indianapolis: Indiana University Press.

Rowe, Kathleen (1995), *The Unruly Woman: Gender and the Genres of Laughter*, Austin: University of Texas Press.

Chapter Twenty Three
The Jerry Springer Show

Jane Roscoe

Production Details

(WCBV/ABC, 1991–)

Creator: Bert Dubow
Host: Jerry Springer
Executive Producer: Richard Dominick
Producers have included: Jennifer Bryne, Melinda Chait, Christi C Harber, Norm Lubow Jennifer Williams, Lisa Bergmen
Directors have included: Greg Klazura

Confessional talk shows have been blamed for turning whole nations into cry-babies, valorising victimhood and exploiting the poor and the marginalised, all in the name of entertainment. *The Jerry Springer Show* is perhaps the most infamous of the genre, outperforming all other American talk shows, broadcast in 190 American markets and sold to over 50 other countries. At its height it was screened every weekday in the US, running with topics such as 'Lesbians on the Rampage', 'Feisty Females', 'Honey, I'm Really a Woman' and 'I've Been Sleeping with my Sister' through to 'My Son is a Nerd and Needs a Make-Over'. As these absurd and sometimes lurid titles suggest, the show appears to go out of its way to be scandalous, shocking and sensational, a mixture of elements that nonetheless makes it compulsive television. Filmed in Chicago, it has taken its host, Jerry Springer (a former lawyer, news anchorman, politician and Mayor of Cincinnati), on a journey to the centre of what many would regard as 'Nasty TV' or 'Tabloid Television'.

There has certainly been much public discussion about what *The Jerry Springer Show* says about contemporary American culture and what impact it has had on both audiences and its featured guests. Its host has been the subject of a moral panic on more than one occasion, often prompted by a spilling over of arguments and conflicts presented in the show (Heaton and Wilson, 1995). In August 2000, for example, one of Springer's guests was found murdered just hours after the episode had been broadcast. Fifty-two-year-old Nancy Campbell–Panitz had appeared under the assumption that she was to be reunited with her ex-husband. Instead, she was confronted by her ex-husband and his new wife, who claimed she had been stalking them. Instead of a happy reunion she was publicly humiliated and physically abused. Although not the first time a murder had been linked to a conflict aired on a TV talk show, this provided more evidence to those who regard the show as 'trashy' and dangerous.

To understand the particular dynamics of *The Jerry Springer Show* it is perhaps helpful to situate it first within the general genre of the confessional talk show as a whole. Since the early 1990s, talk shows have prompted a number of academic reconsiderations. In part, this has come about due to various transformations of the genre and the public sphere. One line of thought positioned talk shows at the forefront of a new form of 'participatory citizenship' or a display of 'emotional democracy'. Here the talk show is conceptualised as a new form of public sphere in which the old dichotomies of public/private, expert/lay person and rational/emotional are challenged and recon-figured. In this new space, talk shows become a place in which experts are challenged, the ordinary person can confront a politician face-to-face and common knowledge takes centre stage (Livingstone and Lunt, 1994). As Jane Shattuc has put it, 'These con-fessional talk shows, whether the topic is transsexuality, incest, interracial sex or wife beating, took up the feminist slogan of the "personal is the political" and gave it a com-mercial forum' (Shattuc, 2001, 84). However, other critics are more cynical about the 'democratic' potential of the form, arguing that the genre, by commodifying human behaviour, is simply exploitative and inherently repressive. As Jon Dovey has put it, '[i]s it any surprise that an economic system that offers us personal power only through consumer choice should also offer the often unattainable goal of personal liberation through "quick fix" psychic solutions...?' (Dovey, 2000, 121).

The Jerry Springer Show clearly illustrates this debate by firstly borrowing many of its conventions from the more 'therapeutic' examples of the genre and then extending them. Like many other examples of the genre, each show is constructed around a par-ticular social or emotional issue. Be it marital problems, sex changes, sibling rivalry or bad bosses, Springer takes it to the extreme. The issues and participants are set up for maximum drama and conflict. Participants are actively sought who represent the opposing sides of the issue/conflict. And while each episode sets up a problem, the show is not constructed around the resolution of the problem. Rather, the focus is based around the *problem display* and, in particular, the paradoxical representation of certain types of behaviour. On the one hand, it presents certain people and activities within a discourse of tolerance and liberalism ('Let's talk about sex workers, their motivations, worries, experiences. We want to understand'). Yet it also functions to identify, exploit and control deviant behaviour, and so such activities are usually condemned by audiences ('I hate your sexy job' and so on).

Audience participation is certainly central to both the concept and the success of talk shows as a whole. However, the audience participation in *The Jerry Springer Show* seems far removed from this context of a reasonable exchange of views and information. His studio audience diss, hiss, shout, jump around and generally make their views heard as loudly as possible. They talk over and tease guests or actively challenge them so that it is not a fair exchange of views but rather a fight for attention. The audience is also there to play 'jury' to this display of deviance. It is the audience who set the moral tone, deciding what is acceptable and how far anyone is allowed to go. As such, it creates an arena where the display of a problem is simply more dramatic and entertaining than its actual resolution. This means that the participants and their problems threaten to become less important in the show than audience reaction. As Jon Dovey puts it, more recent programmes in the genre 'have weakened the narrative-therapeutic res-olution drive in favour of a repetition of difference in very short segments in which the guests themselves are given very little air time' (2000, 117).

As such, Springer, while far from neutral, is placed in the established talk show host role of moderator. Yet he himself sees his role more akin to that of a 'ringmaster' (the title of his 1999 autobiography – [Springer, 1999]), implying that the show itself is a modern-day freak show or human circus. While the people who come on the show do seem 'freakish' (they are paraded out in front of the studio audience, who quickly follow the cues by expressing their likes and dislikes), he also clearly works the crowd, encouraging them to chant his name, 'Je-*rry*! Je-*rry*! Je-*rry*!' He also moves between the guests and the audiences (studio and at home), prompting them to go further, pushing them to reveal more details, forcing them to justify and explain their behaviour. He also embodies that liberal-conservative paradox by encouraging guests to open up, and seems at times to care about them genuinely and show concern for what they have been through. Yet he can quickly turn it round, to the delight of the audience, with a pointed question or observation.

Another crucial way in which *The Jerry Springer Show* is different from earlier examples of the genre is that it was the first to allow actual physical fights. In fact, audiences now expect a fight and guests are primed to engage in physical contact. However, it all seems very well managed; before any real harm can be done, Springer's bouncers rush in to break up the action. As a result, there has inevitably been accusa-tion of fakery, critics arguing that the whole thing is stage-managed. Whether it is staged or not, what the show appears to reinforce is the notion that violence is a way to solve problems. It provides a public space in which the rational is rejected in favour of the irrational, the physical response favoured over an intellectual engagement, and all of this is presented for audience approval and enjoyment (Dovey, 2000). By 1998 there were certainly a number of protests and calls for Springer to clean up his show and discourage violence, and from late 1998 greater restraint has clearly been shown.

The producers of *The Jerry Springer Show* would obviously claim that the participants are all real (as opposed to paid actors) and that their experiences are all authentic. Indeed, participants are seemingly identified and located through a number of strategies. At the end of episodes, the host raises an issue to be dealt with in a future show and asks viewers to call in if they have a connection to this topic. Producers also use guests who have already appeared in a show as leads to other possible people and stories. The studio audience themselves also provide a pool of potential guests, and it is not unusual for experts to be used for recruitment purposes (Heaton and Wilson, 1995). However, producers do admit to coaching and preparing the participants for the show. To be 'good talent', they need to show emotion, they have to be passionate, angry or sorry (Joyner, 1995). Springer himself admits that he encourages guests to be as outrageous as possible and to act up if necessary to get the attention of both the studio audience and television viewers at home. It is clearly a crucial part of the show and it is probably the real reason people tend to watch it. Unlike the 'therapeutic' and 'public service' ethos that is clearly meant to construct and legitimate *The Oprah Winfrey Show* (ABC, 1986–) and so on, the spectacle of the participant's pain and humiliation is unproblematically served up to the studio and television audience as 'entertainment' (White, 1992 and Shattuc, 1997).

Although *Springer* is very much about the display of the problem rather than a search for solution, there is an attempt at some kind of resolution. This usually comes through Springer's ending comments that frequently take a high moral tone. Just as a judge sums up at the end of a hearing, so too Springer attempts to draw together the elements of the show and produce a narrative of closure. He is often patronising in these final words (and you almost expect a 'don't try this at home, kids'), yet his objective is to convince us he really does care. His tone suggests that while he may have enjoyed the stage(ed) antics, there is an important and serious lesson to be learnt. It is a moral indicator of the status quo, and we are left in no confusion as to what or whom is right and wrong. But whether or not we are to read this final address (and perhaps the show as a whole) ironically is open to debate. However, what is clear is that perhaps more than any other programme, *The Jerry Springer Show* (coming as it did before **Big Brother** [Endemol, 1999–]) was the first and most provocative example of the 'reality genre' to harness both the 'voyeuristic' and the 'exploitative' tendencies that now seemingly define so much of contemporary television.

QUESTIONS TO CONSIDER

- How does *The Jerry Springer Show* obey many of the conventional characteristics of the traditional confessional talk show? In what ways does it transcend these boundaries and for what effect?

- Do you think *The Jerry Springer Show* is any less 'therapeutic' than other confessional talk shows or is it just more 'honest' in openly displaying its entertainment values?

- What role do you think the audience plays in *The Jerry Springer Show*? What sort of function do you think Jerry's presence plays in the show's overall dynamic?

- What purpose do you think Jerry's final address to camera plays? Do you think its high moral tone provides a suitable ending for such a show?

- Do you think it is morally right to use people's pain and humiliation as a means of entertainment? In what ways do you think its host and producers would defend their show against accusations of exploitation?

RECOMMENDED READING

Myers, Greg (2001), 'I'm Out of It; You Guys Argue': Making an Issue of It on *The Jerry Springer Show*' in Tolsen, Andrew (ed.), *Television Talk Shows: Discourse, Performance, Spectacle*, New Jersey and London: Lawrence Erlbaum Associates, Publishers.
Shattuc, Jane (1997), *The Talking Cure: TV Talk Shows and Women*, London: Routledge.
White, Mimi (1992), *Tele-advising: Therapeutic Discourse in American Television*, Chapel Hill: University of North Carolina Press.

Chapter Twenty Four □

Marty

Jason Jacobs

Production Details

(NBC, 1953)

Writer: Paddy Chayefsky
Director: Delbert Mann
Producer: Fred Coe

Cast includes:

Marty (Rod Steiger)
Clara (Nancy Marchand)
Marty's Mother (Esther Minciotti)
Angie (Joe Mantell)
Aunt Catherine (Augusta Ciolli)
Virginia (Betsy Palmer)
Tommy (Lee Philips)

According to Charles Barr, 'If there is a canon of classic TV plays, then *Marty*, written by Paddy Chayefsky and directed by Delbert Mann, certainly belongs to it' (1996, 47). First transmitted in May 1953 as part of the *Philco-Goodyear Television Playhouse* anthology series on NBC, *Marty* won several industry awards and has since been recognised as one of the finest examples of early television drama. This early single play is about Marty, a butcher (played by Rod Steiger), who has never had a girlfriend and who is under pressure from his mother, family and friends to settle down with a wife. Part of its appeal was in the way it attended to local and ethnicised groups – his family is clearly coded as Italian-American – while developing universal themes of loneliness and isolation. Marty believes he is doomed to be single: as he says to his friend Angie, 'I'm thirty-six years of age, I've been looking for a girl every Saturday night of my life, you know? I'm a fat little ugly guy and girls don't go for me, that's all … Everybody says to me 'Whenareyegonnagetmarried? Whenareyegonnagetmarried? Whenareyegonnagetmarried?' I wanna get married – don't you think I wanna get married? I wanna get married'.

Under pressure from his mother to find a girl, instead of watching Sid Caesar on television, Marty visits the Waverly Ballroom, a local dance club-cum-pick-up joint. After being rejected by a girl, he is approached by a sleazy guy who is looking for help: 'Listen, I got hooked up on a blind date tonight, and I got a dog, see? And while I was here I met up with some nice-looking chick and I'd like to figure out some way of getting rid of the dog. I give you five bucks to take the dog home for me'. Marty rejects the offer, but the man's cruel misogyny and explicit, brutal commodification of the woman seems to touch something deep in him (he later describes himself as a 'professor of pain'). He asks the 'dog' – Clara (Nancy Marchand, later to become Tony Soprano's mother in *The Sopranos* [HBO, 1999–]) to dance, and they eventually agree to go to the movies together, despite pressure from Marty's male friends to call it off.

Marty was produced by Fred Coe, who had begun working for *Philco-Goodyear Television Playhouse* in 1948 and had gained a reputation for using unknown writers and directors; according to Tino Balio, Coe was responsible for 'setting anthology drama on a course that established it as the most prestigious format on live television' (1997, 390). Delbert Mann, who was later awarded the Oscar for Best Direction for the film version of *Marty* (1954), had worked with Coe in theatre and in 1949 began directing for *Philco*. Susan R Gibberman notes that Mann's style was minimal (1997, 994):

> *Cameras are fairly static and actors are staged within the frame. At Coe's direction, close-ups were used only to emphasise something or if there was a dramatic reason for doing so. The static camera is particularly effective in the* Marty *dance sequence, which Mann filmed with one camera and no editing. Actors were carefully choreographed to turn to the camera when they needed to be seen. Combined with the crowded, relatively small set, the static camera focused the audience's attention on the characters and their sense of uneasiness in the situation.*

Paddy Chayefsky was one of the well-known writers of television drama in the 1950s, alongside Rod Serling, Horton Foote, Reginald Rose and Tad Mosel. He began working for Coe in 1952 and produced a string of TV plays, including *Holiday* (NBC, 1953), *The Mother* (NBC, 1954) and *Bachelor Party* (NBC, 1955). With these Chayefsky gained a reputation for original scripts that explored the ordinary and intimate worlds of lonely characters. His biographies signal that much of the material for his plays was derived from his own experience, something that became much more common, particularly in the UK drama anthology series of the late 1950s, such as *Armchair Theatre* (ITV, 1956–74). Chayefsky's concern with what he called 'the marvellous world of the ordinary' seemed to many critics ideally suited to the medium of television, particularly in so far as it signalled a distance from what they perceived as the starry escapism of Hollywood movies. *Marty* was a fine example of this interest in the everyday, since one of its central themes is concerned with how 'ugly' people, often from lower-middle-class backgrounds, escape loneliness in a world that seems to confine the expression of their emotions.

Originally called *Love Story*, *Marty* was written and rehearsed very quickly, with Chayefsky finishing the last act and giving it to the cast in the middle of the five-day rehearsal. Some critics have pointed out that the 'limitations' of live production in the early days opened up a space for aesthetic experimentation (Caughie, 2000 and Jacobs, 2000) and some self-referentiality (Barr, 1996). However, as John Caldwell points out, the limitations of early television drama were often showcased as markers of achievement in themselves (1995, 48–9):

> *Even in serious, quality artistic offerings like* Marty, *technical limitations were not only evident, but they became a kind of badge of honour. Poorly diffused pools of light and shadow abound in* Marty. *Focus and depth of field were problems as actors moved in real time; the sets were clearly inexpensive and minimal; and luminance levels changed noticeably as the actors walked from one side of the set to another ... 'The show that you are watching' could, as it were, fall apart at any moment ... The whole point, in fact, was to show how much one could do with very little. Live anthology drama wore the then-limited and meagre televisual apparatus as a badge of dramatic honour and prestige.*

Nevertheless, the necessity of live production can force choices on the director that open up new expressive possibilities. For example, Mann decided to shoot the dance scene with one camera, because the set was too small for two; but the result was dramatically satisfying and Mann used it again in the film version, where the same constraints did not apply.

On the surface, the play seems a charming story about loneliness and love, but there is a darker side to *Marty*, most of which comes from the extraordinary performance of Rod Steiger. Steiger was a pupil of the Actor's Studio, which under the guidance of Lee Strasberg had developed the Method system. David Russell describes the Method as 'a system of thinking, as much of acting, at whose heart lies an emphasis on personal solitude, psychological trauma, internal sickness and repression and, in response to this, regression and frustration, sexual or otherwise' (2000, 39). Rod Steiger's acting is exemplary in this respect and demonstrates how the control of childish raw emotion can produce psychological ambiguity.

We see this in an important scene where Marty takes Clara home after the dance. Even today it is distinctly uncomfortable for the viewer to watch. Marty turns on the light in his empty home and ushers her inside. The fact that they are alone in his house creates an awkward tension that is potently clear to both of them. Marty's inept attempts to strike up a conversation with Clara are redolent of Travis Bickle's (Robert De Niro) wooing of Betsy (Cybill Shepard) in *Taxi Driver* (Scorsese, 1976). He discusses the price and cut of steak, then tells her to relax before making a clumsy attempt to kiss her. There is an instant of struggle as he holds her by the shoulders: 'Please just gimme ... No. Just – please – ... all I want is a little kiss ...' Rejected, Marty retreats to a chair and begins to cry, seeing this as another marker on his road of rejection and loneliness. But Clara is understanding and manages to bring him out of his isolated self-pity. Nevertheless, this scene serves to underline the fact that Marty's desperation is a product of sexual appetite as well as existential desire for companionship that he can barely control.

Chapter Twenty Five
Middlemarch

Robin Nelson

Production Details

(BBC1, 1994)

Original novel: George Eliot (Mary Ann, later Marian, Evans)
Screenplay: Andrew Davies
Executive Producer, BBC: Michael Wearing
Executive Producer, WGBH: Rebecca Eaton
Producer: Louis Marks
Director: Anthony Page
Lighting Cameraman: Brian Trufano
Production Designer: Gerry Scott
Music: Christopher Gunning, Stanley Myers

Cast includes:

Dorothea Brooke (Juliet Aubrey)
Rev. Edward Casaubon (Patrick Malahide)
Dr Tertius (Douglas Hodge)
Arthur Brooke (Robert Hardy)
Nicholas Bulstrode (Peter Jeffrey)
Mr Standish (Ronald Hines)
Fred Vincy (Jonathan Firth)
Mrs Cadwallader (Elizabeth Spriggs)
Rosamond Vincy (Trevyn McDowell)
Will Ladislaw (Rufus Sewell)
Mary Garth (Rachel Power)
Sir James Chettem (Julian Wadham)
Voice of George Eliot (Judy Dench)

The television dramatisation of George Eliot's *Middlemarch* (1871–2) in part typifies the BBC tradition of adapting classics of English literature for the small screen. Such period dramas are a peculiarly British production phenomenon, though they find an audience in America and beyond. Indeed, without financial support from abroad, it is unlikely that the large budgets required to produce serials of the scope of *Middlemarch* could be found. In fact, this production was co-funded by WGBH, Boston, and the average cost of each of the six episodes was around £1 million. Funding conditions have implications for the look of such period dramas since, as screenwriter Andrew Davies observes, fingernails must be clean for the American market. Costs are high since generic expectations of 'quality' production values are great amongst the prospective audience. In this context, 'quality' involves a conflation of economic capital in terms of a cinematic mode of production with sumptuous *mise-en-scène* and the high cultural capital derived from the place of certain English novels in the canon of English literature (*Middlemarch* is regarded by many as the archetypal nineteenth century English novel of intellectual weight and moral seriousness).

Settings, costumes and furnishings, besides being historically accurate, are expected to be lavish in materials and anticipated to include an English stately home. In these respects, *Middlemarch* does not disappoint. The country parks and houses (Lowick, Freshitt Hall, Stone Court) top the attractive, but provincial, stone-built rural town of Stamford, chosen to represent Eliot's middle England. The entire town was made over to remove any sign of modern life. The historical research of architecture and materials and the painstaking realisation of the settings, avoiding any give-away signs to break the illusion, inevitably take much time and money. In addition to locations, period dramas typically involve a large cast, and Britain has developed a tradition of character actors who even look as though they belong to another age. The cast of *Middlemarch* includes Michael Hordern, Peter Jeffrey, Robert Hardy and Elizabeth Spriggs, as well as younger, less established but reputable performers. Whilst 'star quality' can be an audience draw, there is some advantage in avoiding big names for key roles where a significant part of the audience will have their own image of the characters from reading the novel. Arguably the casting of *Middlemarch* struck a fine balance.

The process of adaptation for TV drama of a 1,000-page novel representing an entire society, albeit of a provincial English town, inevitably involved editing. The original *Middlemarch* was itself serialised, each magazine edition focusing largely on one aspect of the complex narrative and offering a lengthy story segment. Contemporary TV drama typically interweaves narrative strands, affording quick cuts between one story and another to hold the attention of a range of viewers (Nelson, 1996). Producer Michael Wearing offered a key to the restructuring of the adaptation, affording an insight into that generic thinking which informs television production, when he suggested that Lydgate's arrival in Middlemarch resembled an outsider riding into town in a Western.

The idea of people with a mission riding horses towards their goal allows the core narratives, involving two parallel stories of love and ambition, to be introduced with iconographic power and verbal economy at the outset. Sequences of the stagecoach bearing Dr Lydgate are intercut with those of Dorothea Brooke galloping with her sister through the countryside. The dynamism of this action contrasts with images of grazing sheep and a slow-paced rural life underscored by music based on Vaughan Williams' variation of Tallis, connoting 'Englishness'. With the arrival of Lydgate's coach, the arrangement increases in tempo to herald a sense of disturbance implied by impending reforms but, in television audience terms, offering a hook to catch people's attention. As such, editing, sound score and iconic imagery have been mobilised in the process of adaptation to make *Middlemarch* a text of its time, just as the original novel was a text shaped by production conditions in the mid-nineteenth century.

As one might expect of a period drama of this sort, there are inevitably love stories in *Middlemarch*. In particular, they centre on the young idealists, Dr Lydgate and Dorothea Brooke. Lydgate is a doctor with a reforming zeal in medicine that does not stretch to gender politics. He marries the attractive but flighty Rosamund Vincy and lives to regret it. Dorothea chafes against the constraints on women in Victorian society. Initially she seeks an outlet for her intelligence and social conscience in supporting the research of her dryly academic husband, Reverend Casaubon. On his death, Casaubon writes a codicil into his will precluding his widow's inheritance should she marry his cousin, Will Ladislaw, to whom Dorothea is attracted. Ultimately, Dorothea and Ladislaw forsake the inheritance and marry, and the circumstances of their union are underlined by the marriage of more minor characters, Mary Garth and Fred Vincy. The latter disappoints his family in refusing a profession in the clergy to marry his true love of modest origins.

Thus, although *Middlemarch* has the romantic 'happy endings' required of the historical romance aspect of the period drama genre, passion is tempered by economic conditions. In fact, the specific love stories are located in a range of broader concerns, perhaps hinted at in the opening sequence when the Industrial Revolution is evidenced in the building of the railway and Lydgate's approving observation – 'the future'. Indeed, Lydgate's medical reforms were proposed to alleviate a downside of commercial progress in providing healthcare for those whose displacement from agriculture to towns like Middlemarch saw poverty, disease and slum-dwelling. Dorothea similarly dreams of a miniature welfare state over a century before Britain saw its implementation. Even the romance aspect of her story, her sexual attraction to Will Ladislaw set against the loveless marriage to Casaubon, raises questions of female sexuality and, ultimately, legal questions of women's freedom under law to determine their own destiny. What makes *Middlemarch* stand out, then, from the BBC period drama tradition is the retention of the social and philosophical aspects of the original novel, the clear location of the core narratives against broader English society prior to the Reform Act of 1832.

Episode 4, for example, serves to illustrate how *Middlemarch* subtly sustains the broader historical and social context in which the personal relationships are set. It opens with an overheard remark that, 'the tide is turning, my fine Tory gentleman'. The ensuing conversation on Middlemarch main street continues, 'That's revolution'; 'Couldn't happen here'; 'Happened in France'. A more overtly political discussion between Dorothea's uncle, Arthur Brooke, and Ladislaw follows at *The Pioneeer* newspaper office. Brooke is proposing to stand as a Reform candidate in the forthcoming election and Ladislaw is acting as his agent. Evoking the issue of the abolition of slavery, Brooke observes:

> Wilberforce ... all fine and good. Criminal law reform, long overdue. But I don't want to go the whole hog and give the vote to every Tom, Dick and Harry. That would be changing the balance of the constitution. D'you see?

Ladislaw replies with frustrated irony, 'But we want to change the balance of the constitution: that's what reform's about'. This series of dialogues, simply effected in standard shot/reverse shot, illustrates the economy of the adaptation. Not all viewers, of course, will pick up fully on the references to Wilberforce and the French Revolution, but they afford an historical texture available on several levels. The drama, however, is rooted in character and situation; Brooke is played by Robert Hardy as a genial, bumbling but benevolent English gentleman, well-intentioned, perhaps, but ultimately clueless. At the hustings to which this opening sequence of episode 4 is leading, Brooke is shouted down and pelted with eggs.

Not only does episode 4 economically locate the political history of *Middlemarch*, but through well-structured juxtapositions in the intercutting it also draws parallels of personal narratives involving social issues. In another street conversation, grocer Mawmsey informs Lydgate that he has not prescribed his wife's 'strengthening medicine'. Lydgate observes that it is medically useless and its prescription serves only to bolster the incomes of doctors who are inadequately remunerated under the current system. Cut to: Lydgate finds himself as a married man slipping rapidly into debt. Cut to: the luckless but admirable Farebrother being rewarded with an advantageous living on the recommendation of none other than the struggling Lydgate. Lydgate is lent money by the hypocritical Bulstrode, whose purchase of Stone Court crowns his social ascendancy. Moving on to the cliffhanger ending of the episode, however, another contrast brings the ominous arrival of Raffles, holder of the outwardly pious Bulstrode's dark secret.

Whilst these are all narrative aspects of the source novel, the judicious selection and structuring, along with economic transposition from page to screen, is what makes *Middlemarch* uncommonly worth watching. Davies and the production team use contemporary television forms to advantage. More than pace and range of viewer interests is achieved in the adaptation. Built around the key ingredients of romance narrative and an attractively visual look, a new version of the novel's structural parallelism makes the TV serial more than the sum of its parts, conveying something of that warp and weft of an entire society famously achieved in Eliot's novel. Celia Brooke's preoccupation with cooing – and inviting everybody else to coo – over baby Arthur in the midst of this rich mix serves at once as a measure of interests and another strand in the weft.

Until the very end when a voice-over pulls together possible loose threads in the narrative strands, *Middlemarch* holds to the conventions of television naturalism, offering the illusion of a coherent world. There is no meta-narrative voice where George Eliot's is so evident in the novel. Indeed, Andrew Davies finds Eliot's voice too intrusive and judgemental and aimed for the television adaptation to give life to those characters Eliot did not favour. However, television naturalism is never a neutral view of a world, and the discursive position of the adaptation, broadly aligned with Eliot's sympathies in the novel, is discernible. In another strand intercut in episode 4, Sir James Chettam, an aristocrat with a 'natural right' to dominion, rails against the oppressive terms of Casaubon's will whilst sustaining male chauvinism in acting as rightful protector of his wronged sister-in-law, Dorothea. Although Chettam opposes reform, the presentation of him otherwise echoes that of Brooke in representing a stolid, well-heeled, bourgeois-aristocratic Englishness, so comfortable and self-satisfied with its lot that fundamental reform is not only undesirable but literally unthinkable. By mobilising resonant ironies in the intercutting of narratives, the production team of *Middlemarch* manages overall to convey those qualities of English conservatism that, as George Eliot saw it, hindered the progress of political and social reform.

Few television serials aim to capture the condition of England. Such totalising visions are not popular in an age of partial and multiple perspectives. But *Middlemarch* offers such a vision, inclusive of romance and fine bonnets as aspects of daily living but not perhaps as the stuff of life itself.

QUESTIONS TO CONSIDER

- What features sustain period drama as a mainstay of UK TV drama production?
- To what extent does TV *Middlemarch* sacrifice historical context to foreground love interest?
- How does a 'realist' approach to shooting the novel allow viewers insights into characters' thoughts and feelings?
- How do you think an American audience might view this adaptation of *Middlemarch*? In what ways may they perceive it differently to a British audience?
- How wide a range of functions does the music soundtrack of *Middlemarch* serve?

RECOMMENDED READING

BBC Education (1994), *Middlemarch: A Viewer's Guide*, London: BBC Education.

Giddings, Robert (1990), *Screening the Novel: The Theory and Practice of Literary Dramatization*, Basingstoke: Macmillan.

Nelson, Robin (1997), 'Framing the Real: *Oranges, Middlemarch, X-Files*' in *TV Drama in Transition: Forms, Values and Cultural Change*, Basingstoke: Macmillan.

Chapter Twenty Six

The Monkees

KJ Donnelly

Production Details

(NBC, 1966–8)

Creators: Bob Rafelson, Bert Schneider
Directors (most common): James Frawley, Bob Rafelson, Bruce Kessler, Alex Singer
Music producer (1966): Don Kirshner

Cast includes:

The Monkees: Davy Jones (vocals), Mike Nesmith (guitar), Peter Tork (bass guitar), Micky Dolenz (drums)

The Monkees was a 'zany' comedy regarding the adventures of an amiable rock group that play music and live communally. The series ran to only 58 episodes, but its reputation has been bolstered by constant reruns and worldwide sales, boosted in the 1990s by video sales supported by the group reforming and touring. The show appeared to be a new phenomenon: a television comedy that was also a pop music show. However, it should be noted that the programme's constituents had proven very successful in the cinema since the coming of sound, with musical comedies mixing big personalities, drama and songs that could be sold as an appendage to the package. In terms of television precedents perhaps there were few, but the logic of the mix bears out Todd Gitlin's description of the 'recombinant form' of television, where elements that have proven successful in different types of programme are combined to create new shows or new formats (1983, 78). *The Monkees* certainly went some way towards influencing the aesthetic development of pop promo films, as well as accelerating television product placement (the marketing of products within television shows; see also *Big Brother* [Endemol, 1999–), in this case, largely to the more suggestible pre-teen audiences.

In September 1965, producers Bob Rafelson and Bert Schneider of Screen Gems (a subsidiary of Hollywood studio Columbia) advertised for actors and musicians. The subsequent auditions were filmed and then rated by audiences (the screen tests for *The Monkees* were shown later as appendices to the programmes). NBC purchased the show from Screen Gems/Columbia in January of 1966 and it was broadcast eight

are moments when the denial of the group's bubblegum pedigree becomes fevered, such as when a succession of still screen images holds on a famous image of a man being shot in Vietnam. However, the film was a commercial disaster, clearly alienating its young audience, while the group were seemingly not 'serious' enough to appeal to a sophisticated 'rock' audience. The wholehearted desire to differentiate from the television series was probably undermined by the fact that the second season of the show was still in reruns on NBC at the time of *Head*'s release.

Hard on the heels of *Head*'s failure came a television special for NBC, called *33⅓ Revolutions Per Monkee* (1969). Masterminded by British, Oxford-educated TV pop music veteran, Jack Good, who had made *Oh Boy!* (ITV, 1958–9) in Britain and *Shindig* (ABC, 1964–6) in the USA, it was finished before Christmas of 1968 but was not broadcast until April 14, 1969. An hour long, it included special guests such as Jerry Lee Lewis, Fats Domino, Little Richard, Julie Driscoll, Brian Auger and The Trinity, among others. Despite including some mainstream pop music, the story that held it all together persisted in The Monkees' quest for respectability through mocking their manufactured status. In the programme, the group are made in large test tubes and have no individual identities, being called simply 'Monkee no. 1', 'Monkee no. 2', etc. Their mission is world domination through commercial exploitation.

After the group's demise in 1970, Nesmith was the only member to have a hit solo record, with the single 'Rio' in 1976. He also had a promo made for the single, something of a pioneering activity at the time. In 1986, the group reunited for a tour, celebrating their 20th anniversary, and despite MTV broadcasting the series to stimulate interest, Mike Nesmith refused to join the other three. He was rich enough not to bother, being the heir to the copyright on liquid paper, owning a successful pop promo company and producing a couple of films. Nesmith had an on-off relationship with the group, as they made intermittent concert tours over the next decade or so. However, he did join them for their next television project, an hour-long television special called *Hey Hey It's The Monkees*, which was broadcast on ABC on February 17, 1997.

QUESTIONS TO CONSIDER

- What similarities can you find between *The Monkees* and films like *A Hard Day's Night* and *Help!*? To what extent do you think the show was trying to copy these earlier films?
- How important is *The Monkees'* blend of distinct characters to its success? Can you find similarities between other bands like The Beatles, The Spice Girls or S Club 7?
- What is the role of television in relation to the promotion of pop music? Do you think *The Monkees* television show was more than simply an 'advertisement' for their records?
- What is the relation of television to the selling of products? Can you find examples in *The Monkees* of 'product placement'?
- What are the similarities to and differences of *The Monkees* to more recent manufactured TV pop shows like *Pop Stars*?

RECOMMENDED READING

Goostree, Laura (1988), 'The Monkees and the Deconstruction of Television Realism' in *Journal of Popular Film and Television*, Vol. 16, No. 2, Summer.

Ramaeker, Paul B (2001), ' "You Think They Call us Plastic *Now* ...": The Monkees and *Head*' in Pamela Robertson Wojcik and Arthur Knight, (eds.), *Soundtrack Available: Essays on Film and Popular Music*, Durham: Duke University Press.

Reilly, Edward, McManus, Maggie and Chadwick, William (eds.) (1993), *The Monkees: A Manufactured Image: The Ultimate Reference Guide to Monkees Memories and Memorabilia*, New York: Popular Culture Ink.

Chapter Twenty Seven

Monty Python's Flying Circus

Brett Mills

Production Details

(BBC, 1969–74)

(Note: the fourth series of the programme, in which John Cleese did not appear, while commonly known as *Monty Python's Flying Circus*, is officially called only *Monty Python*.)

Conceived and written by: Graham Chapman, John Cleese, Terry Jones, Eric Idle, Michael Palin
Animation: Terry Gilliam
Producer: John Howard Davies
Director: Ian McNaughton

Performers:

Graham Chapman
John Cleese
Carol Cleveland
Terry Gilliam
Eric Idle
Terry Jones
Michael Palin

The very first episode of *Monty Python's Flying Circus*, broadcast to a tiny, late-night audience on October 5, 1969, contains the funniest joke ever written, a gag so funny that anyone who hears it dies laughing. The military, realising its potential, use the joke in warfare, with soldiers marching through woods reciting it in German while surrounded by hysteria-induced Nazis falling from trees. For an unheard-of comedy show containing relative unknowns it is an audacious and apt sketch, perfectly encapsulating the themes and methods employed throughout the series and which mean that, still today, it is seen as a significant watershed in broadcast comedy.

The programme arose out of – and is symbolic of – significant shifts in British society and culture throughout the 1950s and 1960s. Carpenter (2000) constructs a social history of the era in which post-war drabness began to be questioned by a range of

Oxbridge graduates, who discovered during National Service that what they had been told about the natural ways in which Britain should be understood and governed were no longer viable. A whole range of playwrights and novelists – soon dubbed the 'Angry Young Men' – were inspired to rage against British political and social structures, with the most famous example being John Osborne's play *Look Back in Anger* (1956). This led to a widespread satire boom, inspired by probably the most influential piece of British comedy of the last century: Alan Bennett, Peter Cook, Jonathan Miller and Dudley Moore's theatrical revue *Beyond the Fringe* (1961).

The members of the *Monty Python* team arose from this comedic history. Cleese, Chapman, Idle, Jones and Palin had all worked to various degrees on the popular *The Frost Report* (BBC, 1966–7), David Frost's live series in which a different aspect of British society – class, education, Parliament, and so on – was discussed and mocked every week. Idle, Jones and Palin collaborated on the children's series *Do Not Adjust Your Set* (ITV, 1968 and 1969), in which the standard conventions of television began to be undermined and in which, in the last few episodes, the American animator Terry Gilliam began to display his work. Chapman and Cleese worked closely on *At Last the 1948 Show* (ITV, 1967), in which Idle also appeared sporadically. All of these series garnered cult followings among audiences sympathetic to popular culture that acknowledged the conventions of its form and used comedy to highlight the absurdity of a range of authorities. But it was the producer Barry Took who brought the *Monty Python* team together from their various projects to work on a series, even though, as Took admits, 'the BBC was terribly worried about these people' (cited in Perry, 1983, 43).

What resulted was what has been described as 'A series of crucial importance in the development of comedy, not just on British TV but on a global scale and in various media … [which] … invented a new genre' (Lewisohn, 1998, 449). Influencing its content and format above all else was the team's desire to escape 'the tyranny of the punch line' (Wilmut, 1980, 197). As writers on other shows where good sketches were abandoned as unworkable because a suitable pay-off could not be found, the *Monty Python* team were determined to discard such restrictions, thus opening out the direction in which sketches could develop, a technique with a direct ancestry in Spike Milligan's long-running *Q* (BBC 1969–80) series (Lewisohn, 1998, 438, 449). Yet while Milligan's series resulted in a clutch of random unrelated sketches, *Monty Python's Flying Circus* instead offered some sort of coherence and narrative through Gilliam's animation sequences. Other techniques included the appearance of Chapman's military officer into sketches to end them, complaining that they were 'too silly', or, most blatantly, Cleese's desk-bound presenter bluntly announcing, 'And now for something completely different'.

By abandoning this hitherto limiting requirement, sketches on *Monty Python's Flying Circus* were capable of encompassing virtually any content; the most used adjective for the programme is 'surreal'. However, this is a lazy way of describing the programme's concerns which, while not as didactically satirical as much of that which preceded it,

131

relies on satire's questioning of authority for much of its punch. What makes the programme's focus less obviously classically satirical is that 'it represents a *social* critique and is not narrowly concerned with politics or politicians' (Wagg, 1992, 269). It therefore plays with, and undermines, a whole range of social norms which its contributors, from suburban, middle-class, university-educated backgrounds, had found to be stifling while they grew up, and representative of deference to authority in adulthood. Many of the sketches attack middle-class culture generally, most obviously in the recurring images of bowler-hatted, pinstripe-suit-wearing civil servants performing ridiculous antics with deferential seriousness. So while the famous 'Ministry of Silly Walks' sketch clearly relies on Cleese's genius for physical comedy (also employed in his [with Connie Booth] phenomenally praised sitcom, *Fawlty Towers* [BBC, 1975–9]) for much of its actual comic moments, the sketch as a whole works because it attacks the pomposity with which government departments go about their business, using the public's taxes to do so.

Similarly, *Monty Python's Flying Circus* attacks the politics of authority by engaging with the norms of culture itself. While a number of programmes had played around with the conventions of television (and, post-Python, Idle took this even further in *Rutland Weekend Television* [BBC, 1975–6]), *Python* instead used the medium's formats to question the high/low culture divide. Thus 'in one spoof TV show contestants have to summarize seven works of Marcel Proust in fifteen seconds each; in another, questions on football and pop music are put to Karl Marx, Lenin, Mao Zedong and Che Guevara' (Wagg, 1992, 271). This has led to debates as to whether *Monty Python's Flying Circus* requires an educated audience for its jokes to make any sense, meaning that the satire only functions for those who are being mocked (Neale and Krutnik, 1990, 207). Wilmut rejects such a reading, stating that 'any feeling of "intellectualism" is in fact a clever optical illusion' (1980, 217) and that only a general understanding of cultural divides is necessary for the sketches' effectivity. Whatever, such comedy clearly represents the team's rejection of the norms of culture which their education had tried to force upon them.

Another aspect of the series' comedy which is often explored is its cruelty (Wagg, 1992, 270). In doing so it revelled in, and made fun of, the physicality of the human experience that much of British society attempts to deny. Bishop (1990) relates this to Bakhtin's notion of the carnivalesque (1984), in which humour's social role is seen as a celebration of the physical, and 'death and human destruction are a comic grotesque image' (Bishop, 1990, 59). By allowing such discrete concepts to rub up against each other, the series perhaps gets the nearest to nihilist comedy that has ever been seen on television (Thompson, 1982).

It is perhaps surprising then, that, unlike the vast majority of British comedy, the series managed to become a significant success in America. Miller (2000) outlines the history of the programme in the US, in which he questions the assumption that the programme appealed to an educated, older, middle-class audience for whom the references were more likely to have meaning. Instead, the programme was popular in a range of areas, whether rural or urban, and was picked up by the burgeoning undergraduate population for whom it represented the comic extension of American counter-culture already being mined by acts such as Richard Pryor and George Carlin. Indeed, Miller argues that central to its appeal – and the appeal of much British programming in America – was that it was not a product of the commercial American broadcasting system. In that sense, its very 'Britishness' made it radical. In addition, the programme's constant undermining of authority figures mirrored audiences' continued campaigning against the government over issues such as Vietnam and race problems. Miller finds 'Several utterances of "our-own-ness" ' (ibid.) in which American audiences not only felt the series reflected their relationship with authority, but, in response, claimed ownership over the programme and the politics it espoused. This was evidenced in American responses to the *Monty Python* stage shows in New York in 1976 and Los Angeles in 1980, where 'they would applaud a sketch upon recognizing it, laugh a moderate amount through it, and then clap and cheer enthusiastically at the end' (Wilmut, 1980, 222). Here audiences weren't finding such comedy funny anymore, but instead applauding its existence and acknowledging their relationship with it.

However, there are those for whom the programme represents some of the worst of comedy and, specifically, the British comedy industry. Many have criticised the series' portrayal of women, in which the only female characters are either screechy old harridans played by one of the male cast in drag, or a 'sexpot' (usually played by Carol Cleveland) who has little function other than being the object of male desire (Banks and Swift, 1987). Similarly, critics have seen the programme's overt cleverness as patronising to its audience and upholding the legitimacy of such knowledge. Laughing at, and being a fan of, the programme has a certain kind of 'snob merit' (Miller, 2000, 137) which allows viewers to display their intellectualism. The American television critic Cleveland Amory similarly sees the use of obscure references as merely a method by the team to legitimise what is, in essence, nothing more than silly undergraduate humour; the programme is an example, then, of what he calls 'overgraduate humour' (1975, 32). None of this has prevented the series from having its spin-offs. As a team, four films have been produced: *Monty Python and the Holy Grail* (Terry Jones and Terry Gilliam, 1974), *Monty Python's Life of Brian* (Terry Jones, 1979), *Monty Python Live at the Hollywood Bowl* (Terry Hughes, 1982) and *Monty Python's Meaning of Life* (Terry Jones, 1983), with *Monty Python's Life of Brian* one of the most controversial films of all time.

In some ways, it is difficult to see the influence of *Monty Python's Flying Circus* on contemporary comedy, precisely because the team took their concerns and comedic style to their legitimate conclusion, leaving nothing for successors to do. After all, if your series contains the funniest joke ever written, how are other comedians going to top that? And, even though it should have a health warning on it, here is the World's Funniest Joke, in German, of course:

Venn ist das nurnstuck git und Slotermeyer?
Ja! Beigerhund das oder die Flipperwaldt gersput.

QUESTIONS TO CONSIDER

- Does the series, as intended, always avoid punchlines? If so, what is funny in the series and how are sketches brought to an end? Are these methods as pleasurable as those found in 'conventional' sketch shows?

- Is the programme merely 'overgraduate humour', or something more sophisticated than that? Is there any social or personal value to the programme's use of 'silliness'?

- Does the series constitute a satirical attack on authority and government? If so, what kinds of alternative solutions does the series offer? Is it possible to gain pleasure from the series without accepting it as satire?

- Is there something uniquely 'British' about this kind of humour? How is 'British' humour different to that in other cultures? Which other British series use such humour?

- How does the programme engage with both high and popular culture? By bringing these two areas together, what does the series do to our assumptions about culture generally?

- What kinds of portrayals of women exist in the programme? Is the series sexist, with everything presented from a male point of view? Do you think audiences would see such portrayals differently now to when they were first recorded?

RECOMMENDED READING

Perry, George (1983), *Life of Python*, London: Pavilion Books.

Thompson, John O (1982), *Monty Python: Complete and Utter Theory of the Grotesque*, London: British Film Institute.

Wagg, Stephen (1992), 'You've Never Had it so Silly: the Politics of British Satirical Comedy from Beyond the Fringe to Spitting Image' in D Strinati and S Wagg (eds.), *Come on Down? Popular Media Culture in Post-War Britain*, London and New York: Routledge.

Chapter Twenty Eight

The Moon Landing

Gary R Edgerton

Production Details

(Network Pool Coverage, 1969)

The system of pooling footage and live feeds among the three American television networks was first devised by veteran NBC producer, Roy Neal, in 1960 at the outset of Project Mercury. It was ABC-TV's turn to coordinate the coverage for the Apollo 11 'Moon Landing'.

ABC (American Broadcasting Company) anchor: Frank Reynolds; analyst: Jules Bergman (news science editor)
CBS (Columbia Broadcasting System) anchor: Walter Cronkite; analyst: Walter M Schirra (former astronaut)
NBC (National Broadcasting Company) anchor: Frank McGee; co-anchors: Chet Huntley, David Brinkley

---

The moon landing was a global television event of epic proportions. Forty million or nearly 70 per cent of the total number of television households in the US were tuned in at the moment that Neil A Armstrong took his first steps on the lunar surface. These Americans were joined by an estimated 425 million more viewers from 49 other countries. The entire Apollo 11 mission started with the lift-off of a Saturn V rocket at Cape Kennedy in Florida on Wednesday, July 16, 1969 and ended with the splashdown and recovery (by the aircraft carrier USS *Hornet*) of the command module (Columbia) on the following Thursday, July 24 in the Pacific Ocean. Highlights were covered on TV and radio throughout the 9 days, but the core telecast took place over 31 continuous hours during July 20 and 21, when the much smaller lunar module (Eagle) disengaged from Columbia and landed on the moon, carrying mission commander Armstrong and Eagle pilot Edwin E ('Buzz') Aldrin, Jr. These two men explored the lunar surface for 2 hours and 14 minutes, while Columbia pilot Michael Collins orbited the moon, waiting for their eventual return.

Considering its global coverage, it is not surprising that the moon landing became a perfect opportunity for political propaganda purposes. Its larger significance certainly becomes more evident when viewed through the lens of the Cold War. Although the Americans created the National Aeronautics and Space Administration (NASA) in 1958, they spent the early years of the space programme chasing the Russians. Russia had launched Sputnik 1 (meaning 'traveller', an artificial satellite that was the first to orbit the earth) on October 4, 1957. One month later, they sent up Sputnik 2, containing a dog named Laika, the first living creature to travel in space. But the real triumph came on April 12, 1961, when Soviet cosmonaut Yuri Gagarin became the first human to journey into orbit and return safely. However, on May 25, 1961, newly elected President John F Kennedy issued a public challenge to his fellow citizens before a joint session of Congress. 'I believe', he announced, 'this nation should commit itself to achieving the goal, before this decade is out, of landing a man on the moon and returning him safely to earth'. Space had emerged, then, as 'the new battleground in the Cold War' (Chaikin, 1994, 2), where the first superpower to reach the moon would definitively demonstrate its scientific and technological superiority over its political rival for the whole world to see via television.

The widespread reaction to the moon landing was certainly as complicated and divided as the era itself. 'The 1960s had seen the assassination of one president (Kennedy) and the ruining of another through the war in Vietnam (Johnson). Civil strife tore at the nation's colleges, and race riots set fire to its cities', recounts journalism historian Bruce J Evensen, '[b]ut the moon landing seemed to suggest that a brighter future was still possible' (1999, 154). So in full view of hundreds of millions of spectators worldwide, Armstrong and Aldrin planted an American flag into the lunar surface, just before a call came during 'a two-minute radio hookup' from President Richard M Nixon, offering the entire Apollo 11 crew hearty congratulations from the Oval Office of the White House. Nixon's live image was inserted into the upper left-hand corner of television screens around the globe as he told the astronauts that 'because of what you have done, the heavens have become a part of man's world. And as you talk to us from the Sea of Tranquility, it inspires us to redouble our efforts to bring peace and tranquility to earth' (Rugaber, 1969). In *Tube of Plenty*, eminent broadcast historian Erik Barnouw wrote that '[a]ll over the world, the moon landing took the Vietnam war off the front pages and – at least temporarily – out of the minds of men' (1990, 427). Still Nixon's aforementioned comments provide a subtle reminder that all was not calm and contented at home, despite the unprecedented accomplishments of the Apollo 11 mission.

In retrospect, the space race was tailor-made for television. More than anything, the moon landing functioned as the climactic episode in a kind of continuing miniseries which extended from the telecasting of six Mercury (1961–3), ten Gemini (1965–6), and seven Apollo missions (1967–9), before culminating with the moon landing. The shorter Mercury and Gemini space flights, especially, were covered from start to finish before rapt audiences in the tens of millions watching on small portable TVs in schools and at work, as well as on bigger screen console models at home. Each of these individual space launches was a television news special in its own right, coming as they did on a semi-regular basis every three to six months, flush with the inherent drama of a slowly orchestrated countdown, an explosive lift-off, a vicarious journey into space, enhanced by cameras positioned outside and later inside the capsules, and usually a traditional happy ending complete with a stirring splashdown and recovery. What made these telecasts all the more compelling was the palpable sense of danger about them. Occasionally disasters did happen, as with Apollo 1 on January 27, 1967, when three astronauts were literally burned alive while being trapped inside their space capsule sitting atop a massive Saturn 1B booster rocket on the launch pad at Cape Kennedy. This ever present sense of danger was a part of every mission. None of the half billion people watching Apollo 11 could ever be sure whether or not the moon landing would ultimately end in triumph or tragedy. This uncertainty made for an early and unusually compelling brand of reality programming.

The climax of the moon landing occurred at approximately 10.55 EDT on July 20, when Neil Armstrong slowly descended the ladder attached to the landing platform of lunar module as he stepped ever closer towards the surface of the moon. Pausing a third of the way down, he 'pull[ed] a D-shaped handle, opening a storage bay and exposing the lens of a black-and-white (RCA) camera', which would telecast his movements from that point onward (Barnouw, 1990, 424). (The actual landing on the moon was not captured live on camera. Instead the Columbia Broadcasting System invested in '[f]ull-scale models of the command and lunar modules, manned by CBS reporters and NASA advisers, duplicat[ing] the actions of the astronauts in a quarter-acre studio' for TV audiences around the world [Evensen, 1999, 153]). However, once Armstrong activated Eagle's camera, the signal was transmitted to the orbiting command module, Columbia, then to three enormous earth-bound antennae in Australia, Spain and California, where it was relayed to NASA in Houston and, finally, to the networks. Within '1.3 seconds' Armstrong appeared almost luminescent against the dull grey background, moving as if in slow motion in his shiny white spacesuit (Barnouw, 1990, 425). He lightly jumped off the last rung of the ladder at the end of his descent, famously remarking as his boot landed safely on the surface of the moon: 'That's one small step for man, one giant leap for mankind.'

However, the drama of the moon landing was generated more by the extraordinary nature of the event itself than by its visual aesthetics. The vivid studio transmissions of a grey and yellow-coloured Eagle replica which preceded the actual touchdown greatly contrasted with the somewhat ghostly and indistinct black and white images that were first telecast from the lunar surface. Shot with a fixed lens and perspective, these static and hazy pictures harkened back to the earliest days of experimental television. Fifteen minutes after Armstrong's initial departure from Eagle, Buzz Aldrin became the second human being to walk on the moon. For more than a half-hour, these two astronauts tested their mobility according to the moon's gravity, took photographs of each other, inspected the spacecraft, and set up a second black and white RCA camera on a tripod some 60 feet away, pointing back at them and the lunar module.

The overall textual quality of the moon landing noticeably improved with this second standing TV camera and its closer angled lens. Armstrong and Aldrin's movements were now much clearer, even occasionally capturing brief glimpses of their faces, as each astronaut learned to walk anew, negotiating the lighter gravitational pull of the moon along with the unfamiliar weight and mass of their oversized backpacks. The most elementary tasks obviously took the maximum effort out of them. For example, Armstrong and Aldrin spent much of the remainder of the moonwalk collecting 20 pounds of rock samples, before struggling together for over 10 minutes simply to hoist these few bags of minerals back into the hatchway of their spacecraft. Such mundane tasks and their rudimentary black and white televised portrayals were never memorable in and of themselves, but the unprecedented setting and the novelty of live satellite transmissions from outer space made the moon landing extraordinarily exciting TV.

Six more Apollo missions (12 to 17) proceeded on schedule, five of which resulted in ten more astronauts walking on the moon before television cameras. The size of the audiences to these subsequent telecasts waned, however, as worries increased over social problems and the prolonged conflict in Vietnam. Funding was finally rescinded for the last three planned Apollo space fights (18 through 20), causing their ultimate cancellation as the space race came to an end. Thanks to television, though, Apollo 11 provided human beings around the world with the opportunity to look at the earth in a wholly new way. Television was evidently contributing to a growing global self-awareness, even as Cold War tensions were being acted out in the moon landing for hundreds of millions of people to watch in July 1969 and to reflect upon quietly afterwards. An estimated worldwide television viewership of 528 million people had watched the event, the largest audience for any TV programme up to that point. The accompanying radio listenership increased the aggregate total to nearly one billion, providing a broadcast audience of approximately a quarter of the earth's population. The moon landing was clearly a watershed experience for humankind, both fulfilling an ancient dream as well as signalling the extraterrestrial reach and power of television as never before.

QUESTIONS TO CONSIDER

- In what ways did television and the space programme grow up together? How is the moon landing an indication of TV maturing from a national to an international medium?
- What viewer identification strategies and conventional narrative formulas were employed in the televised presentation of the moon landing?
- How can the moon landing be seen as a vestige of the Cold War?
- How does the moon landing compare and contrast with the kind of reality programming that is common today?
- What were the various audience reactions to the moon landing in July 1969? How do you feel personally about this global television event in retrospect?

RECOMMENDED READING

Barnouw, Erik (1990, second revised edition), *Tube of Plenty: The Evolution of American Television*, New York: Oxford University Press, 422–8.

Evensen, Bruce J, 'Moon Landing' in Michael D Murray (ed.) (1999), *Encyclopedia of Television News*, Phoenix, AR: Oryx Press, 153–5.

Paterson, Chris, 'Space Program and Television' in Horace Newcomb (ed.) (1997), *Museum of Broadcast Communications Encyclopedia of Television*, Volume 3, Chicago and London: Fitzroy Dearborn Publishers, 1536–9.

Chapter Twenty Nine

Neighbours

Ros Jennings

Production Details

(Grundy, 1985–)

Creator/Executive Producer: Reg Watson
Directors have included: Chris Adshead, Judith John-Story, Nicholas Bufalo
Executive producers have included: Marie Trevor, Don Battye
Producers have included: Sue Masters, Philip East, Magaret Slarke
Writers have included: Christine Madefferi, Betty Zuin, Geoffrey Truman
Theme Music: Tony Hatch

Cast has included:

Madge Bishop (Anne Charleston)
Helen Daniels (Anne Haddy)
Jim Robinson (Alan Dale)
Charlene Robinson (Kylie Minogue)
Scott Robinson (Darius Perkins/Jason Donovan)
Henry Ramsey (Craig MacLachlan)
Joe Mangel (Mark Little)
Mrs Mangel (Vivean Gray)
Mike Young (Guy Pearce)
Harold Bishop (Ian Smith)
Beth Brennan/Willis (Natalie Imbruglia)
Felicity Scully (Holly Valance)

Produced by the Grundy Organisation in Melbourne, *Neighbours* was first screened in Australia in March 1985. Since then, it has confirmed itself both as Australia's most popular domestically produced soap and also Australian television's greatest international success (at its peak it was exported to around 25 countries). In particular, it proved to be a distinctively post-colonial triumph by establishing itself as a mainstay of the BBC's programming in Britain. Indeed, as Stephen Crofts suggests, it 'proved to be sufficiently compulsive viewing to be one of only two scheduled TV programmes to survive the carpet bombing of Gulf War coverage on UK television on the war's first day, January 18, 1991' (1995, 99). Between 1986 and 1993 (when the soap opera achieved its peak viewing figures), *Neighbours* had an impact on British television culture that reached way beyond its £27,000 a week cost. The serial also had a far-reaching effect on popular culture by giving first exposure to young talent, producing actors such as Guy Pearce (who has gone on to a substantial career in Hollywood) and providing the springboard for a wealth of internationally successful pop singers, such as Jason Donovan, Natalie Imbruglia, Holly Valance and the incomparable Kylie Minogue.

The creator of *Neighbours* was Brisbane-born television writer and producer, Reg Watson. Like many young Australians in the late 1950s and early 1960s, he travelled to Britain because of work limitations in Australia (domestic Australian television did not get off the ground until 1956 and its early years were very much dominated by American and British imports). While working for ATV in London, Watson wrote early episodes of the ground-breaking medical drama *Emergency Ward Ten* (ATV, 1957–67). His most important work in Britain was, perhaps, in his role as producer and also principal writer of the original *Crossroads* (ITV, 1964–88) (a long-running, popular – though critically reviled – British soap opera based in a fictitious motel in the Midlands). When he returned to Australia in 1977, he capitalised on his expertise in British television serials by joining the Grundy Organisation to take on responsibility for serial development. His early successes for Grundy included *The Restless Years* (1983–6) and *Sons and Daughters* (1981–7).

The Grundy Organisation played an important part in Australia's outward reach by creating and marketing attractive drama packages for overseas networks. As Tom O'Regan has argued, 'Australian television drama has a "double face", its medium size makes it more outward looking' (1993, 59). In particular their efforts resulted in the effective penetration of the British market in the late 1980s and early 1990s. A crucial aspect of this successful endeavour was that 'the price [was] right' so-to-speak, in that it cost the BBC around £27,000 for a week's worth of episodes of *Neighbours* compared to £40,000 per half-hour episode of its own domestically produced soap, *EastEnders* (BBC, 1982–). In the economic climate of deregulation and greater financial accountability of the 1980s that was initiated by Margaret Thatcher's Conservative Government, *Neighbours* allowed the BBC to take action to ensure that it remained an important player in British television broadcasting, despite the fact that it had been opened up to unprecedented levels of competition.

Neighbours was broadcast for the first time on BBC1 in October 1986, using a system known as 'stripping'. Originally, this meant that the programme went out at 1.30 pm five days a week (Monday to Friday) and was repeated at 9.05 am the next morning. After a year of being 'stripped' its popularity was so great that it was decided to drop the morning screening and rescreen the lunchtime episode in the early evening. This mechanism of scheduling was copied by ITV when they introduced their own Australian soap, *Home and Away* (Seven) in 1990. Rather than compete directly with *Neighbours*, ITV created the opportunity for a twice-daily package of Australian soap by choosing to broadcast it immediately following *Neighbours*.

Late 1980s Britain proved to be especially receptive to *Neighbours*. In a cultural climate of political conservatism, negative equity and high unemployment, this upbeat Australian serial captured the British public imagination. It was certainly felt that the relative affluence of average Australian people would attract a British audience. As Barry Brown (from the BBC's Purchased Programme Department) has put it, 'I thought it would appeal to women because it is a classless society. Living standards in Australia are high, and it's good to see ordinary people like Max the plumber or Des Clarke the young baker, living well without money problems' (cited by Selby and Cowdery, 1995, 181).

This was also the peak of the power of the tabloid press in the UK and what Crofts (1995) has described as the teen sex appeal of *Neighbours* became the topic of mass coverage and mass circulation in the tabloids. This resulted in the creation of popular celebrities and, more especially, idols for the serial's many young viewers. *Neighbours* was certainly a pioneer in opening up a new youth market for soap operas and was to have profound effects on the character range of British domestically produced soaps in the years that followed. In fact, by 1988 it had become the most popular children's and young adults' programme on British television. This was partially due to its concentration of younger characters in the regular cast as opposed to the elderly and middle-aged ones so prevalent in British soaps. The explicit targeting of a youth audience was capitalised on through the policy of 'stripping' the serial and rescheduling the repeated episode for the early evening so that it could be a part of an everyday schedule of viewing and not just confined to school holidays.

Germaine Greer famously described *Neighbours* as representing the 'world of the detergent commercial' (Greer cited by Crofts, 1995, 101). It certainly broke with the gritty social realism that had shaped British soap serials such as **Coronation Street** (Granada, 1960–) and *EastEnders*, and as Dorothy Hobson (2003) has argued, *Neighbours* was a new type of soap for Britain because it presented families who actually like each other and are not afraid of displaying affection. The usual conventions of gossip, rumour, family, kinship, romance and community were in evidence, but as Crofts (1995) has outlined in his excellent analysis of ten textual reasons for its widespread success, there was enough variation to give the serial a new spin on soap life. While being on the one hand extremely conservative in its values (e.g. as Crofts argues, its unrebellious youth 'uphold sensible adult values' [1995, 100]), the programme did portray its female characters doing paid work that was somewhat alternative to stereotypical notions of femininity (e.g. Kylie Minogue's character Charlene was a mechanic). Also, the safe but rather enclosed world of a suburban Australian close was in one sense confining (any viewer quickly learnt that leaving Ramsay Street to go out into the Australian bush would result in disaster) but, to the British viewer, it was especially appealing in its dominant codes of depoliticised middle-class citizenship (Crofts, 1995, 100). This was, perhaps, the communication of the serial's Australian dimension or specificities and this was also a strong element of the show's appeal in Britain.

As Cunningham and Miller have argued, *Neighbours* offers 'dreams of ordinary people in a land of opportunity' (1994, 129–30), and this is reinforced by the sunshine and space that the typical suburban Australian plot affords in terms of residence and lifestyle possibilities for 'ordinary' people, in stark contrast to those available in Britain. The location, Erinsborough (an anagram of the serial's title, *Neighbours*) stands both in Australia and abroad as a non-specific signifier of Australia. Although made in and loosely associated with Melbourne, it does not reflect the reality of Melbourne's cultural diversity. *Neighbours* is a programme that represses difference in favour of wholesome community values. This worked particularly well in Thatcher's Britain and, because of the cultural competitiveness between Australia's major cities (particularly Sydney and Melbourne), the non-specific fictional location of Erinsborough also worked well to attract national audiences within Australia. As a result of *Neighbours*, Australia became one of the most desirable holiday destinations for young people in Britain but, conversely, also lead to the notion of an Australian invasion of British television, with *Neighbours* becoming the vanguard of an Australian 'cycle' in British programming, with series like *Prisoner: Cell Block H* (Grundy, 1989–93), *Flying Doctors* (9 Network, Crawford, 1986–91) and also numerous miniseries such as *Return to Eden* (Hanna Barbera, 1993) and *Bodyline* (10 Network, 1984) doing very well in the early 1990s.

QUESTIONS TO CONSIDER

- Why do you think *Neighbours* has become such an important Australian export, particularly in the UK?
- What do you think are the major differences between *Neighbours* and a traditional British soap opera like *Coronation Street* and *EastEnders*?
- Can you think of ways in which *Neighbours* has affected soap operas in and outside of Australia?
- Do you think it is fair to describe *Neighbours* as inherently 'conservative'? Identify aspects of it that you think might attempt to actually subvert traditional stereotypes.
- What aspects of Australian life do you think *Neighbours* refuses to reflect? In what ways might you think it offers a less than comprehensive view of contemporary Australia?

RECOMMENDED READING

Crofts, Stephen (1995), 'Global Neighbours?' in Robert C Allen (ed.), *To Be Continued… Soap Operas Around the World*, London and New York: Routledge.

McKee, Alan (2002), 'Neighbours: National Niceness' in *Australian Television: A Genealogy of Great Moments*, Australia and New Zealand: Oxford University Press.

Selby, Keith and Cowdery Ron (1995), 'The TV Soap: *Neighbours*' in Keith Selby and Ron Cowdery, *How to Study Television*, London and New York: Macmillan.

Chapter Thirty

News at Ten

Glen Creeber

Production Details

(ITN, 1967–99; 2000–)

(A very short list of prominent individuals in its history)

Newscasters:

Andrew Gardner, Reginald Bosanquet, Sandy Gall, Leonard Parkin, Alastair Burnet, Gordon Honeycombe, Anna Ford, Selina Scott, Pamela Armstrong, Martyn Lewis, Carol Barnes, Alastair Stewart, Fiona Armstrong, Trevor McDonald, Julia Sommerville, Mark Austen, Andrea Catherwood

Reporters:

George Fitch, Michael Nicolson, Peter Sissons, Peter Snow, Sandy Gall, Peter Fairley, Richard Lindley, Gerald Seymour, Geoffrey Archer, Norman Rees, John Suchet, Jon Snow, Carol Barnes, Michael Brunson, Paul Davies, Desmond Hamill, Ian Glover-James, Lawrence McGinty, Brent Sadler, Peter Sharp, David Chater, Penny Marshall, Ian Williams, Robert Moore, Andrew Simmons, Colin Baker, Joan Thirkettle, Mark Austen, John Irvine, Terry Lloyd

Programme Editors:

David Nicholas, Sue Tinson, Jill Chisholm, Nigel Dacre, Geoffrey Cox, Nigel Ryan

---

Although the BBC has gained an international reputation for their news programmes, it was actually the first commercial channel (ITV and its subsidiary ITN – Independent Television News) that brought about some of the most important changes and developments in television news reporting in Britain. In particular, *News at Ten* produced many of the transformations in television news in the UK that viewers now take for granted. Before it, no British TV news bulletin had ever been longer than 15 minutes. In contrast, *News at Ten*'s new 30-minute slot finally allowed news stories to be developed in greater detail, while also giving the programme-makers the opportunity to utilise recent developments in technology (not least the arrival of pictures by satellite from around the world). Above all, *News at Ten* deliberately set out to make the news more

144

accessible and relevant to its viewers without losing the 'seriousness' of the BBC. As Jeremy Potter puts it, '*News at Ten* was designed to appeal to the readers of serious and popular newspapers alike' (1990, 122).

Before the introduction of commercial television in 1955, the BBC had tended to take a sombre and overly cautious approach to the news. Fearing that a face on-screen would somehow 'taint' its impartiality, the channel simply relayed the late evening radio news over a blank screen or over a single photograph of Big Ben (Crisell, 1997, 92). However, with the arrival of ITN in September 1955, news*casters* (rather than news*readers*, which apparently did not suggest their active role in writing scripts) were proudly displayed on-screen, clearly constructing them as *personalities* rather than disembodied voices. Christopher Chataway (originally an athlete who had won the BBC's 'Sports Personality of the Year' in 1954), Robin Day (hard-hitting, authoritative journalist) and Barbara Mandell (the first women to read the news on British television) were young, energetic and relatively (at least by the stuffy standards of the BBC) informal. Added to this, ITN introduced the Vox Pops (members of the public giving their views straight to the camera) and the reporter package (reporters giving their own commentary from the field), as well as encouraging more confrontational interview techniques.

This dramatic and accessible style of presentation was clearly an important component of *News at Ten*'s original success. After its initial three-month trial it soon became a fixed presence in the evening schedules. Exactly a year after its first edition it occupied three of the top four positions in the British television charts and nightly audiences of around 12 million were commonplace. Its title music ('Arabesque' composed by Johnny Pearson) became instantly recognisable, while the Big Ben 'bongs' between the headlines during its opening sequence quickly became a trademark of the programme, a device that clearly added to the dramatic tension upon which it built much of its appeal. As Justin Lewis points out, *News at Ten*'s opening sequence ensures viewer involvement by producing a traditional piece of suspense, creating an 'enigma/resolution structure that characterises most TV or cinematic fiction …' (Lewis, 1985, 214). To add to this sense of drama, the programme also continued its mission to make news stories as interesting and understandable as possible, increasing audience involvement (Selby and Cowdery, 1995, 130).

During the 1970s *News at Ten* was still very primitive, with graphics such as maps and tables simply made out of cardboard and Letraset (Stanley, 1999, 177). Having stories beamed in via satellite was still very expensive and film could take a day or so to arrive from the other side of the world. However, despite these difficulties, crucial world events such as the Russian invasion of Czechoslovakia, the Biafran and the Vietnam Wars were reported by ITN crews sent out to film the action. But it was the Yom Kippur War in 1973 that really marked a turning point for the programme. The improvements in satellite technology meant that for the first time viewers could see the pictures of a major foreign news story on the day they had been filmed. This meant that Michael Nicholson and Gerald Seymour's graphic reports of the war

145

could finally be seen a day before the newspapers had time to print their account. But as well as gaining praise for its international reporting, applause was also given to the programme's coverage of home events. In February 1974 its studio director Diana Edwards-Jones became the first woman to direct an election night, later winning a Royal Television Society award for outstanding creative achievement behind the camera.

Soon *News at Ten* was developing a style of presenting and reporting that its viewers would recognise today. In particular, research quickly showed that audiences had a tendency to switch over or off during the commercial break. As a result, news stories were not always run in sequence of their 'newsworthiness', but one or two important and interesting stories would be left over for the second section of the programme. Short trailers of stories to come (known as 'pre-commercials' or 'pre-coms') were also included before the advertisements, encouraging viewers to stay tuned. Dramatic announcements such as 'Coming up after the break…' also helped to ensure that viewers did not switch over. Added to this, the second half of the programme frequently included a 'special report' commissioned in advance about a current and continuing story. These were not particularly 'newsworthy', but they would offer more detail to an interesting or intriguing story such as 'the mystery of corn circles, animal cruelty, or rhino hunting in Africa' (Harrison, 2000, 96). In conclusion, *News at Ten*'s famous 'And finally…' story at its end was constructed to leave audiences on a *positive* and light-hearted note before saying goodnight.

However, despite the programme's success it gradually became clear that *News at Ten* found it increasingly difficult to survive the changes that were taking place in British broadcasting after the 1980s. Changes in technology such as the introduction of ENG (Electronic News Gathering) meant that more news was now available quicker, cheaper and easier than before. The proliferation of new cable and satellite channels also increased competition. Twenty-four-hour cable news channels such as the Atlanta-based CNN (Cable News Network) and the British-based Sky News meant that viewers relied less on the late terrestrial programme for their nightly news update.

Detailed audience research in the United States revealed that in such a competitive climate news programmes had to become more 'entertaining' and 'dynamic' if they were to hold on to their audiences. As a result, *News at Ten* called in an American consultant in 1992 to restructure their bulletins. As Patricia Holland explains, 'The set became brighter, the items shorter and more personal. Audience research revealed that Trevor McDonald was the newscaster who inspired the "greatest confidence" in the audience. Hence Trevor became the *News at Ten* Anchor' (Holland, 1997, 190). As a result, accusations of 'dumbing-down' were inevitably directed at the programme, many critics arguing that it had become more interested in securing audience appeal than reporting important stories in an accessible manner. Some critics even ironically referred to the programme as the 'Trevor McDonald Show', mocking its new commercially and personality-driven agenda.

Yet little seemed to stop the general decline in *News at Ten*'s audience ratings during the 1990s. In particular, ITV claimed that there was a big switch off of its audience at 10 pm, particularly when films or feature-length dramas that began after the 9 pm watershed had to be interrupted by the news halfway. There was, however, great pressure for the news to remain at 10 pm, not least from John Major, the then Prime Minister. Despite these pressures, the ITC (Independent Television Committee) finally gave in to ITV's insistence to reschedule the programme, but only if it maintained its commitment to 'public service values'.

Amidst much controversy, the last *News at Ten* was finally broadcast on the 5th March, 1999. However, the change of the late evening news to 11 pm was regarded as a public disaster for ITN, with the ITC eventually accusing the network of 'failing to stem an unacceptable decline in ratings for the replacement news bulletins' (cited by Tumber, 2001, 104). Despite ITV's committed insistence to bring the *News at Ten* to an end, the programme was finally reinstated in 2000. By this time, however, the BBC's *Nine O'Clock News* had controversially changed its time to 10 pm, ironically increasing competition for terrestrial news during a time in the schedules that ITV had originally made their own. Interestingly, during the war in Iraq in 2003 the main ITN news bulletin was transmitted at nine o'clock, no doubt hoping to claim the BBC's earlier spot.

As we move into the twenty-first century, all news programmes are now under increasing attack from commercial pressures, forcing the genre to sustain audiences as securely as drama and entertainment have done in the past. It was with this commercial agenda clearly in mind that new terms for *News at Ten* were negotiated when it finally returned to the ITV schedule. The programme now has to broadcast on only 3 nights a week; the network has also been granted an extra 2½ minutes of peak-time advertising slots, an increased number of commercial breaks throughout the programme and 20 seconds of programme promotions in the centre breaks (Tumber, 2001, 104–5). These compromises mean that *News at Ten*'s future is perhaps more secure than it once was, although how long it will remain in its current form is uncertain in the present climate. However, for the time being at least, *News at Ten* continues a tradition of accessible but authoritative programming that has helped to set the agenda for television news in Britain for well over 30 years.

QUESTIONS TO CONSIDER

- When *News at Ten* first started in 1967 it quickly gained a reputation for producing accessible but hard-hitting news coverage. Do you still think this is true? In what ways do you think the programme may have changed over the years?

- Analyse *News at Ten*'s opening sequence. What role do you think the music, graphics and presentation of the headlines play? Why do you think it is that despite the considerable changes made to the programme over the years the Big Ben clock and its 'bongs' have remained virtually intact?

- Compare an edition of ITN's *News at Ten* with the BBC's *Ten O'Clock News* from the same day. Make a note of such points as the language of the newscasters, the running order of the stories, the set design and the time devoted to each item. What differences and similarities can you find and how do you account for them?
- How far do you think *News at Ten* is now personality-led? What do its critics imply when they call it the 'Trevor McDonald Show'?
- Do you think *News at Ten* will be able to remain as and where it is over the next 30 years? What changes do you envisage for its future and why?

RECOMMENDED READING

Potter, Jeremy (1990), 'Independent Television News' in *Independent Television in Britain*, Vol. 4, London and New York Macmillan.

Selby, Keith and Cowdery, Ron (1995), 'Analysing a TV news broadcast: *News at Ten*' in *How to Study Television*, London: Macmillan.

Tumber, Howard (2001), '10 pm and all that: The battle over UK TV news' in Michael Bromley (ed.), *No News is Bad News: Radio, Television and the Public*, London and New York: Longman.

Chapter Thirty One

The Olympic Games

Rod Brookes

Production Details

(Various national broadcasters)

Organisers: The International Olympic Committee

The Olympic Games is routinely celebrated, not least by its organisers the International Olympic Committee (IOC), as the television event that brings the 'global village' together through shared appreciation of the universal ideals embodied in athletic competition, transcending racial, national and religious differences. According to the IOC's website, 'television is the engine that has driven the growth of the Olympic Movement'. Following the Mexico Olympics of 1968 – the first Olympics to be broadcast live in colour – each subsequent Summer Games has seen an exponential rise in the revenue generated by the sale of television and sponsorship rights, so that from 1984 onwards the right to host the Olympic Games has been transformed from a loss-making liability to a prize so lucrative that bidding cities have been prepared to go to great lengths to win it. Correspondingly, the IOC has grown into a powerful international non-government organisation, with a turnover greater than the GDP of many small nations; it has had a President, in Juan Antonio Samaranch, who saw himself as equivalent in status to world leaders; and it has been able to exert significant economic and political power through awarding the privilege of hosting the Summer and Winter Olympics with all the economic benefits involved, conferring recognition on emerging nations, etc.

Producing television coverage of the Olympic Games has now become a massive undertaking. The Sydney Olympic Broadcasting Organisation claimed that it had televised more than 3,400 hours of live coverage of the 2000 Olympics, covering 300 events, using more than 900 cameras and 400 video tape machines, employing 3,500 personnel, and working with more than 12,000 personnel from rights-holding broadcasters. Finally, the audience for the Olympics is the largest for a regularly occurring television event. The organisers of the 2000 Sydney Olympics estimated a worldwide television audience of 3.7 billion, an increase from 3 billion over the Atlanta Olympics four years previously (although it should be noted that these estimates are probably exaggerated and certainly unverifiable – there is no reliable audience research on Olympic viewing figures in Africa outside South Africa). Clearly, the Olympic Games should be regarded as one of the most important – if not *the* most important – global television events.

But analysing the Olympic Games as a television *text* introduces a major practical problem: the version of the Olympics viewers in different nations see will differ, in some cases quite drastically, depending on the degree of customisation adopted by national rights-holding broadcasters in their Olympic presentation. And this makes problematic the idea of the Olympics as bringing the world together through a simultaneous act of television consumption.

Officially, the Olympic Charter requires that the international television signal provided by the host nation's broadcaster covering the various events – consisting of visual feed including live action, real-time and slow-motion replays, natural sound and optional graphics – should be as neutral as possible: for example, equal time should be devoted to each competitor as they are lining up for the start of track events. Hence, there should not be any bias in the time allocated to athletes of any particular nation or part of the world. However, each rights-holding broadcaster can then customise the international signal to a greater or lesser extent. Unlike the **FIFA World Cup** (various national broadcasters, 1930–), national broadcasters have the option of purchasing unilateral camera positions in Olympic arenas that they can use to supplement the live universal signal through additional footage: additional close-ups of their own nation's athletes, interviews conducted by their own star presenters, etc.

The degree of customisation of the international feed by different national broadcasters depends on the degree of financial resources available. The BBC sent more than 350 staff to the Sydney Olympics – more than the number of British athletes competing – to provide additional footage and reporting at a cost of £35 million (Wells, 2000). By contrast, the coverage of the Sydney Olympics seen by most viewers in Africa was restricted to the form of edited highlights produced by a partnership consisting of the African continental rights-holder URTNA (the union of African public broadcasters) and the French broadcaster Canal France International. African broadcasters can barely afford the costs of live transmission of the games for a few minutes each day, let alone those involved in sending personnel to provide supplementary footage and reporting. More dependent on the 'neutral' international signal, African viewers were denied the degree of focus on their own national athletes enjoyed by viewers in the developed nations (Abele, 2001).

But a huge difference in access to resources is not the only reason why viewers in different nations saw different texts of the Sydney Olympics. Despite sending 2,000 of its own staff to the Olympics – six times the BBC's cohort – viewers of US network NBC, like most African viewers, also saw the Olympics in the form of edited highlights, but for a very different reason: the notoriously market-driven approach to covering television sport in the US. NBC had invested $705 million for the US TV rights, accounting for more than half the total revenue the IOC generated through the sale of TV rights overall, and was not about to see such a huge investment wasted because most of the prestigious events were scheduled to take place while US viewers were asleep. Hence live coverage – usually by far the most valuable for broadcasters and advertisers – was sacrificed, and NBC delayed all its coverage until prime time, when it was shown in the form of heavily packaged edited highlights. Further, NBC regards the Olympic Games as potentially representing the 'holy grail' of sports marketing: the sports event that will finally prove popular with the majority of female viewers. NBC's coverage of the 1996 Atlanta games betrayed rather stereotypical assumptions about what women might want from sports coverage through adopting a 'soap opera' approach to presentation (Andrews, 1998; Borcila, 2000; Chisholm, 1999; Eastman and Billings, 1999; Heywood, 2000; Toohey, 1997; Tuggle and Owen, 1999).

For the 2000 Olympics, then, NBC filmed in advance biographical sketches of US athletes, highlighting any personal tragedies to be overcome through athletic endeavour. Typically NBC's coverage consisted of recorded highlights of the day's action, involving US medal contenders sandwiched between mini-soap operas about their lives. The presentation of NBC's edited highlights was heavy on 'human interest', but the humans that NBC was interested in were almost exclusively American. Further, NBC's coverage was heavily dominated by 'prime-time' sports – swimming, gymnastics, baseball and track and field athletics – to the effective exclusion of the rest (Arlidge, 2000).

By contrast, the BBC treats its coverage of the Olympic Games as an *international* event as central to its public service remit, clearing the usual schedules to broadcast as many events as possible live, even sports which are usually of little interest to British fans or in which British competitors have little chance of success. Nevertheless, in an increasingly competitive television environment, the BBC still has to demonstrate that it is serving a significant proportion of the available audience in order to secure investment, particularly on its main channel BBC1. Whilst Olympic athletics can usually be relied upon to deliver reasonable audience returns, most other Olympic sports are likely to provide significantly smaller audiences than the programmes that forego their regular slots. Hence, even if the BBC is more 'internationalist' in its coverage than NBC, it still seeks to build its audiences through the tried and tested method of encouraging identification with national representatives through its sports presentation. The most successful example of audience building was the BBC's production of *Gold Fever*, a video-diary series documenting the preparations made by the British men's coxless rowing four in the run-up to the Olympics. This series almost certainly contributed to a sizeable audience of seven million for their eventual victory, despite being held in the early hours of the morning.

The tension between internationalism and nationalism in the BBC's Olympic coverage can be illustrated by an analysis of its presentation of one of the most important evenings of the 2000 Sydney Olympics athletics: Monday, September 25. For the BBC, the main stories of the evening were either concerned with the continuing achievements of a pair of established global superstars (Cathy Freeman and Michael Johnson in the women's and men's 400 metres) or with the increasing success attained by British athletes. The editing of the presentation reflects these priorities.

Take, for example, the women's 400 metres, in which Australian-aboriginal athlete Cathy Freeman and British athletes Katharine Merry and Donna Fraser were all competing. Cathy Freeman's victory had already been anticipated as the biggest story of the games. Ten days previously, Cathy Freeman had lit the Olympic torch at the end of an opening ceremony, the main theme of which was that the Sydney Olympics marked the final culmination of a process of reconciliation between Australia's white European, aboriginal and recent immigrant populations, which had been long and difficult but nevertheless had finally been *achieved* (clearly a problematic idea, see Godwell, 2000; Moragas Spa et al., 1995; Tomlinson, 1996, 2000). As she embarked on her victory lap carrying the Australian flag, the presentation cut between close-ups of an emotional Freeman and medium- and long-range shots of a full stadium of cheering spectators also waving Australian flags. One camera was directed at Freeman's mother in the front row, and close-ups of her smiling face had already featured several times in this sequence. Finally, Freeman goes over to embrace her mother. Through cutting between an aboriginal Australian athlete, her mother and a crowd of cheering Australians, this sequence reinforces the organisers' message that the Olympic Games marked the resolution of past conflicts.

At the same time, the BBC's coverage was also interested in the British representatives, as usual using the international feed for the immediate line-up and race uninterrupted, but inserting into this feed its own extra footage of Katharine Merry warming up before the race and herself doing a lap of honour afterwards. By contrast, the winner of the silver medal, Jamaican Lorraine Graham, is virtually ignored. Whether or not she did a lap of honour the BBC viewer will have no idea.

Attempting to analyse the Olympic Games as a television text is very revealing about the complexities and contradictions of our supposedly global media culture. Ostensibly it is a global event that most of the population of the world with access to a television set consumes simultaneously. Yet the form of television presentation of the Olympic Games and the context in which it is viewed can differ markedly depending on the location of the viewer.

QUESTIONS TO CONSIDER

- In analysing an Olympic telecast, how easy is it to distinguish between images provided by the international signal as opposed to the channel's own cameras?
- Why does the BBC insist on televising the Olympic Games when some of the events get lower ratings than the programmes they have made way for?
- To what extent is the performance of British/American athletes the main story of BBC/NBC television presentation of Olympic events?
- In what way does television coverage of the Olympic Games use 'human interest' to aid viewer identification with particular athletes?

- What characteristics of 'soap opera' can you recognise in your own country's packaging of the Olympic Games?

RECOMMENDED READING

Miller, Toby, Lawrence, Geoffrey A, McKay, Jim, Rowe, David (eds.) (2001), *Globalization and Sport: Playing the World*, London: Sage.

Moragas Spa, M de, Rivenburgh, NK and Larson, JF (1995), *Television in the Olympics*, London: John Libbey.

Schaffer, K and Smith, S (eds.) (2000), *The Olympics at the Millennium*, Piscataway, NJ: Rutgers University Press.

Chapter Thirty Two

Popstars

Jane Roscoe

Production Details

(Screentime, 2001–)

Originally created by Jonathan Dowling

Popstars was originally developed in New Zealand by Jonathan Dowling, with the first series broadcast in 1999. After its modest success the rights were sold to Screentime who developed the idea and sold it on around the world. It has to date been sold to 36 countries, with many having already broadcast a second series. Spin-offs have followed, like *Pop Idol* (Thames Television, 2001), which was developed in the UK by Simon Fuller (once manager of The Spice Girls, sometimes known as 'Svengali Spice') and Nigel Lythgoe (controller of Entertainment at London Weekend Television) for their production company 19TV; while *Popstars: The Rivals* (ITV, 2002) and *American Idol* (Fox, 2002) have also proved phenomenally successful. All these shows take as their focus the popular music industry and give a behind-the-scenes view of the processes involved in the journey from 'wannabe' to pop commodity. They are structured around the interactions between pop singers and their relationships with their management and other industry personnel. Although it is not consciously set up as an exposé of the music industry, through the focus on the everyday aspects of the process, much is revealed. They all start with the audition process and end with a live concert. There is nothing new about manufactured pop (see **The Monkees** [NBC, 1966–8]), but what is new is that these new reality shows allow us to watch the *process* of manufacturing popular music for the first time.

Popstars and *Pop Idol* draw on the conventions of docusoap by building narratives around key characters. The focus is on the emotional highs and lows, personality clashes and the relationships between individual performers and the industry. Like many docusoaps they take us behind the scenes of an industry, making visible the mundane, everyday aspects of the world of pop. In *Popstars* we are given access to the lives of the band members and, in doing so, we are privy to their personal interactions, arguments and, most importantly, their showdowns with their management. The form relies on the 'naturally occurring drama' of these situations to propel the narrative and maintain viewer interest. However, this so-called naturally occurring drama needs some help and direction. In fact, the transformation of the everyday person into a 'popstar' takes a number of stages, with each stage forming the basis of an episode. For example, creating an image becomes the focus when the band is selected. Here, stylists, make-up artists, hairdressers and designers are brought in to create a look for the band. While it might seem as though the band members have some say in their final appearance, they actually have little say as to what they wear and how they look. They are sent to voice-coaches and take dance classes. Rather than their talent being natural, it seems that it is entirely constructed. Yet at every turn, it makes visible the processes of manufacture.

Performance is central to *Popstars*. There are a number of ways in which we can talk about performance within these formats. We have the obvious point about the actual performance of the bands, but there are other layers of performance, for example, the auditions were not just about whether they could sing, but whether they had what it takes to 'a star'. They had to have the right personality, the right look and the right attitude. This is explicitly performed for the camera and the audience through the ways in which the participants move, dress and behave around the other 'hopefuls'. It is an exercise in showing how to *behave* like a star. At other levels it is possible to think about the format as providing a forum for the performance of gender and ethnicity too. Popular music has long been associated with particular versions of masculinity and femininity and as a site in which issues of race and class have been explored. These performances, while not explicitly foregrounded are central to the format. Discourses of gender, class and race also permeate the make-over process, in terms of how they are dressed and taught to move. For example, the first Australian series band 'Bardot' were presented as an uneasy mix of sex and denial. The young women were dressed to capture the gaze of the male eye, while at the same time attempting to engage their real audience – the very young girls. Yet, it is exactly this mix of girl and woman, which so often typifies the teenage experience, that is a central concern of popular music. At another level it is this performance of gender and sexuality that makes the series so compelling.

The audition process is certainly central to the format of these shows, and as the format has developed so the second and third series seem to spend longer and longer on this part of the narrative. The ratings figures for these episodes suggest that audiences enjoy watching people being routinely humiliated by the judges and other hopefuls (a factor, it has to be said, that was often crucial to the popularity of earlier television talent shows such as *New Faces* [ITV, 1973–8]). However, *Popstars* frequently and deliberately includes the auditions of people who display little or no talent at all, their ritual humiliation simply served up as entertainment for audiences. The judges are caught on camera rolling their eyes, sniggering and generally being brutal towards those who have little hope of making it. *Popstars* is also different from earlier television talent shows in the sense that we get to know certain individuals in almost 'intimate' detail. As the audition process proceeds it is extended through strategies such as including mini-narratives on the final shortlisted hopefuls. Here we meet their friends and family, who fill us in on why they are deserving of fame, fortune and this opportunity for success. As well as extending an already popular segment of the series, it allows viewers to develop a connection with these individuals and allow possible identification ('they are just like me' or 'that could be me').

The use of stereotyped characters is also a way to develop a context in which drama may 'naturally' occur. It also provides a way for audiences to quickly engage and identify with the characters. For example, in the original New Zealand version, the band members were (like The Monkees and The Spice Girls) explicitly stereotyped and often encouraged to play up to those roles. Keri was blond and petite and regarded as the innocent 'baby' of the group. Carly was overtly sexual in behaviour toward the camera and was presented as the 'vamp'. Meagan, because of her real-life role as a mother, was seen to be the reliable, sensible maternal figure. Erika was presented as strong-willed, bossy and a bitch, and finally, Joe, who, due to her larger-than-life physical characteristics, seemed to play the dual roles of 'outsider' and the 'real woman'. The performance of these roles provided a number of opportunities for conflict both within the group and between them and others.

The central question most frequently asked about these programmes is: 'Are they anything more than examples of the comodification of pop music and youth?' Certainly, the real people and real talent are packaged as a spectacle for the pleasure and entertainment of a popular audience. It is structured and edited to maximise the entertainment value (Bruzzi, 2000), yet, such formats may have opened up spaces in the public sphere in which to explore certain notions about popular culture, gender, race and class. They have certainly brought a new audience to non-fiction – an audience that has traditionally watched prime-time soaps and sitcoms, not documen- taries. And as with *Big Brother* (Endemol, 1999–), there is also an 'interactive' element to these shows which facilitates viewer involvement, perhaps giving audiences the illusion that they can either 'make or break' an individual. Although not unique in earlier television talent shows like *Opportunity Knocks* (ITV, 1956–78) (where Hughie Green's famous 'clapometer' would record the studio audience's applause and viewers were asked to send in their votes on a postcard), it clearly brought the role of the viewer to the fore in the selection process.

Shows like *Popstars* work to provide a fast-track on the music industry career path, and not just for those who end up as the winners. The judges, often those whose careers have seen better days, have the chance to relaunch themselves and reconnect with a younger audience. The televisions series is also a way to build a specific audience for the music. The image is now so central to popular music that it is almost possible (and the format testifies to this) to have a successful band with a fan base, even before they have released a single. In *Popstars*, then, the series is used as a promotional tool and for the purpose of building a fan base. By the time the single comes out – it is almost certain it will hit the number one spot.

There have been a number of variations since this first series in New Zealand. *Popstars* around the world have tried all-girl bands, all-male bands and mixed bands. In New Zealand a spin-off series created an all-maori band, and a UK spin-off *Popstars: The Rivals* created a girl band (Girls Aloud) and a boy band (One True Voice) and then pitted them against each other. In many countries the single released at the end of the series has topped the local charts. In the UK 'the rivals' went head to head for the number one position in the Christmas 2002 charts (the girls won). Although a different format, *Fame Academy* (BBC, 2002–) can be seen as a response to the success of *Popstars*. Here, a group of talented young people live together in a hothouse environment designed to nurture and develop their raw talent. Bringing together elements of *Popstars* and **Big Brother**, the audience gets to decide who will win and who will be voted out along the way. At its core, though, is the same objective as *Popstars*, that is, to create a successful pop commodity.

These formats allow the audience a say in the development of the narrative and, like **Big Brother**, allows a new relationship to be built between the producers, the 'popstars' and the audience. Audienceship for such formats can be seen as an expression or enactment of culture (Nightingale, 1996) or perhaps, in John Hartley's (1999) terms, an example of power viewing: an assertive and sophisticated notion of viewing in which initial pleasure can also be transformed into critical engagement. As such, formats rely on and expect viewers to be conversant with the notion that it is at once both highly constructed and unscripted, and this may be a useful way in which to understand their popularity. It both allows us to identify with the pop dream, have a hand in selecting the 'next big thing' and critically engage with the notion of manufactured pop if we should so wish.

QUESTIONS TO CONSIDER

- How have programmes like *Popstars* and *Pop Idol* developed the original conventions of earlier talent shows like *Opportunity Knocks* and *New Faces*? What characteristics are familiar and what has the show changed or modified?

- What elements of docusoap has a programme like *Popstars* appropriated? How are audiences drawn into the human drama of the narrative?

- What notions of gender, race and class are implicitly alluded to in the make-over process of the band? How much choice do you think individual members have in the way they are presented by the programme?

- Do you think *Popstars* offers its audience anything other than simply the commodification of pop music and youth? How much room do you think there is in the show for individual talent to emerge?

- How have other shows developed and adapted the original format of *Popstars*? Do you think there will come a time when the novelty of such shows will no longer be sufficient to attract audiences?

RECOMMENDED READING

(No critical work directly relevant for study of this programme was available at the time of writing, although academic articles can be expected. For general reading see below.)

Dovey, Jon (2000), 'McDox 'R' Us – docusoap and the Triumph of Trivia' in Jon Dovey, *Freakshow: First Person Media and Factual Television*, London: Pluto Press.

Kilborn, R and Izod, J (1997), *Introduction to Television Documentary*, Manchester: Manchester University Press.

Malone, Maria (2001), *Popstars: The Making of Hear-Say*, London: Andre Deutsch.

Chapter Thirty Three

Prime Suspect

Glen Creeber

Production Details (series 1)

(Granada Television, 1991)

Writer: Lynda La Plante
Director: Christopher Menaul
Producer: Ron Lever
Executive Producer: Sally Head

Cast includes:

DCI Jane Tennison (Helen Mirren)
DS Bill Otley (Tom Bell)
DCI John Shefford (John Forgeham)
George Marlow (John Bowe)
Moyra Henson (Zoë Wanamaker)

The first *Prime Suspect* serial consisted of two two-hour episodes shown on consecutive evenings and was originally broadcast in Britain on the April 7 and 8, 1991 to wide public and critical acclaim. It subsequently won numerous awards, including a BAFTA for Best Drama Serial, and was later developed into four further instalments, finally ending with *Prime Suspect 5* in 1996 (although at the time of writing a new series is apparently in production). Despite its writer Lynda La Plante being strongly associated with the drama as a whole, she only wrote *Prime Suspect 1* and *Prime Suspect 3* and simply provided the story outline for *Prime Suspect 2*. However, it is perhaps testament to the depth of her original script and Helen Mirren's skills as an actress that the character of Detective Chief Inspector (later Superintendent) Jane Tennison gradually gained a life of her own, dominating and determining the whole focus of the series.

La Plante was originally trained at Royal Academy of Dramatic Arts (RADA) and started her career as an actress in television and on the stage. It was while playing a prostitute in one of the first British female cop shows, *The Gentle Touch* (LWT, 1980–4), that she finally vowed to 'write something better' (cited by Sean Day-Lewis, 1998, 81). After a number of rejections (including one from the female police series *Juliet Bravo* [BBC, 1980–5]), her script about a group of women who lost their husbands in a bank robbery was finally accepted by Thames Television. *Widows* (Thames, 1983) typically involved the inverting of a traditional male genre, with their bereaved wives successfully carrying on the job started by their late husbands. However, despite numerous credits to her name (such as *Widows II* [Thames, 1985], *Civvies* [BBC, 1992], *The Governor* (ITV, 1995–6), and *Trial and Retribution* [ITV, 1997–]), it is still probably *Prime Suspect* for which she is best known.

As with the majority of La Plante's work, *Prime Suspect* was based on a considerable amount of prior planning and research. In particular, she famously 'shadowed' real-life Detective Chief Inspector Jackie Malton, following her for 6 months as she watched her take charge of 45 detectives, interview killers and attend autopsies (Haywood, 1996, 107–8). Indeed, many critics applauded the new sense of realism that the drama brought to the police genre as a whole. Reflecting La Plante's own meticulous research, its unflinching portrayal of the police autopsy soon became an essential requirement of many detective serials, particularly *Silent Witness* (BBC/A&E, 1996–), which also included an unmistakably 'Tennisonesque' female protagonist played by Amanda Burton. Similarly, the serial's relentless representation of squalor and violence broke new boundaries in television drama generally. This quality of realism and production was continued with *Prime Suspect 2*, in which the subject of racism temporarily supplanted the issue of sexism. Continuing this socially led agenda, other issues in the series have included homosexuality, paedophilia, drug addition, male prostitution and child abuse.

However, *Prime Suspect* is probably best known today for the way that it attempted to subvert the inherent maleness and masculinity of the British cop show. Although *Juliet Bravo*, *The Gentle Touch* (LWT, 1980–4) and **Cagney and Lacey** (CBS, 1981–8) had already given leading roles to women police officers, *Prime Suspect* was seen as one of the most successful attempts at critiquing and possibly reinventing the traditional police genre. When the classic male chauvinist DCI John Shefford dies of a heart attack only a few minutes into the first episode, Tennison (at her insistence) is reluctantly given the job of heading the murder investigation. Despite tough opposition from Shefford's remaining crew, particularly the overtly sexist Bill Otley, she finally solves the case and in the process gradually earns the respect of her male colleagues. In this way, the conventional male police drama is set up and then gradually deconstructed, Tennison fighting both the blatant prejudices of the police force and the implicit prejudices of the police genre in her attempt to be accepted on an equal level with the men.

Perhaps inevitably, critics have argued that such a quest has Tennison take on many of the characteristics of the traditional *male* detective. She chain-smokes, drinks, swears and displays anything but a 'gentle touch'. Typically, she finds it almost impossible to sustain a successful relationship (her partner leaves her halfway through the first story) and is clearly obsessed, driven and ruthlessly ambitious. Indeed, some commentators have suggested that Tennison clearly had to abandon a great deal of her 'femininity' in pursuit of her professional success. According to Mary Eaton, 'Close inspection shows that the triumphs achieved by Tennison are bought at a high price; a successful detective but not a successful woman' (1995, 175). Similarly, Charlotte Brunsdon has argued that the drama serial carries out an ingenious 'balancing act' that – despite its overtly feminist intentions – still manages to preserve many of the basic ingredients of the traditional male text. By the end of the drama, Brunsdon argues, Tennison is 'fully integrated into the language of the lads' (1998, 234).

Yet, despite her apparent 'masculinisation', some critics have argued that Tennison still manages to retain important aspects of her 'femininity'. Indeed, Tennison's knowledge of female behaviour is actually crucial to gradually solving the murder case. It is, for example, her understanding of boutique clothes that first alerts her to the misidentification of the original body by Shefford and his team (who hurry the investigation in an attempt to break a previous police record and conceal Shefford's apparent relationship with the victim). Similarly, her determination to talk to a number of prostitutes at a pub in Oldham brings with it an important breakthrough, a stark contrast to the way the women were treated by the male officers. Finally, it is Tennison's female 'gofer' that eventually makes the 'feminine' connection between all the victims and their 'Nu-Nails' nail extensions, a crucial clue to eventually putting Marlow in the dock (Brunsdon, 1998, 233–4). Examples such as these suggest that despite her apparently 'masculinised' persona, the traditionally 'feminine' aspects of Tennison's personality are still crucial for actually solving the case. As Sandra Tomc puts it, '*Prime Suspect* emphasizes its vilification of "patriarchy" through its presentation of Tennison herself, whose qualities as a *woman* accentuate the flaws of the male-centred system around her' (1995, 49, emphasis in the original).

This narrative ambiguity is further heightened by many of the visual elements of the drama itself. Christopher Menaul's direction of the first series – with its dark streets, hard-boiled detectives, low-key lighting, mumbled dialogue, butchered female bodies and claustrophobic interiors – is clearly reminiscent of aspects of the classic crime genre, particularly *film noir*. Such a generic tradition may even be implicitly alluded to by the name of Tennison's first prime suspect, the serial killer George Marlow (John Bowe), perhaps an implicit reference to Raymond Chandler's Philip Marlowe, the hard-boiled detective of classic crime novels and movies like *The Big Sleep* (Hawks, 1946) and *Farewell, My Lovely* (Richards, 1974) (Creeber, 2001, 152–5). Shefford is certainly an embodiment of such a tradition, a tough, individualistic cop in the mould of *The Sweeney's* (ITV, 1975–82) Jack Regan (John Thaw) who, as Geoffrey Hurd points out, was partly derived from the 'American crime writers and the gangster thriller movies of the 1930s and 1940s' (Hurd, 1981, 61; see also Clarke, 1986).

Seen in this light, it is possible to conceive *Prime Suspect* as a self-reflexive attempt to explore and investigate the type of masculine dynamics that critics have argued typified the traditional crime genre. Indeed, the *film noir* tradition has frequently been critiqued by feminist film critics like E Ann Kaplan for its 'sexist' portrayal of strong (often sexualised) women. 'The hero's success or not', she argues, 'depends on the

Chapter Thirty Four

The Prisoner

Matt Hills

Production Details

(Everyman Films, for ITC Productions, ITV, 1967–8)

Created by: Patrick McGoohan
Executive Producer: Patrick McGoohan
Producer: David Tomblin
Writers have included: George Markstein, David Tomblin, Anthony Skene, Vincent Tilsley, Terence Feely, Patrick McGoohan
Directors have included: Don Chaffey, Pat Jackson, David Tomblin, Patrick McGoohan

Cast includes:

Number Six (Patrick McGoohan)
Number Two (Colin Gordon/Clifford Evans/Mary Morris/John Sharpe/Peter Wyngarde/Guy Doleman/Leo McKern)
The Butler (Angelo Muscat)

Like **Doctor Who** (BBC, 1963–89), **Star Trek** (NBC, 1966–9) and **The Twilight Zone** (CBS, 1959–87), *The Prisoner* has become one of a number of TV programmes considered to be 'cult', meaning that it has a dedicated fan following that continues to appreciate its merits some 35 years after it was originally broadcast (Jenkins, 1992). Rather like **Star Trek**, *The Prisoner* has an author figure – this time in the shape of Patrick McGoohan. And resembling the case of Rod Serling in **The Twilight Zone**, McGoohan the televisual author was also McGoohan the performer (or star, even) in his own programme. These factors – a loyal fandom helping to secure the show's place in TV history and a star with an unusual degree of authorial, creative control – go to make *The Prisoner* a key television text.

The Prisoner's basic narrative premise is that a secret agent (played by McGoohan) has attempted to resign from his job, taking vital information with him. In order to prevent this resignation and its possible consequences, the agent is abducted (presumably by his paymasters) and imprisoned in a strange place known only as The Village. Kept here, the secret agent's loyalty, knowledge and psychology are all put to the test in various ways. Which of his fellow prisoners can he trust, and who is working to try and get information out of him or to gauge who he has really been working for? Along with other inhabitants of The Village, this prisoner is given a code, 'Number Six'. We never find out his real name. The scenario of Number Six's resignation is conveyed visually in the opening credit sequence of the programme's first episode, 'Arrival', and revisited in the closing sequence of the last episode.

At the time of creating and making *The Prisoner*, McGoohan had just starred in a highly successful British spy/adventure series called *Danger Man* (ITV, 1960–9) (eventually retitled *Secret Agent* [CBS, 1965] in the US), and American advance publicity surrounding his new venture speculated that Number Six was the same spy character that McGoohan had played in *Danger Man/Secret Agent*, one John Drake (Miller, 2000, 44). American press reviews of *The Prisoner* therefore largely attempted to cue audience interpretations by relating the show to McGoohan's prior success. However, *The Prisoner* is clearly not a textual continuation of this earlier show; it has a tone, narrative world and *mise-en-scène* all of its own, and it is never textually suggested that 'Number Six' is in fact the John Drake character (Miller, 2000, 44).

Part of *The Prisoner*'s distinctiveness emerges through the mysteries that its narrative premise leaves in place. We never learn just who 'Number Six' really is, nor exactly who his captors and controllers in The Village are. We are never sure where The Village is located, or what information Number Six possesses that is so important to his captors (who are also numbered: Number One is The Village's ultimate authority, and Number Six battles against different seconds in command in various episodes). So much of the programme's narrative is left unstated or implied that the show has been described as 'surely the most enigmatic TV series ever made and one whose meaning continues to be debated by cultists and academicians alike' (Chapman, 2002, 49). By leaving its format so very open to audience speculation and explanation, *The Prisoner* prefigured the 'endlessly deferred narratives' (Hills, 2002, 134–5) of later cult TV shows like **Twin Peaks** (ABC, 1990–1), working to withhold clear narrative resolutions. Narrative non-resolution is certainly one way in which *The Prisoner* has invited and sustained its cult following. As David Buxton has observed, 'viewers were invited to draw their own conclusions, a prospect that excited a cult minority but undoubtedly bewildered most' (1990, 95).

Another dimension of the show's cult appeal lies in its setting. By using the strange architecture found in the Welsh town of Portmeirion as a location for The Village, the programme achieved a surreal look, but one which also conveyed the solidity of an actual location. Portmeirion works to sustain the programme's cult following by providing a real location that fans can visit, perhaps to recreate scenes from the show (Hills, 2002, chapter 7). And Portmeirion's architectural style conveys a paradoxically real-seeming artificiality that fits well with *The Prisoner*'s thematic emphasis on designed, managed and controlled environments (Freeman, 1999, 59). Indeed, the role that Portmeirion played in creating *The Prisoner*'s striking visual style is recognised in John Hartley's term 'Portmeirionisation'. For TV scholar Hartley, 'Portmeirionisation' is the process through which '[p]laces start to look real, authentic, and genuine only when they approximate most accurately to their fictionalisation on TV' (Hartley, 1999, 220). Although Hartley's argument here is somewhat 'postmodern' – places seem 'real' to us only due to their mediated representations – the fact that he chooses Portmeirion to consider the relationship between actual locations and their media images illustrates that *The Prisoner* and its weirdly 'artificial/real' setting continue to possess cultural resonance for academics as much as for fans of the show.

As well as boasting a mysterious narrative and a highly open, enigmatic format, *The Prisoner* ended with a fragmented and elusive conclusion. The final episode of the show's 17-episode run revealed the identity of The Village's controller, Number One, but the precise meaning of this revelation is still hotly debated by fans. *The Official Prisoner Companion* notes that 'Those who insist on finding meaning in *The Prisoner* must begin their inquiry with the most persistent enigma of the series: the identity of Number One' (White and Ali, 1988, 164). The last episode, 'Fall Out', briefly unmasks Number One, showing that he is actually Number Six. But since it is also Number Six himself who is doing the unmasking, this doesn't seem to work as any kind of 'realist' conclusion, prompting allegorical readings that interpret the show as a battle between good and evil aspects of one psyche, or as a struggle between civilised/animalistic impulses (White and Ali, 1988, 165–6). And *The Prisoner*'s extreme openness as a text does not just revolve around this one narrative question. Other interpretations of the programme have read it in relation to its 1960s context (Gregory, 1997, 177):

> *'Fall Out' is … in its use of 'hallucinatory' imagery, music and dialogue, clearly influenced by the 'psychedelic' era which was still virtually current while it was being made. As a reflection of that era it stands comparison with albums like The Beatles'* Sergeant Pepper *(1967)… or films such as Dennis Hopper's* Easy Rider *(1968).*

Not only adopting the surrealist and psychedelic tone of a strand of 1960s popular culture, *The Prisoner* also thematically portrays 'the Establishment' as an oppressive cultural force via images of The Village and its numbered, brainwashed inhabitants under constant surveillance. To an extent, then, *The Prisoner* takes themes of oppression and revolution (and the individual versus society), but partly depoliticises them by rendering them separate from any clear political or cultural referents. As telefantasy, it depicts struggles for individuality or cultural power, but only in a decontextualised way that does not obviously link back to 'real-world' political struggles. Although the show can be viewed as subversive in so far as it offers a critique of the mass media and social conformity, this 'subversion' can also be interpreted as a conservative defence of cultural elites and their need to remain above or outside of 'the masses'. David Buxton's analysis of the programme is telling in this respect (Buxton, 1990, 96):

> The Prisoner *suffers … from an ideological thinness, an obsessive concern with individual freedom in a setting that is too facile to allow the issue to be treated with sufficient complexity. … [A] 'radical'-minded anxiety over state interference in private life and the use of the media to manipulate citizens into a dull conformity spills over into a conservative attack on the welfare state itself, seen as effacing the individual personality into a mere number.*

Buxton's argument is that *The Prisoner* presents a view of the world that appeals primarily to an educated middle-class audience, enabling this audience to conservatively reject what they construe as the 'mindless consumption habits of the masses' (1990, 96). If this is so, then to suggest that the show was or is especially 'subversive' rather misses the point that its decontextualised themes of individualism can be taken to support a wide range of political positions, both radical and, as Buxton stresses, culturally conservative.

Further interpretations of *The Prisoner* have discussed it as 'postmodern' television (Booker, 2002). The way in which the programme addresses serious philosophical concerns of individualism – or, at the very least, the way in which it attempts to do so – within the format of a popular TV series has prompted some critics to suggest that '*The Prisoner* can be seen as anticipating the "postmodern" erosion of traditional frontiers dividing "high" and "mass" culture' (Osgerby, Gough-Yates and Wells, 2001, 25). However, this notion that *The Prisoner* blurred the boundaries of 'high' and 'mass' culture can be analysed without invoking the theoretical machinery of 'postmodernism'. For instance, the programme's 'philosophical' tone has also been discussed in relation to its author-creator, Patrick McGoohan (see Osgerby, Gough-Yates and Wells, 2001, 25). Rather than breaking down the barriers between 'high' and 'mass' culture as 'postmodern' TV, *The Prisoner*'s distinctiveness can be thought of as a matter of TV authorship, given that McGoohan had an unusually large degree of control over the show as a result of his earlier success with *Danger Man*. He not only created and executive produced *The Prisoner*, but also starred in it as the lead character, while writing, directing and, on occasion, even re-editing episodes. By simultaneously taking on such a remarkable series of institutional roles, McGoohan was arguably able to steer *The Prisoner* as far more of a 'televisionary' (Carrazé and Oswald, 1990) than is typically the case in TV series production (see also Lewis and Stempel, 1993, 7).

The show's relatively short run of 17 episodes was another factor that allowed McGoohan to retain a very high degree of creative control in comparison to long-running key TV texts like **Doctor Who** and **Star Trek**. By fusing enigmatic, allegorical and philosophical elements with the spy genre, McGoohan ensured that *The Prisoner* would fascinate at least one fraction of its audience, albeit a 'cult minority', thereby becoming a leading example of cult television (Gregory, 1997, chapter 8) rather than a challenge to cultural lines of division between 'high' and 'mass' culture. We will probably not be seeing its like again, not least because the combination of roles performed by McGoohan was, and still is, remarkable for a popular TV series.

QUESTIONS TO CONSIDER

- Why has *The Prisoner* been thought of as 'subversive' TV? Is this a reasonable assessment of the show's politics?
- What textual qualities have sustained and supported *The Prisoner*'s cult status?

- What different interpretations of *The Prisoner* can you produce? Which do you think is the most convincing, and why?
- How useful is the concept of 'postmodernism' when trying to understand the appeal and success of *The Prisoner*?
- *The Prisoner* is often considered to have been 'authored' by its star, Patrick McGoohan. How important do you think this unusual co-attribution of stardom and authorship has been to sustaining *The Prisoner*'s reputation as a key TV text?

RECOMMENDED READING

Buxton, David (1990), chapter 3 of *From The Avengers to Miami Vice: Form and Ideology in Television Series*, Manchester and New York: Manchester University Press.

Gregory, Chris (1997), *Be Seeing You… Decoding The Prisoner*, Luton: University of Luton Press.

Miller, Jeffrey S (2000), chapter 2 of *Something Completely Different: British Television and American Culture*, Minneapolis and London: University of Minnesota Press.

Chapter Thirty Five ☐

Queer as Folk

Glen Creeber

Production Details

Queer as Folk (UK, Channel Four, 1999–2000)

Directors: Charles McDougall/Sarah Harding, Menhaj Hfcuda
Writer/Co-Producer: Russell T Davies
Executive Producer: Nicola Shindler
Associate Producer: Tome Sherry
Designer: Claire Kenny
Director of Photography: Nigel Walters
Editor: Tony Cranstoun/Tony Ham
Composer: Murry Gold

Cast includes:

Stuart Jones (Aidan Gillen)
Vince Tyler (Craig Kelly)
Nathan Maloney (Charlie Hunnam)
Hazel Tyler (Denise Black)
Sonna Clarke (Carla Henry)
Alexander Perry (Antony Cotton)
Phil Delaney (Peter O'Brien)

Queer as Folk (USA, Showtime, 2000–)

Based on the British series created by: Russell T Davies
Developed for American television by: Ron Cowen, Daniel Lipman
Director: Kevin Inch
Writer: Richard Kramer
Executive Producers: Tony Jonas, Ron Cowen, Daniel Lipman

Cast includes:

Brian Kinney (Gale Harold)
Michael Novotny (Hal Sparks)
Justin (Randy Harrison)
Emmett (Peter Paige)

Ted (Scott Lowell)
Debbie Novotny (Sharon Gless)
Melanie (Michelle Clunie)
Lindsay (Thea Gill)

The original *Queer as Folk* was made by the Red Production Company and appeared on British television's Channel Four, its 8 episodes, each of 40 minutes, running from February 23 to April 13, 1999. After its widespread success, a second series was quickly commissioned, *Queer as Folk 2: Same Men, New Tricks*, which was first screened on Channel Four in February 2000. Shown in more than 13 different countries, the original British serial was later developed into an American version, also called *Queer as Folk*, now into its second series and originally backed by Hollywood director Joel Schumacher. Although it was initially regarded as a toned-down version of the British serial, some critics argued that the sheer breadth of the American series (now clocking up over 40 episodes) has meant that it has been able to develop characters and story-lines far beyond the original. For many, one of the highlights of the American version was Sharon Gless (originally of **Cagney and Lacey** [CBS, 1981–9] fame) putting in a virtuoso performance as Michael's (Vince in the UK) mother.

Set in Manchester's vibrant gay scene and transferred to Pittsburgh for the American version, both dramas became notorious for their explicit treatment of homosexuality, in particular their frequently graphic portrayal of gay sex. In Britain the controversy particularly focused on the scene of two men, one of them a 15-year-old schoolboy (changed to 17 for the American version) and the other a man twice his age, having sex in the opening episode. This sequence was particularly sensitive in Britain as its first broadcast coincided with the Labour Government's plan of lowering the homo-sexual age of consent to 16. One gay viewer argued that scenes such as these could fuel homophobic fears about the seduction of vulnerable young boys by older predatory men (Channel Four, 2000). Others accused the drama of reinforcing stereotypes of all gay men as pill-popping, sex-obsessed 'disco bunnies', while many criticised the drama's lack of any fully rounded lesbian characters (Collins, 2000, 7). But perhaps the most extreme reaction to the drama came from Australia, where all of its terrestrial channels refused to broadcast it, fearing that it could be regarded as child pornography. When pay TV Foxtel did finally screen it, a separate channel had to be created so as to ensure that no children could accidentally tune in (McKee, 2002, 235).

However, the programme-makers have continually defended the drama, arguing that it never set out to represent the entire gay community. Alistair Pegg, the editor of *Pink Paper* argued that, 'It is not representative and it is not a public information film about being gay, it's about three gay men who happen to be real, interesting characters' (cited by Gibson, 1999). According to its original creator, Russell T Davies, he began writing the script thinking he should be representative and include *every* aspect of gay culture but soon realised that would make for very uninteresting drama. 'In the end', he argued, 'I realised I had to focus – to find good characters, good stories and to hell with representation' (Davies, 1999, 6). In fact, the American version even came complete with a warning at its conclusion that the series did *not* attempt to represent the entire gay populace (Keller, 2002, 2).

Despite these limitations, *Queer as Folk* was nonetheless seen as a real attempt to break away from the way homosexuals had tended to be depicted on television in the past. In particular, there is little apology made for the way they choose to live their lives and express their desires. As James Keller (2002, 1) has put it:

> *The characters in* Queer as Folk *exhibit little of the shame and self-loathing that is staple in the mainstream depictions of gays and lesbians, nor do they make an effort to apologise for their behaviour to the uninitiated and the unsympathetic. The show is a strident affirm-ation of the personal choices of a collection of young adults.*

Part of this lack of apology is explicitly made in the way the show famously showed same-sex desire.

Before *Queer as Folk*, gay and lesbian characters had seldom been shown displaying affection on television, sometimes provoking controversy with just the merest of touches. Even as late as the 1990s, the sitcom *Roseanne* (ABC, 1988–97) in the US and the soap opera *Brookside* (Channel Four, 1982–) in the UK both came under fire for showing two women simply kissing. Added to this, AIDS-focused American TV dramas such as *An Early Frost* (NBC, 1985), and *In the Gloaming* (HBO, 1997), and the Hollywood movie *Philadelphia* (Demme, 1993) were accused of making their central gay characters too 'straight', forcing them to 'imitate middle-class, middle-aged heterosexuality in order to be accepted' (Gauntlett, 2002, 87).

In contrast, *Queer as Folk* appeared to make little apology for its explicit treatment of gay life, gay sensibilities and (most famously) same-gender desire. In the first episode of the British version, Stuart and Nathan indulge in hot, sweaty, passionate French kissing – later moving on to oral sex, anal intercourse and even 'rimming' i.e. the stimu-lation of the anus with the tongue. With both men naked, covered in sweat, Nathan's legs are thrown over Stuart's shoulders as he penetrates him. 'I can feel him now', Nathan later tells his best friend at school, '... it's like he's left a space. He's still there' (Davies, 1999, 41). As explicit as such a portrayal of gay sex was, Russell T Davies has argued that it was simply a component of the story, an element of the drama that was probably less shocking than many aspects of the narrative that failed to attract attention. As he told Alan McKee (2002, 240):

> *With the sex scenes in episode one it's story, it's as simple as that. I mean, it's a boy getting his mind fucked as he's buggered ... it's fascinating that verbally in the same episode, there's a monologue to camera from Stuart where he describes having sex with a gym teacher when he was twelve. No one ever mentions that – there's no fuss about that ... But you*

don't see a naked arse in that – so therefore you don't panic. It's the nakedness that people panic about and I found that absolutely fascinating, that passed everyone by and that's actually far more shocking.

The very look of the drama also seemed to self-consciously break free of the 'serious' and heavy-handed way that homosexuality had tended to be represented by television in the past. The bright, blurred orange city lights of the opening British credits and the bouncy, high-octane music of Murry Gold's catchy theme tune, certainly lends a more buoyant atmosphere to the drama than the world-weary tones provided by Bruce Springsteen's melodic but sombre theme to *Philadelphia*. Added touches such as Vince's opening appearance addressing the audience in front of a luminous yellow background only heightened the brilliance of a *mise-en-scène* already saturated in colour. As its executive producer Nicola Shindler has explained, such a look was blatantly borrowed from the colourful, high production values of American television drama such as *Ally McBeal* (Fox TV, 1997–2001) and *L.A. Law* (NBC, 1986–94). Shooting everything with very long lenses also meant that everyone in the foreground was made to look 'sharp' while the background remained somewhat 'beautiful' (cited by Channel Four, 2000). According to Glen Creeber, then, the very look of the series 'can be seen as a crucial part of the drama's own "camp" aesthetic; a colourful, accelerated, vibrant and flamboyant sensibility that refused to betray its own playful sense of the world …' (forthcoming).

This is not to say that 'issues' such as homophobia and the dangers of gay promiscuity are not addressed by the drama. Indeed, Nathan's (Justin in the US) 'coming out' story is filled with all the clichés of school bullying, unsympathetic teachers and bigoted fathers, with the American version even having Justin hospitalised after a vicious homophobic attack. And although safe sex is not foregrounded in the British series (Brian does offer a message of safe sex in the US version [Keller, 2002, 2]), some of the dangers of casual sex are still addressed, one character dying of a heroin overdose after picking up a stranger late one night. However, the way these issues are dealt with is never allowed to become too serious – the sheer fun, energy and excitement of the contemporary gay scene seldom allowed to be eclipsed entirely. As a result, the drama tends to show different aspects of urban gay life without necessarily concentrating on the negative side of this particular lifestyle. Indeed, perhaps the great strength of both the British and American versions is that viewers get to know these characters in intimate detail so rather than simply seeing them as 'gay characters' (and therefore emblematic of certain 'gay issues'), their sexuality eventually becomes only a small (although important) part of their complex psychological make-up. As a result, we are given a more emotionally sophisticated and ideologically ambiguous insight into their behaviour and lifestyle as a whole.

Queer as Folk also showed gay characters consistently fighting back (often humorously) against homophobia, refusing to become mere victims of heterosexual prejudice and ignorance. In typically 'camp' style, Nathan uses a karaoke microphone to reveal a 'queer-bashing' school bully in front of an entire gay club. But perhaps the most dramatic statement of all comes from Stuart, who drives a brand new Jeep into a glass showroom after listening to homophobic jibes from the sales assistant. Added to this, the hypocrisy of the heterosexual world is consistently revealed, Stuart (Brian in the US) seducing a number of married men who claim to be 'straight', even when they are having sex with him in the office toilets. As such, these gay characters are consistently seen refusing to be determined by the restrictive and frequently hypocritical standards of heterosexual society; providing an unapologetic, honest and positively assertive gay role model for a new century. While the series may not have represented the entire gay world, it certainly went a long way in finally dramatising aspects of gay life never presented on British and American television before.

QUESTIONS TO CONSIDER

- Do you think the sex scenes in the drama were necessary? Do you think there would have been less controversy if the characters were heterosexual?

- Do you agree with Russell T Davies' claim that, as the writer, he had to concentrate on the 'drama' rather than the 'issues'?

- Is the drama's refusal to explicitly deal with issues such as 'safe sex' justified? Should more have been done to warn viewers about the dangers of drug taking and unprotected sex?

- Explain how the drama actually may have perpetuated common myths (and fears) about homosexual men. Do you think it is possible that it may have done more harm than good in its depiction of contemporary gay life?

- How are the lesbian characters portrayed in the drama? Do you think their characters should have been more developed in the British version? If so, why?

- Do you think Nathan's/Justin's 'coming out' story is a realistic portrayal of a young gay man's struggle to be accepted? Do you think it provides a positive role model for younger gay or lesbian viewers?

RECOMMENDED READING

Channel Four (2000), *What the Folk?* (documentary on *Queer as Folk*) included in Channel Four/Red Productions, *Queer as Folk 2: Same Men, New Tricks*, DVD.

Creeber Glen (2004), '*Queer as Folk*' in Creeber Glen, *Next Week On ...: Television Drama in the Age of Serial Fiction*, London: British Film Institution.

McKee, Alan (2002), 'Interview with Russell T Davies', *Continuum: Journal of Media & Cultural Studies*, Vol. 16 No. 2, July, 235–44.

Chapter Thirty Six

September 11, 2001

Justin Lewis

Production Details

(Various international networks)

In terms of brutality or loss of human life, the events of September 11, 2001 in the US were horrific but not entirely unprecedented. The recent history of humankind is replete with disasters, atrocities and massacres: from the dropping of an atomic bomb on Japan to the killing fields of Cambodia; from the genocide in Rwanda to the Union Carbide gas leak in Bhopal; from the Indonesian invasion of East Timor to the government-sponsored massacres in Central America. What made September 11, 2001 so extraordinary *as a television news event* was less its scale than its circumstance. It happened in the most powerful country in the world and in the very heart of the military industrial complex (the Pentagon) and in a city (New York) that is both the centre of media empires and the backdrop for countless media images. Moreover, it exceeded every conceivable measure of news value (Harrison, 2001, 114–16) – to such an extent that many of those in the West watching events unfold on their television sets found it hard to describe in news terms. For some, the only available reference point for such audacious, lurid excess came not from Bhopal or Oklahoma City but Hollywood. As Mehdi Semati put it, 'geo-political and cultural worlds came together on September 11 in a lethal and monstrous moment of blockbuster imagination' (Semati, 2002, 214).

It was not just that it was unexpected or shocking in its simplicity, or that, being both hijack and suicide bombing several times over, it was more deadly than other terrorist attacks. For in the cold, hard currency of news value we know that an event is more significant if it is captured on film or video, if it involves Americans or Western Europeans, if it is a singular act of terrorism rather than a routine act of war, if it kills quickly rather than slowly, and if it fits into a simple narrative of international geopolitics rather than (like the Oklahoma City bombing) a more uncomfortable set of domestic contradictions. In the longer term, it was this last aspect that made the attacks on the World Trade Center and the Pentagon so compelling as a TV news story. Before the dust had settled, and certainly before any culpability became clear, even the comparatively sober BBC was asking what bloody act of punishment or revenge might be sanctioned by such an attack. In the US, reporters quickly countered the egregious drama of the terrorist attack with anticipation of what to come: as Peter Jennings of ABC news opined: 'the response is going to have to be massive if it is be effective' (Kellner, 2002, 148).

The same questions were asked after the bombing of the federal building in Oklahoma City as a succession of television 'experts' and TV reporters suggested that the atrocity had, as the CBS news reporter put it, 'middle eastern terrorism written all over it'. But when the perpetrators turned out *not* to fit the Orientalist stereotype, the story lost its urgency and edge. It no longer had the capacity to make the political earth move – to prompt, for example, big increases in military budgets or presidential approval ratings. Indeed, the bomber's rhetoric bore an awkward resemblance to some of the more vociferous language coming from the majority party in the US Congress. While it made little difference to the hundreds of victims, Timothy McVeigh's guilt meant no war of retribution, no rush to legislate, no bombing campaigns, no shifts in the geopolitical map. The attacks on the World Trade Center and the Pentagon, on the other hand, sanctioned all of these things.

What followed, in quick succession, was not only the full-scale wars in Afghanistan and Iraq, but the creation of a rationale for future wars. The 'war against terrorism', with its shady, almost unfathomable adversaries and its ruthlessly high stakes is the closest the US has come to replicating the tactics and terms of the Cold War. What happened on September 11, 2001, thereby set in motion a series of responses which defined the whole framework of US television news coverage in the weeks and months that followed (and, to a lesser extent, news coverage elsewhere). Domestic and international politics were either overshadowed or redefined. Put simply, if it wasn't connected to the attack on September 11 or the war on terrorism, it wasn't news.

So it was that a series of news stories with their own narratives, some of which turned out to have little or no direct connection to the attacks on the World Trade Center and the Pentagon, dominated network news. September 11 defined everything from the anthrax letters to the plunging stock market and the rising death toll in the Israeli/Palestinian conflict. The anthrax scare, like the Oklahoma bombing, became less newsworthy as the terrorist's identity got closer to home. But for many weeks it was, regardless of lack of evidence, constantly linked to the notion of a sinister foreign threat. The effect of September 11 on the economy was also sucked into the subsequent mood of insecurity and paranoia, even though the economic consequences had nothing to do with the actual attacks themselves, but the fear of more to come (with a consequent dip in the talismanic barometer of 'consumer confidence'). President Bush was thus able to urge Americans to go shopping as an act of patriotic duty. And the Palestinian/Israeli conflict was reduced to the value-laden mathematics of the war on terrorism, attention focusing on the Israeli victims of suicide bombing rather than the more numerous Palestinian victims of the Israeli army.

It is, in this respect, hard to overstate the power of September 11 as a television news event, to such an extent that it is difficult to make observations about risk and response without seeming banal. Thus the logic for significantly increasing the US military budget (already gargantuan by comparison with the rest of the world) appeared inexorable, even though the whole modus operandi of terrorism is to bypass conventional military defences. The scale of the response, in other words, had more to do with the enormity of September 11 as a *media moment* than with a more dispassionate assessment of the security of people or nations. To understand the nature and power of TV news agendas, it is worth reminding ourselves that, even in 2001, terrorism comes a long way down the list of things putting lives at risk. In the US, handguns and cars are routinely more deadly than all the terrorist networks combined. And in the world as a whole, millions die every year from preventable diseases, lack of access to food and clean water, and from an environment made more hazardous with every passing decade by climate change.

It is commonplace to observe that television news, with its eye on the present, is poor at providing people with much in the way of historical context (Lewis, 2001). And yet the cultural and political framework that emerged from news coverage in the wake of September 11 was both an appeal for historical understanding and, simultaneously, a denial of it. If America suffered what *The Times* called (on the day after the attack) a 'loss of its innocence', there followed a desire to understand what the US had done that could possibly inspire such hatred. This desire was stunted by the discursive structure of US network news, which was so tightly bound to censorious notions of patriotism (McChesney, 2002; Kellner, 2002) that it was difficult to venture any explanation that might involve any examination of US foreign policy.

The only permissible explanations for what happened on September 11 were those based on the psychology of envy or the culture of totalitarian fundamentalism. Invariably, discussions of cause and motive were structured around a dichotomy in which the US is associated with freedom, democracy and human rights and its adversaries (notably the terrorists and their sympathisers) with their suppression. The US news media, in this sense, followed President Bush's lead when, in his speech to Congress on September 20, he suggested that what was to come was a battle between the freedom-loving world and 'those governed by fear … who want to destroy our wealth and freedoms'. Antipathy towards the US was thus seen as, at best, an outbreak of avarice or cultural psychosis and, more commonly, as a straightforward expression of evil.

This analysis was sustained by the main operational historical metaphor for the 'war against terrorism'. In news coverage in the US and Britain, this was *not* the invidious history of US or British foreign policy in the Middle East, but the more distant and more morally uplifting history of World War Two, with all its powerful Hollywood echoes. In both the US and the British news coverage, the war against Hitler and Nazism was invoked more persistently than any other historical or explanatory narrative (Lewis, 2002). The logic of this analogy was fiercely partisan, the implication being that this, too, was a clash between good and evil, and that such an evil could only be beaten by military force.

What this made less visible – particularly in the US news media – was a series of more plausible histories and explanations. Most notable was the absence of the long list of instances in which the US and other Western governments have aided, supported or promoted oppressive, unjust or brutal regimes all over the world, and that it is, in fact, US government support for those who 'govern by fear' (whether in Saudi Arabia or the West Bank) that is the source of such anger. In the news climate following September 11, to retrieve these histories was to risk being denounced as 'anti-American' and, in the US, such voices were confined to the Internet. It is, perhaps, indicative of the source and pattern of international news flows that this perspective was replicated in many parts of the increasingly interconnected global media system. In Brazil, for example, while press coverage offered a more diverse range of perspectives, television 'had little to say about the historical context of the ... war on Afghanistan' (Baiocchi, 2002).

Perhaps the most distinctive alternative TV voice to emerge after September 11 was the Al Jazeera satellite network, based in Qatar. Although Al Jazeera was denounced by many in the US as a mouthpiece for terrorist propaganda, its reporters had access to parts of the region that few Western TV networks could rival. What is clear, however, is that all media have a vested interest in the way they present and codify certain news stories. Because of the tragic and global significance of the events that took place in America on September 11, 2001, this particular news story became (and continues to be) a site of intense ideological and political contention.

QUESTIONS TO CONSIDER

- List as many of the prominent 'news values' as possible that made the events of September 11, 2001 such an internationally important news story.
- Assess whether or not you think the events deserved to get the sort of coverage they did. How do you think it may have been covered and reported if a similar event had taken place *outside* of the US or Europe?
- Did the events of September 11, 2001 represent an increase in terrorist incidents worldwide, or was it a one-off, singular event?
- How do you think the television news coverage surrounding the events and after may have simplified the political and historical context of the attack?
- How do you think television presented the US in the wake of September 11, 2001? In what ways do you think it may have played a part in advocating and sustaining George Bush's 'war on terrorism'?

RECOMMENDED READING

Chomsky, Noam (2001), *9–11*, New York: Seven Stories Press.

Lewis, Justin, Maxwell, R and Miller, Toby (eds.) (2002), special issue of *Television and New Media*, Vol. 3, No. 2.

Zelizer, Barbie and Allan, Stuart (eds.) (2002), *Journalism After September 11*, London and New York: Routledge.

Chapter Thirty Seven

The Simpsons

Brett Mills

Production Details

(Fox [Gracie Films/20th Century Fox], 1989–)

Creator: Matt Groening
Developed by: James L Brooks, Matt Groening, Sam Simon
Executive Producers: Mike Scully, Bill Oakley, John Weinstein and others
Producers: John Vitti, Conan O'Brien, J Michael Mendel, Richard Sakai and others
Writers: John Swartzwelder, Sam Simon and others
Directors: Mark Kirkland, David Silverman, Rich Moore and others
Animation Company: Klasky-Csupo (1989–91), Film Roman (1992–)
Theme Music: Danny Elfman
Musical Direction: Alf Clausen

Cast includes:

Homer Simpson, Grampa Simpson, Krusty the Klown, Barney, Groudskeeper Willie, Mayor Quimby and others (Dan Castellaneta)
Marge Simpson, Patty Bouvier, Selma Bouvier and others (Julie Kavner)
Bart Simpson, Nelson Muntz, Todd Flanders, Rod Flanders, Mrs Wiggum and others (Nancy Cartwright)
Lisa Simpson (Yeardley Smith)
Montgomery Burns, Smithers, Principal Skinner, Reverend Lovejoy, Otto, Kent Brockman and others (Harry Shearer)
Moe, Apu, Chief Wiggum, Professor Frink and others (Hank Azaria)

In 1990, American politicians, religious leaders, schoolteachers and other moral guardians declared war on an ordinary working-class family from Springfield. Seeing the five members of the family as not only representing the worst of contemporary America but also capable of dragging civilised society down with them, through the influence of television, clothes bearing their catchphrases were banned from schools and President George Bush called for America to embrace older, more traditional values. Worst of all, most of the antisocial behaviour being meted out on society by the family emanated from the 10-year-old son, whose parents seemed powerless – or, indeed, unwilling – to offer any punishment or correction. The fuss seems unbelievable now; particularly as all this venom was directed towards a fictional, four-fingered, yellow-skinned, cartoon family, on a fledgling TV network (Fox). In the early 1990s, *The Simpsons* had finally arrived: over a decade later the show is still with us, a part of American – and global – culture. It is a phenomenon which *Time* magazine called 'the best TV show of the century' (cited by Bhattacharya, 2000, 18).

The origins of *The Simpsons* are well documented (for example, Bhattacharya, 2000; Erickson, 1995; Hilton-Morrow and McMahan, 2003). The creator, Matt Groening, had achieved underground success with his cartoon strip *Life in Hell*, and attracted the attentions of Hollywood producer James L Brooks. Brooks, responsible for a raft of innovative and popular American comedies such as *The Mary Tyler Moore Show* (CBS, 1970–7), *Taxi* (ABC and NBC, 1978–83) and *Rhoda* (CBS, 1974–8), as well as directing the feature films *Terms of Endearment* (1983), *Broadcast News* (1987) and the Oscar-winning *As Good as it Gets* (1997), was looking for animation shorts for the struggling *The Tracey Ullman Show* (Fox, 1987–90). Brooks expected Groening to offer an animated version of *Life in Hell*. Instead, Groening, worried that he was risking his one successful venture on a television transfer, came up with the Simpson family – father Homer, mother Marge, and children Bart, Lisa and Maggie – all except Bart named after Groening's real family. The animation shorts were successful and popular, and the poorly performing Fox network, on the lookout for innovative and brand-defining shows, commissioned a series of full half-hour episodes (see Hilton-Morrow and McMahan, 2003 for the fuller story). *The Simpsons'* first story – 'The Simpsons Roasting on a Open Fire' – encapsulated much of what was to come, being a Christmas special of a series that hadn't even aired yet.

The Simpsons proper is quite different to the shorts it grew out of, both visually and in content. Both clearly develop from Groening's counter-culture credentials and paranoid responses to authority, which can be evidenced in *Life in Hell*. However, the series proper also incorporates Brooks' trademark character-driven comedy and willingness to experiment with the interplay of comedy and tragedy, strong narratives and delving into characters' emotional motivations and responses. Precisely who is responsible for the coherent narrative tone and social ideology that is seen in *The Simpsons* is a topic of much debate (Erickson, 1995, 449), though it is most likely that it is the interplay between Groening and Brooks, in conjunction with other producers, writers and directors, that results in the programme as is. Whatever, *The Simpsons* remains a phenomenally collaborative process, with a wealth of production crew, performers and animators, and a lengthy production process spread across more than one continent.

The initial hostile reactions to *The Simpsons* are only understandable in relation to contemporaneous television comedy. In the late 1980s, American television was dominated by **The Cosby Show** (NBC, 1984–92), a sitcom which, while radical in terms of presenting a successful, middle-class African-American family, clearly believed 'in parental authority, male primacy, old-fashioned sexual morals, monetary caution' and 'respect for elders' (Jones, 1992, 260). In doing so it never questioned the primacy of the family unit, instead offering middle-class lifestyles as the epitome of the American dream. More importantly, it reduced politics to the purely personal and familial, as any social problem bigger than that within the home couldn't comically be dealt with by the characters' homilies (Jones, 1992, 261). *The Cosby Show* reflected the social attitudes of the 1980s and the return in America to traditional notions of the family.

The Simpsons, on the other hand, offered the family as a site of contestation, battle, unhappiness and – most confusingly for conservative readings – still a solid unit for whom familial roles are understood and adhered to. Yet such familial stability rested on the absurdity of parents – the laziness of Homer and the unimaginativeness of Marge – as well as the willingness of the children – the inventive Bart and the clearly phenomenally intelligent Lisa – to accept their parents as failures. Here was a family in which father certainly didn't know best. For many this was acceptable as long as it resulted in the collapse of the family. The fact that the Simpsons remain a coherent, loving unit, while failing to conform to the conventions of the family, undermines the authority of adults, the superiority of parents and the inferiority of children. Worse, by contrasting the Simpson family with their God-loving, authority-respecting, constantly happy neighbours, the Flanders, and finding the Simpsons to be the more coherent and sympathetic unit, the programme acknowledged 'follies and imperfections in even apparently ideal families' (Newman, 1996, 28).

The initial hostility towards the programme rested on this tension and is epitomised by the show's initial star: Bart. Glynn (1996) outlines readings of Bart made by a number of groups and individuals for whom conventional notions of society and family are of import. He notes how fear of the programme rested squarely on the assumption that 'animated narratives constructed from the perspective of the fourth grade hellion Bart were sure to produce a new generation of rebellious underachievers who are "proud of it, man", and not about to back down in the face of proper authority' (Glynn, 1996, 63). On a broader scale, *The Simpsons* offered a threatening world-view by explicitly linking the difficulties faced by an 'average' family to bigger themes of work and politics. So, while in *The Cosby Show* problems and resolutions are found and sorted within the home, *The Simpsons* offers a broader social critique, positioning the Simpson family as only one among many, and at the mercy of those in power who, in Groening's words, 'might not always have your best interests at heart' (cited in Bhattacharya, 2000, 19). In doing so, it heralded a new age of working-class comedy which explored the relationship between individual and society, as seen in *Roseanne* (ABC, 1988–97) and *Married … with Children* (Fox, 1987–97). It also, importantly, put the Fox network on the map, a channel-defining programme which marked it as different to CBS, NBC and ABC.

A decade later, the programme 'still represents the worst in television for many parents' (Alters, 2003, 165). It also addresses specific audiences unlike other series

(Hilton-Morrow and McMahan, 2003, 83), resulting in a bidding war between the BBC, Channel Four and Channel Five in 2002 for the UK broadcast rights (with Channel Four the eventual winner). It's commonly argued that the success of 'family' series such as *The Simpsons* rests on its 'double coding'; that is, the text is structured to offer different pleasures for different audiences (Wells, 1998b, 225). The argument goes that while adults can enjoy the intertextual references and satirical jibes at government, children instead get pleasure from the bright colours, the speed of the action and the slapstick violence. Indeed, Groening himself notes that 'No matter how clever you are, you've got to have Homer slam into a brick wall at some point' (cited in Bhattacharya, 2000, 23). While Farley (2003, 152) rightly questions such simplistic notions of 'adult' and 'childish' pleasures, it's clear that *The Simpsons* encompasses a range of jokes, on a variety of subjects, unseen in the majority of comedy, or, indeed, television.

Furthermore, the immediate and lasting success of *The Simpsons* raises questions as to why animation was unseen in American prime time for nearly two decades, since the end of *The Flintstones* (ABC, 1960–6; NBC, 1967–70). Indeed, the 1990s can be seen as a decade in which animation had a renaissance, not only on television, but within popular culture more generally. It's virtually inconceivable that series such as *South Park* (Comedy Central, 1997–), *Beavis and Butt-Head* (MTV, 1993–7), *King of the Hill* (Fox, 1997–) and Groening's own *Futurama* (Fox, 1999–2002) in America, and *Stressed Eric* (BBC2, 1998) and *Pond Life* (Channel Four, 1996) in Britain, would ever have been commissioned – or watched – if *The Simpsons* hadn't made adult animation a viable form of programming again. Wells argues that this development is 'an inevitable product of the cultural influence exerted by the "baby-boomer" generation' (2002, 86), which has resulted in audiences and programme-makers versed in the language of television generally and animation specifically, for whom high/low cultural distinctions, which might result in guilt for adults enjoying something as traditionally 'low' as cartoons, have no meaning (Furniss, 1998). Certainly, *The Simpsons* offers pleasures to those with much 'teleliteracy' (Bianculli, 1992, 175–83), with its constant references to other shows and films. This has led to the programme being seen as emblematic of 'postmodern' television, in which there is 'a hyperawareness on the part of the text itself of its cultural status, function, and history' (Collins, 1992, 335), and a 'seemingly symbiotic relationship with television itself' (Wells, 2002, 97). This reached its apotheosis when President Bush announced that America needed fewer families like the Simpsons and more like the Waltons. Bart, at home, watching Bush on television, turned to his family: 'Hey, we're just like the Waltons. We're waiting for an end to the depression too' (Flew, 1994, 14).

QUESTIONS TO CONSIDER

- Is *The Simpsons* a sitcom? Compare it to other sitcoms, in terms of character and narrative.
- Are Bart and Homer Simpson bad role models? How do they respond as characters to their roles within their families and at school/work?

- What does the programme say about gender differences within families? How are Marge, Lisa and Maggie different to Bart and Homer? Is the programme sexist in its portrayals of women?
- What is the programme able to do that non-animated sitcoms can't do? Look at the kinds of stories that are told, the depiction of characters and the types of jokes that are made.
- How does *The Simpsons* reflect Matt Groening's statement that those in authority 'might not always have your best interests at heart'? Look at its portrayal of authority figures such as Mayor Quimby, Principal Skinner and Chief Wiggum.
- What audience do you think the programme is made for? Are there different pleasures on offer for children and adults? Why might this be so?

RECOMMENDED READING

Thanks to Rebecca Farley and Tim Robins for assistance with articles and readings.

Glynn, Kevin (1996), 'Bartmania: the Social Reception of an Unruly Image', *Camera Obscura*, 38, 61–90.

Irwin, William, Conard, Mark T and Skoble, Aeon J (eds.) (2001), *The Simpsons and Philosophy: the D'oh! of Homer*, Chicago and La Salle: Open Court.

Pinsky, Mark (2001), *The Gospel According to the Simpsons: The Spiritual Life of the World's Most Animated Family*, Westminster: John Knox Press.

Chapter Thirty Eight

The Singing Detective

Catrin Prys

Production Details

(BBC, 1986)

Writer: Dennis Potter
Director: Jon Amiel
Producers: Kenith Trodd, John Harris
Choreographer: Quinny Sacks
Designer: Jim Clay
Make-up designer: Francesca Hannon

Cast includes:

PE Marlow (Michael Gambon)
Philip [aged 9] (Lyndon Davies)
Nicola (Janet Suzman)
Mark Binney/Finney/Raymond (Patrick Malahide)
Nurse Mills (Joanne Whalley)
Dr Gibbon (Bill Paterson)
Mr Marlow (Jim Carter)
Mrs Marlow (Alison Steadman)

The Singing Detective, first broadcast on BBC1 between November 17 and December 21, 1986, is regularly hailed by critics as its writer Dennis Potter's masterpiece; a striking and brilliant culmination of all his main themes and preoccupations. Made in association with the Australian Broadcasting Corporation, *The Singing Detective* unravelled before viewers' eyes for six weeks, its final episode attracting an audience of six million in the UK. Its success in Britain was also mirrored in countries like Sweden and Germany, and later, in 1988 it was shown on a few PBS stations in the US. Marvin Kitman of New York's *Newsday* called it: '... the most fantastic program I've seen in my eighteen years as a TV critic ... the kind of program that comes along and permanently changes the parameters of what TV drama can do and reclaims TV as a creative medium' (cited by Carpenter, 1998, 511).

According to Glen Creeber, *The Singing Detective*, 'is best understood as the sensational continuation of themes and structural techniques which Potter had been pursuing and developing since the early 1960s' (1998, 168). Without doubt, the serial is a fascinating reworking of the techniques and thematic concerns with which the writer had been experimenting since his days as a BBC dramatist in the 1960s. Single plays such as *Stand Up Nigel Barton* (BBC, 1965), *Where the Buffalo Roam* (BBC, 1966) and *Moonlight on the Highway* (ITV, 1969) are all early examples of how Potter utilised the narrative of television drama as a journey into the deepest realms of the human (mostly male) psyche. In particular, Potter employed flashbacks, direct address to camera, fragmentation of time and space and Eisensteinian montage (Cook, 1995, 26–32) to explore frequently difficult and complex emotional terrain. *Moonlight on the Highway* (which dealt with child sexual abuse, a brave topic for TV drama in 1969) was also the first to foreground, what would, most notably in *Pennies From Heaven* (BBC, 1978) and *The Singing Detective*, become a Potter trademark – characters unexpectedly bursting into songs from the 1930s and 1940s (and eventually the 1950s in *Lipstick on Your Collar* [Channel 4, 1993]). Thus, from the outset, Potter's drama stood out from the usual televisual flow by broaching difficult and sometimes controversial themes and by presenting stylistic challenges to the comfortable tenets of naturalism (Caughie, 2000, 81–124).

Directed by Jon Amiel and produced by Kenith Trodd and John Harris, *The Singing Detective* is a fascinating, intricate serial centered around a pulp-fiction author named Philip Marlow. Suffering from an acute form of psoriatic arthropathy (a dreadful combination of psoriasis and arthritis that causes painful limbs and terrible blistering of the skin), Philip is literally a prisoner inside his own skin and bones. The action progresses through an array of experimental techniques such as childhood flashbacks and characters 'lip-synching' to popular music of the 1930s, as well as cleverly interwoven artistic genres that are used to reveal Philip's deep-rooted anxieties and obsessions. Seen in this context, *The Singing Detective* is a serial preoccupied with the internal workings of Philip Marlow's mind. The dramatic techniques employed by the drama all contribute to deflect the attention of the viewer from the superficial externals of naturalism and towards the inner reality of the character's psyche.

Indeed, an internal logic is at the very core of *The Singing Detective*. Despite the initial narrative confusion into which the viewer is plunged, the structural dynamic of the serial is reassuringly simple to follow, bearing in mind that all the colliding narrative levels actually take place *inside* Marlow's tortured mind (Creeber, 1998, 169). Through flashbacks we learn of his mother's infidelity (he witnessed her having sex with a stranger in his childhood forest), and of his feelings of isolation and guilt when she finally commits suicide. Confined to his hospital bed in the present, he continually rewrites, in his head, his own detective story (also called *The Singing Detective*), and incorrectly imagines that his wife, Nicola, is conspiring to steal the rights to the screenplay of the novel. We also witness Philip suffering from severe hallucinations: as his body temperature soars out of control, he imagines people around him suddenly bursting into song and dance routines.

Potter's expressionistic approach and style has most frequently been labelled by critics as 'non-naturalistic', but other terms such as 'psychological realism' perhaps more aptly convey the interior landscape of the drama (Cook, 1995, 26–32). Consequently, Potter's work has sometimes been described as merely formulaic or 'tricksy', implying that his experimental techniques were only deployed in an attempt to shock the viewer or simply to create public controversy. However, in *The Singing Detective*, Potter's pioneering techniques clearly came from a *need* to represent its central protagonist's mind in its full and frequently desperate and unstable condition. Marlow struggles to make sense of his memories, desires and deep-rooted feelings of guilt and betrayal – factors that require constant acknowledgement and re-examination of past events and future consequences. Thus, by submerging the viewer in an expressionistic, non-naturalistic, multi-layered narrative milieu, the serial dramatically reveals its central protagonist's inner psychology rather than simply portraying the external and chronological realities of his life. Only by shattering a naturalist or realist mode of storytelling could it delve into areas of such fragmented psychological complexity, presenting the viewer with an alternative and sometimes shocking singular vision.

For example, if we look at Marlow's rewriting of his own detective story in his head, we realise how certain factors clearly represent his psychological obsessions. It is interesting and crucial that Potter chose the detective genre for Marlow's pulp novel, bearing in mind that its main premise is to find out 'who done it?' The quest for 'clues' in the *film noir* fantasy is surely a fictional portrayal of his own painstaking process of psychoanalysis and detection; the post-war backdrop of paranoia, darkness and suspicion also an apparent objective correlative of his own soul (notice, of course, he shares his name [minus the 'e'] with Raymond Chandler's own hard-boiled detective). Moreover, *film noir* is always populated with dark, mysterious women and *femmes fatales*, a significant factor considering Philip's fear and loathing of the opposite sex. Sonia, one of the prostitutes/spies in his novel, is certainly dangerous and deceitful, a figure that seemingly represents the protagonist's lack of trust in women in general. Thus, the detective genre, as a whole, serves as a literal mirror for Philip's psychological condition, his mistrust of women and fear of sex. Likewise, the popular songs of the 1930s (the period of Philip's childhood) play a similar role, both in terms of their lyrics and their visual reinterpretation.

The ultimate connection between these conflicting layers of narrative can be found within the childhood flashbacks, in particular the scene when the young Philip spies his mother having sex. Later, we see the child confessing to his mother that he witnessed the act, a confession that not only coincides with him showing her his first psoriatic lesion but also consequently leads to her suicide. His troubled view of sex and women is apparently rooted in these disturbing memories, a view which is confirmed in his discussions with Dr Gibbon, the psychiatrist (Potter, 1986, 53, emphasis in the original):

> *Dr Gibbon:* You don't like women. Do you?
> *Marlow:* Which sort do you mean? Young ones. Old ones. Fat ones. Thin ones. Faithful ones. Slags? Sluts? . . .

Chapter Thirty Nine

The Sopranos

David Lavery

Production Details

(USA, HBO, 1999–)

Writers have included: David Chase, Frank Renzulli, Robin Green, Mitchell Burgess, Terence Winter, Todd A Kessler, Michael Imperioli, Lawrence Konner

Directors have included: David Chase, John Patterson, Allen Coulter, Tim Van Patten, Henry J Bronchtein, Steve Buscemi

Producers have included: David Chase, Ilene Landress, Brad Grey, Mitchell Burgess, Robin Green, Frank Renzulli

Cast includes:

Giacomo Jr. (Jackie Jr.) Aprile (Jason Cerbone)
Richie Aprile (David Proval)
Salvatore (Big Pussy) Bonpensiero (Vincent Pastore)
Artie Bucco (John Ventimiglia)
Ralph Cifaretto (Joe Pantoliano)
Adriana La Cerva (Drew De Meteo)
Dr Jennifer Melfi (Lorraine Bracco)
Christopher Moltisanti (Michael Imperioli)
Johnny (Johnny Sack) Sacramoni (Vincent Curatola)
Anthony (AJ) Soprano, Jr. (Robert Iler)
Carmela Soprano (Edie Falco)
Carrado (Uncle Junior) Soprano (Dominic Chianese)
Janice (Parvati) Soprano (Aida Turturro)
Livia Soprano (Nancy Marchand)
Meadow Soprano (Jamie-Lynn Sigler)
Tony Soprano (James Gandolfini)
Paulie Walnuts (Tony Sirico)

Almost from the beginning – the series premiered on the American premium cable channel HBO in January of 1999 – *The Sopranos* critics have heaped upon it the highest praise. When in 2002 the widely read periodical *TV Guide* published its list of the 50 greatest shows of all time, *The Sopranos* only held fifth place but was the highest ranked dramatic series in television history. Ellen Willis deemed it 'The richest and most compelling piece of television – no, of popular culture – that I've encountered in the past twenty years ... a meditation on the nature of morality, the possibility of redemption, and the legacy of Freud' (2002, 2). The subtitle of Canadian Maurice Yacowar's recent book – *The Sopranos on the Couch: Analyzing Television's Greatest Series* (2002) – assumes its pre-eminence, whilst TV critic Stephen Holden declared that *The Sopranos* was not only the best television drama ever made, 'but episode by episode as good or better than any Hollywood movie to be released in ages ...' (Holden, 2000, ix).

Of course the verdict was not unanimous. Prominent critics like Wolcott (2000) (who had originally praised the series) and Paglia (2001) loudly voiced their loathing of it. Italian-American groups denounced the show for what they believed to be its offensive, grossly stereotyped depiction of Italians as mobsters, mounting letter-writing campaigns, staging boycotts, harassing *Sopranos* cast and crew in their public appearances and even seeking legislative action against the series. Some critics (Lauzen, 2001) were also appalled by what they saw as misogynist tendencies in season three (the rape of Dr Melfi, the brutal murder of a pregnant stripper, the near suicide-by-mobster of Tony's mistress Gloria Trillo). When broadcast uncensored in Canada on CTV, the national Broadcast Standards Council was asked to take action against the series and CTV. The Council's review of *The Sopranos*, however, found the complaints without merit (Johnston, 2002).

The continuing narrative of *The Sopranos* moves back and forth between the suburban nouveau riche and mafia families of a New Jersey crime boss. On the home front, we find Carmela, Tony's long-suffering, morally compromised, but very tough wife; Meadow, his daughter, now a student at Columbia University, who knows very well that her father is not really in the 'waste management' business; Anthony Junior, his bad boy son; his New Age 'shlub' of a sister, the scheming, but now born-again Christian Janice; Uncle 'Junior,' Corrado Soprano, an elderly, easily manipulated Mafioso; and his (now deceased) passive-aggressive monster of a mother, Livia (played by the veteran TV actress Nancy Marchand who was also in **Marty** [NBC, 1953]), who coerces Uncle Junior into ordering a failed hit on Tony, retaliation for putting her in a luxurious retirement home. At the 'office' – Tony and his crew use *The Bada Bing*, a local strip club, as their primary headquarters, although they also convene in the back of Satriale's Pork Store – the regulars include Silvio Dante, manager of the *Bing* and Tony's loyal captain; Paulie Walnuts, an anal-compulsive hit man; and Christopher Moltisanti, Tony's impulsive nephew, a young made man who aspires to write mob dramas for Hollywood. Tony's worlds collide, however, in the office of Dr Jennifer Melfi, where he seeks help for panic attacks. A mob boss in a psychiatrist's office was, in fact, the seed crystal for the series, and Melfi becomes an all-purpose ficelle, interpreting Tony's conscious and unconscious life.

Faced with the challenge of doing a mob story on television, its original creator David Chase understood immediately (as he tells Bogdanovich, 2002) that he would have to redirect the genre 'into the family'. The series' mobsters are all fans of the gangster film genre – Silvio endlessly quotes Michael Corleone (Al Pacino) from *The Godfather* films, Christopher tries his hand at writing an (illiterate) gangster film screenplay, Tony cries while viewing *Public Enemy* (Wellman, 1931), moved to tears by the film's loving mother, so different from his own – and *The Sopranos* is, not surprisingly, intertextual to the core, playing off of predecessor texts in the genre. Indeed, it is possible to map most of the narrative according to the gangster film coordinates outlined by Robert Warshow 40 years ago (Auster, 2002; Pattie, 2002; Remnick, 2001).

But *The Sopranos* operates on a new, smaller scale in a different medium. Glen Creeber has argued that 'the series implicitly critiques the "televisionisation" of the gangster genre – parodying its gradual development (Chase might say decline) from cinematic epic to standard video or television fare … its constant self-reflexive referencing to its own generic history reveal[ing] a television narrative desperately trying to reinvent and re-examine itself' (2002, 125). And Donatelli and Alward (2002, 65) insist that it is possible to view *The Sopranos* as 'a kind of feminist metatext' in which:

> *Tony and his mob friends are 'framed' by rules of domestic television … all their actions … constantly subject to forms of irony and comedy that by now have become inevitably identified with serialised programming. While Tony and his friends may think they're tough, everything that they do is undercut because they are cast in soap opera episodes that deny them the dignity of a full-length Mafia movie, let alone a trilogy.*

The Sopranos has likewise departed from many of the conventions of television drama. Its casting, especially of the balding and overweight James Gandolfini as Tony, was a departure from television norms, as were the characters they portrayed, capable of extreme violence and despicable behaviour. Nor did its narrative style conform to traditional multi-season dramas. Though fans expected some variation on the 'Who shot JR?' (see **Dallas** [CBS, 1978–91]) cliffhanger at the end of season one, Chase and company offered none, nor has the series exhibited any sense of urgency about resolving some of its many narrative arcs. In the introduction to the *Sopranos* scripts, Chase articulates his hope that his series is 'similar to the foreign films I loved as a young adult for their ideas, their mystery, and their ambiguity – for not having the endings spelled out or telling the audience what to think or feel' (Chase, 2002, 11). The series' peerless use of music is likewise distinctive.

In order to produce his 13-episodes-a-year mini-movies, Chase has also demanded more and more time between seasons of *The Sopranos* – time devoted to fine-tuning the writing (each script goes through as many as 10 drafts) and planning for the on-location (in New Jersey) cinematic-style filming. (*The Sopranos* has a rich textual geography which, not surprisingly, has invited the attention of media ecologists [Strate, 2002].) The hiatus between the third and fourth years lasted 16 months. Nor has Chase been willing to agree to an indefinite run for the series. Although *The Sopranos* is now committed to a five-year run, Chase is absolutely determined to then pull the plug on his creation.

Although the major American television networks, all of which passed on the show, have attributed the tremendous success of *The Sopranos* to HBO's cable TV freedom to air nudity and profanity, Chase finds that explanation superficial. It is not bare breasts and obscenities that have set *The Sopranos* apart but, according to its creator, a variety of other factors: the narrative possibilities granted by the absence of commercial interruption, the freedom to allow characters to develop slowly over time and the series' insistence on treating its audience as highly intelligent. As Poniewozik observes, *The Sopranos* expects its viewers to remember details from three years back in an era in which the broadcast networks 'increasingly believe it's highfalutin to air dramas like *24*, that require viewers to remember what happened the week before' (2002, 56) (also see Bishop, 2001).

The Sopranos also assumes that its audience shares its often wicked sense of humour (see, for example, the recently published *The Sopranos Cookbook* [Rucker, 2002]). In several interviews Chase has proclaimed his credo that humour should accrue naturally out of the dramatic material and not be imposed upon it, a doctrine to which the series, full of pratfalls, scatology, puns, malapropisms, funny names and clever allusions (Lavery, 2002, provides a 19-page partial catalogue of *Sopranos* references), is not always faithful. *The Sopranos* is one of the funniest shows on television, however, because it partakes in the great tradition of comedy: its characters are consistently hilarious because they are often clueless, devoid of any insight into themselves and any wisdom about their individual predicaments.

Not governed by the same Nielsen ratings criteria as broadcast programming – for years, HBO's most famous tag line has proclaimed 'It's not TV. It's HBO' – *The Sopranos* has nevertheless garnered the largest audiences in the history of cable. Although only about a third of American homes even receive HBO, the premiere of the second season drew 11 million viewers. A product of 'TV III' – a period in broadcast history that critics roughly begin in 1995, dominated by cable television and the rise of digital programming – *The Sopranos* stands as a nuts-and-bolts triumph of non-network TV and as the show that established once and for all the HBO brand with the viewing public (Rodgers, Epstein and Reeves, 2002; Levinson, 2002). While television executives in the US are now in the process of rediscovering the Least Objectionable Programming theory and building their schedules on its foundation, *The Sopranos* has demonstrated, in the words of James Poniewozik, something quite different: 'Not only will ordinary folks watch a show that demands constant attention, resists easy closure, relies on subtext and is rich with metaphor – they will pay near usurious subscription fees for it' (2002, 56–7).

QUESTIONS TO CONSIDER

- Why have Italian-American defamation groups found *The Sopranos* so offensive? Do you think such criticism is justified?

- Psychoanalysis plays a prominent role in every episode. What contribution does it make to the series' narrative as a whole and how has it contributed to its success?
- How are women portrayed in the series? How are they similar and dissimilar from their counterparts in classic gangster films?
- What features of cable television have contributed to both the economic and artistic success of *The Sopranos*?
- *The Sopranos* is highly dependent upon cultural and pop-cultural references. Can you give some examples and what role do you think they play in the drama as a whole?
- How does the use of music function in *The Sopranos*? Compare it, for example, with the way music is used in contemporary crime movies like *Reservoir Dogs* (Tarantino, 1992).

RECOMMENDED READING

Gabbard, Glen O (2002), *The Psychology of The Sopranos: Love, Death, Desire and Betrayal in America's Favorite Gangster Family*, New York: Basic Books.

Lavery, David (ed.) (2002), *This Thing of Ours: Investigating The Sopranos*, New York: Columbia University Press.

Yacowar, Maurice (2002), *The Sopranos on the Couch: Analyzing Television's Greatest Series*, New York: Continuum.

Chapter Forty

Star Trek

Matt Hills

Production Details

Originally created by: Gene Roddenberry

Executive Producers have included: Ira Behr, Rick Berman, Brannon Braga, Gene Roddenberry, Michael Piller, Jeri Taylor

Directors have included: Marc Daniels, Lawrence Dobkin, James Goldstone, Chip Chalmers, Jonathan Frakes, Robert Weimer, Patrick Stewart, Winrich Kolbe, Kim Friedman, Les Landau, LeVar Burton

Star Trek (original series) (NBC/Paramount, 1966–9)
Cast includes:

Capt. James T Kirk (William Shatner)
Mr Spock (Leonard Nimoy)
Dr Leonard 'Bones' McCoy (DeForest Kelley)
Mr Sulu (George Takei)
Lt. Uhura (Michelle Nichols)

Star Trek: The Next Generation (Syndicated, 1987–94)
Cast includes:

Capt. Jean-Luc Picard (Patrick Stewart)
Cmdr. William Riker (Jonathan Frakes)
Lt. Cmdr Data (Brent Spiner)
Lt. Geordi LaForge (LeVar Burton)
Lt. Worf (Michael Dorn)

Star Trek: Deep Space Nine (Syndicated, 1993–8)
Cast includes:

Capt. Benjamin Sisko (Avery Brooks)
Lt. Cmdr. Jadzia Dax (Terry Farrell)
Lt. Cmdr. Worf (Michael Dorn)
Odo (Rene Auberjonois)
Major Kira Nerys (Nana Visitor)

> *Star Trek: Voyager* (UPN, 1995–2001)
> Cast includes:
>
> Capt. Janeway (Kate Mulgrew)
> First Officer Chakotay (Robert Beltran)
> Security Chief Tuvok (Tim Russ)
> Chief Engineer B'Elanna Torres (Roxann Dawson)
> Seven of Nine (Jeri Ryan)
>
> *Enterprise* (Syndicated, 2001–)
> Cast includes:
>
> Captain Jonathan Archer (Scott Bakula)
> Sub-commander T'Pol (Jolene Blalock)
> Dr Phlox (John Billingsley)
> Ensign Hoshi Sato (Linda Park)
> Ensign Travis Mayweather (Anthony Montgomery)
> Chief Engineer Charles 'Trip' Tucker III (Connor Trinneer)
> Lt. Malcolm Reed (Dominic Keating)

If *Star Trek* is a key television text, then it merits such status by virtue of having become that most amorphous type of television: *a phenomenon* (Gibberman, 1991). TV 'phenomena' combine longevity with cultural influence, seeping out into the culture at large so that viewers who have never seen a programme are still familiar (via intertextual references, publicity and well-known catchphrases such as 'Beam me up, Scotty') with its characters and format. Much like the case of the British SF TV series **Doctor Who** (BBC, 1963–89), *Star Trek* has endured (Hockley, 2001) long beyond its original series. Both have returned from the industry death of cancellation, in large part as a result of their brand recognition and loyal fan followings (Verba, 1996). However, only *Star Trek* has returned and gone on to second, third, fourth and now fifth leases of life in the form of different spin-offs.

Star Trek's status as a TV phenomenon means that it has supported a wide range of merchandising and a film series alongside its television version, as well as many academic publications (Hills, 2000). A meta-textual web of meaning, *Star Trek* has done nothing less than sustain a vast, narrative universe, aiming to coherently develop timelines and alien cultures.

The original series would typically end with a comedic scene on the Enterprise Bridge, closing off that week's narrative and restoring the status quo ready for the crew's next adventure. Stories rarely referred back to previous adventures, although continuity was already present in the form of alien cultures and races (such as Vulcans and Klingons) that audiences gradually learnt more about as the series progressed. However, 'series memory' and the development of continuity became more pronounced as textual qualities from *Star Trek: The Next Generation* onwards, as the show became less focused on stand-alone episodes and, like much American television drama of the 1990s, began to incorporate soap-operatic 'story arcs' or ongoing storylines.

This shift in narrative structure can be linked to changes in the American television industry; whereas the original series was aimed at a mass audience and could not afford to assume that viewers had been avidly tuning in each week, later series not only assumed fan audiences, they sought to reward audience loyalty by building in levels of textual detail and continuity that would repay attentive viewing. The *Star Trek: Deep Space Nine* episode, 'Troubles and Tribble-ations', is a good example of this, since it digitally combines material from an original series episode ('The Trouble with Tribbles') with new footage of *Deep Space Nine* characters. Although it is possible to appreciate the episode without detailed fan knowledge of the original series, such knowledge is rewarded in the form of in-jokes relating to changes in Klingon make-up effects, as Klingon character Lt. Worf refuses to explain why he doesn't look like Klingons from the 1960s series.

The *Star Trek* franchise has been accorded great cultural significance by many critics. Rather than being viewed as an ephemeral part of television's alleged cultural wasteland, the series is often taken as an example of 'authored' popular, genre TV or as an example of 'TV-as-high-culture' (resembling the one-off TV plays or drama popular in the 1960s). Before self-conscious notions of 'quality TV' and 'cult TV' meant that American television drama could routinely be industrially promoted and publicised as 'authored' or 'auteurist', the original series was created, executive produced and sometimes written by Gene Roddenberry. Henry Jenkins (Tulloch and Jenkins, 1995) has analysed how Roddenberry's 'author-function' works to sustain notions of *Star Trek* as valued, important TV, positioning it as a reasonably early example of 'auteurist', popular television for its fans and scholars. The 'author-function' serves as a principle of classification (allowing texts to be grouped together) and as a principle of explanation (explaining textual similarities via recourse to the author's preoccupations or concerns), as well as marking out a sign of value, given that only certain texts in a culture are read as authored (Tulloch and Jenkins, 1995, 188–91).

Roddenberry's name appears to work in each of these ways; it links 'authentic' *Star Trek* to a reading of the show that emphasises its humanism and utopianism, and allows the show to be valued by fans as a progressive, authorial message. When particular episodes of the original series failed to live up to fans' auteurist interpretation of the show, by not reflecting Roddenberry's tolerance for cultural diversity, then these episodes were (Tulloch and Jenkins, 1995, 189):

> described as a 'betrayal' of Roddenberry's personal vision, thereby displacing discomfort with the series content onto some other aspect of the production process (Paramount, the networks, other members of the production team). The tendency is to ascribe the series' virtues to those agents with whom the fans have the most direct personal contact (the producers, the writers, the actors) and to ascribe its faults to forces ... less easily conceptualised in personal terms (the studio, the network, the ratings).

This auteurist type of interpretation therefore leads to a rather simplistic 'good guys' versus 'bad guys' argument, where personal forces of creativity and vision are valued, while impersonal forces of 'the industry' are devalued, as if Gene Roddenberry himself, and *Star Trek*'s later production teams, can somehow be positioned outside the TV industry rather than considered as a part of it.

Whatever the reasons for its cultural 'elevation' by both fans and critics, endless interpretations of the series have focused on its representations of various social and philosophical issues. Most frequently, the *Star Trek* franchise has been valued for its humanist tenets, with alleged religious deities often being exposed in stories as technological trickery or as alien races (Porter and McLaren, 1999; Wagner and Lundeen, 1998). Supposedly conveying anti-organised-religion sentiments, the series has also been read as offering progressive representations of race (Bernardi, 1998; Pounds, 1999). The most frequently cited development here is the fact that a black actress, Michelle Nichols, was cast as one of the original 1960s Enterprise Bridge crew. By suggesting that religion would no longer be significant in mankind's future, and that ethnic and cultural diversity would be embraced, *Star Trek*'s creator Gene Roddenberry's 'vision' has been identified by fans as one of tolerance and 'Infinite Diversity in Infinite Combination'. Consequently, the series has been viewed as upbeat, utopian TV SF, seemingly doing away with ethnic conflict, bigotry, cultural power struggles and racial prejudice.

However, there are a number of limitations to reading *Star Trek* as utopian. Firstly, the programme can simply be interpreted rather differently: that is, as a representation of Cold War tensions, with the Federation's battle against the alien Klingon race coding capitalist/communist and US/USSR tensions. This interpretation was even worked into the film series, where *Star Trek VI: The Undiscovered Country* (Meyer, 1991) seemed to parallel the real-life politics of *glasnost* with its narrative changes in human–Klingon politics. 'To boldly go where no man has gone before' certainly has implicit notions of colonisation that also may have reflected a less than utopian mission on behalf of the Enterprise crew. Secondly, gender representations in the original *Star Trek* were, in general, hardly sophisticated. The programme repeatedly featured women in largely subservient roles and as exotic, scantily clad villains for Captain Kirk to romance. Even by the time of *The Next Generation* in 1987, the show continued to reproduce stereotypes of empathetic femininity via the character Deanna Troi. Indeed, it is not until 1995's *Star Trek: Voyager* that we have a female captain at the helm of the show (Roberts, 1999). And in terms of race, it was only with 1993's *Deep Space Nine* that an African-American Captain, Benjamin Sisko, finally took command.

It is also worth considering just what *Star Trek*'s 'utopian' world-view consists of. Although differences based on caste and creed have supposedly been erased and science has triumphed over religion (something that is challenged in the first *Star Trek* franchise not to have been created and overseen by Roddenberry, *Deep Space Nine*, which adopts a more accepting view of mysticism), *Star Trek* nevertheless presents an exceptionally hierarchical view of communal life. Everyone, from captain to security guard, knows their place. Command is supposedly built on assent and legitimated through the merits and charisma of various captains. But what this apparent meritocracy disguises is that *Star Trek*'s vision of the future is often militaristic (on occasions, Kirk shoots first and asks questions later) and based around an insistence that characters accept a rigidly defined hierarchy and allocation of roles. Being a red-shirted security guard in the original series of *Star Trek*, doomed to die as soon as you beam down to a planet, and lacking any characterisation or even a name, may not be everyone's idea of living in an utopian future.

As a result, academic accounts which accept at face value the cultural status of *Star Trek* as authored (Gregory, 2000) and utopian in intent (or even those that adopt the position that *Star Trek* is akin to 'high culture' in its scope for Shakespearean narrative or humanism [Barrett and Barrett, 2001]), fail to see how bids for cultural value are staged through and around *Star Trek*. Such academic accounts, along with popular readings of *Star Trek* and its 'metaphysics' or philosophy (Hanley, 1997) are in danger of simply affiliating themselves with one particular bid for *Star Trek*'s elevated cultural value. They fail to analyse different constructions and interpretations of the programme by different audiences. And as one of the longest running and most multifaceted programmes in television history, it would indeed be surprising if the *Star Trek* franchise could ever be convincingly reduced to one coherent and comprehensive 'reading'.

QUESTIONS TO CONSIDER

- What differences in narrative structure and aesthetics are there between the five *Star Trek* franchises?
- Does *Star Trek* represent a 'utopian' human future or a militaristic, authoritarian one?
- Look at *Star Trek*'s portrayal of race, status and gender. Do you think its treatment of such issues makes it 'progressive' or 'conservative' in design?
- How do you think the original series may have reflected US foreign policy during the 1960s?
- How has Gene Roddenberry's 'author-function' worked to construct *Star Trek* as culturally valued TV?
- What can the history of *Star Trek* tell us about how fans and producers view the TV industry?

RECOMMENDED READING

Barrett, Michèle and Barrett, Duncan (2001), *Star Trek: The Human Frontier*, Cambridge: Polity Press.
Harrison, Taylor, Projansky, Sarah, Ono, Kent A and Helford, Elyce Rae (eds.) (1996), *Enterprise Zones: Critical Positions on Star Trek*, Boulder, Colorado: Westview Press.
Tulloch, John and Jenkins, Henry (1995), *Science Fiction Audiences: Watching Doctor Who and Star Trek*, London and New York: Routledge.

Chapter Forty One
Sunday and *Bloody Sunday*

John Corner

> **Production Details**
>
> *Bloody Sunday* (NI Productions for Channel Four Drama, January 20, 2002)
> Producer: Mark Redhead
> Writer and Director: Paul Greengrass
>
> Cast includes:
> Ivan Cooper (James Nesbitt)
> Major General Ford (Tim Piggot-Smith)
> Kevin McCorry (Allan Gildea)
> Eamonn McCann (Gerard Crossan)
> Colonel Steele (Chris Villers)
>
> *Sunday* (Granada Film/Hell's Kitchen, January 28, 2002)
> Producer: Gub Neal
> Writer: Jimmy McGovern
> Director: Charles McDougall
>
> Cast includes:
> Major General Ford (Christopher Eccleston)
> Leo Young (Ciarán McMenamin)
> John Young (Barry Mullan)
> Mrs Young (Brid Brennan)

The screening of these two programmes, within days of each other and 30 years after the actual incident in Northern Ireland that they dramatise (since commonly referred to as 'Bloody Sunday'), was a key television event. It projected new and critical versions of what exactly happened on January 30, 1972, when 27 civilians were shot (13 died) by members of the Parachute Regiment during the 'disturbances' surrounding a civil rights march in Londonderry. The incident threw up a range of questions about both political and military intentions and judgements that have lasted through to the recently reopened inquiry, which was still in session in Summer 2002. The judgement of the first inquiry, conducted within days of the incident by

Lord Widgery (the Lord Chief Justice), has been seen increasingly to be faulty and politically managed in its view that no blame could be attached to the army's behaviour.

The programmes were also significant in that they were the first major dramatisations of the issue to be televised. The sensitivity and import of the event itself was such that either one, on its own, was bound to have revived the long-standing British debate about the social and aesthetic legitimacy of drama-documentary formats. Coming together, they generated both a greater public impact as resources for public discussion of the real incident and also a rare opportunity for critical comparison of approach and dramatic design. Although both of them inevitably draw commonly on the increasing range of evidence and testimony to be made public in recent years, following sustained pressure-group activity and independent investigations, they show some marked differences in the way they work up this material into a re-enactment and thereby place the viewer as 'witness' within an unfolding event.

A key question for nearly all drama-documentary based on specific events has been the extent to which imagination joins evidence in the production of the re-enactment (see Corner, 1996, chapter 2 and Paget, 1998, chapter 5 for more detailed commentary; see also *Culloden* [BBC, 1964] and *Cathy Come Home* [BBC, 1966]). This querying of the precise mix of ingredients has been joined by anxiety about the power of the form to suggest itself to viewers as revealed truth, thereby hiding the elements of conjecture and pure invention at work and the consequences these have for judgements. A central problem for both these dramas, then, is what 'spaces' they open up for the re-enactment (*where* do we go, topographically, socially and politically, in following the story?) and how to organise these spaces in time, both in relation to the established chronology of the real event and to the narrative economy of the drama (its tensions, crises and expositional emphases).

Paul Greengrass's design for *Bloody Sunday* clearly turns on his decision to develop his account around a central figure, Ivan Cooper, an MP for the area. Cooper was an organiser of the civil rights march on the day (by the 'Northern Ireland Civil Rights Association') and was continuously involved in the events, including as a direct witness, right through to attendance at the hospital following the shootings and the giving of a press conference at the end of the day. Cooper was played by James Nesbitt, an actor with a very strong and popular television presence at the time, in part due to his role in the comedy drama series *Cold Feet* (Granada for ITV network, 1998–2003). This idea of building the narrative system around a central character played by a known actor who carries attractive values from previous roles (tough yet sensitive, funny, intelligent) is vital to the shape and impact of the drama, effectively pulling the viewer in around a point of strong empathy and even identification.

In each of the four basic phases of the drama (i.e. the build-up to the march, the march itself, the core of the incident and its aftermath in hospitals, homes, the army command centre, etc.) the central character has a quite pivotal position in attempting to avert trouble and then in responding to the tragedy that occurs. For periods, his role is inevitably displaced by a concern with other spaces and with other individuals caught up in the events, but he provides a regular point of reference for 'reading' what happens, his response being the most powerful direct cue the film offers us to guide our own assessment. His position as someone deeply committed to the peaceful route to political reform, who at the end of this Sunday finds it much harder to be critical of those who embrace armed struggle, is crucial for the drama as a whole. It is partly echoed in the transition of one of the young working men portrayed, who is seen to move from a distanced and critical attitude concerning the IRA to being a recruit in the final scene.

In the light of the evidence available, any attempt to portray the army sympathetically would be virtually impossible. However, an interesting aspect of *Bloody Sunday* is the way it depicts a quite sharp division between two senior army officers involved. The senior of the two (Major General Ford) welcomes the involvement of the paratroopers to arrest or shoot the 'young hooligans' thought to be behind much of the trouble in Londonderry. This is part of a new 'get tough' policy. However, the other staff officer, actually in direct command on the day, has reservations about the deployment of the paratroopers at all, a worry he shares with the senior RUC officer present and one that is fully confirmed by what happens. In the middle scenes of the drama, this officer is shown refusing permission for the paratroopers to move in on the streets until the very last minute, when no other options appear to be available.

The effect of this dramatically is to provide what is at least a partly sympathetic figure within the army command and to open up a series of tensions and differences within what initially might seem a unitary space. Substantively, it has the effect of at least complicating any idea that there was a clearly defined prior intention, perhaps originating from London, to carry out the killings. Again, in a way that echoes this tension closer to ground level, one of the paratroopers, a radio operator, is disturbed by the events he has witnessed and the failure to cease fire immediately when ordered. His troubled response to the events contrasts with that of the other men in his platoon. Through a number of deft characterisations surrounding a central figure, a clearly defined foreground of developing public events set against various private spaces and a set of internal tensions additional to the primary division between troops and marchers, *Bloody Sunday* generates strong story values alongside its core and shocking scenes of violence.

In contrast, Jimmy McGovern's *Sunday* does not develop the level of 'public' framing of the event found in *Bloody Sunday*. Instead, it has a strong grounding in the personal and domestic context of the events, embedded, as they are, in the lives of a selection of 'ordinary people'. The closer engagement with the texture of family life certainly brings out a sense of how religious and political tensions impact upon personal, everyday reality. For example, one of the fathers of a young victim of the shooting works for the British Army as a civil servant and there is a romance across the

Protestant–Catholic divide. Throughout, women characters are strongly presented, largely as a result of the domestic emphasis and the consequent reduction of male focus at many points. There are also scenes in a morgue where the directly personal, intimate level of horror involved in recognising a dead loved one is strongly brought out (this might be compared to the more public scenes of grief and chaos in the hospital sequence of *Bloody Sunday*).

Another key feature of *Sunday* is the way in which the shootings are depicted twice, each time at some length. The first depiction occurs within the basic chronology of the narrative. The second occurs through a number of flashbacks as witnesses give evidence to the Widgery inquiry (*Sunday* gives far more attention than *Bloody Sunday* to the nature of the 'whitewash' involved here, giving Widgery himself a strongly negative depiction). This second dramatisation, generated as it is by the traumatic memories of the witnesses, and in particular by the memories of the paratrooper radio operator upset by what he saw, is much stronger in its depiction of what is essentially presented as the murder of the innocent. McGovern's presentation of the army, officers and men, is clearly strongly negative at the level of personal portrayal (a scene in a barracks' bar as the paratroopers joke at television news of the day's events is indicative here). The shootings are seen as part of a clear high-command policy, issuing finally from Downing Street (the then Prime Minister, Edward Heath, is briefly presented) and pursued enthusiastically by senior staff officers (Christopher Eccleston plays the key role of Major General Ford here).

In discussion of the two films, it is not surprising that many critics found the cooler, documentary-like approach of *Bloody Sunday* more acceptable than the more obvious and sometimes heavy evaluations coming through in *Sunday* (less like a documentary for much of its length, primarily because of its basis in domestic settings). However, McGovern's drama was recognised for its own distinctive way of handling the depth of personal tragedy and of highlighting, too, the kind of 'justice' that Widgery's inquiry achieved.

Both programmes intercut newsreel with dramatised sequences at key points, but there was little danger of any viewer being confused about the basic status of what they watched as a dramatisation. The central scenes in both carried a raw force (in some ways the documentary style of *Bloody Sunday* makes it the more shocking) that undoubtedly served to engage people with the event in ways that news and current-affairs programmes could not, given the limitations of available actuality footage. In a sense, both dramas attempted to 'fill in the hole' right at the centre of the event – those minutes during which the paratroopers were deployed on the streets and firing their weapons, minutes which have been the subject of detailed and sometimes contradictory testimony.

The view that drama is an unsuitable medium for developing public knowledge on controversial topics was once again aired in some quarters (again, both Corner, 1995 and Paget, 1998 give some of the history and background to the general debate). Here, both films ran the risk, in their pre- and post-publicity, of under-recognising the

as well as more unexpected artefacts like computer mouse mats… According to the BBC's annual report, £330 million was generated overall during the programme's first two years, with 23 million going directly to the BBC in 1998 (43 per cent of which came from sales of video tapes).

Teletubbies is the brainchild of Anne Wood, who began developing children's stories for a magazine (*Books for Children*) she devised while working as a teacher in the 1960s. In 1982 Wood took up the position of Head of Children's Programmes for the now defunct breakfast television company, TV-AM, where she introduced the puppet character Roland Rat and *Rub a Dub Tub*. Wood left TV-AM in 1984 to set up Ragdoll Limited, which got its first commission from Channel Four and then was commissioned by ITV to make *Rosie and Jim* (Central, 1990–2, 1995–). As a result, Ragdoll quickly gained a reputation for making quality pre-school programmes with an educational emphasis.

In the mid-1990s, the BBC was looking for something aimed at a younger demographic than they had provided before. Working with Andrew Davenport, Wood devised *Teletubbies* as a show that would appeal to the youngest demographic yet addressed by a television programme. According to Wood, 'The BBC wanted a programme for children younger than anyone had ever dared make before' (http://www.ragdoll.co.uk). The result was an innovative programme that achieved instant success – and instant notoriety. As Davenport puts it, 'Everyone seeing it for the first time was aware they were seeing something completely new' (ibid.).

Set in Tellytubbyland (actually a 6-acre lot in the Warwickshire countryside), where big rabbits gambol around plastic flowers, the show is centred on its four central characters, brightly coloured and rotund alien babies that have strange receivers on their heads and television screens on their bellies. The Teletubbies interact with this environment often in response to an off-screen voice coming from a Voice Trumpet in the ground that directs, encourages and responds to their behaviour. Sometimes they play in their underground bunker, the Tubbytronic Superdome, where they sleep and make 'TubbyToast' and 'TubbyCustard', or chase their cleaning machine with a life of its own, the Noo-Noo (often the 'naughteee Noo-Noo'). These antics are structured around regular recurring events. The most significant of these is the windmill on the hill that acts as a conduit between the real world and Tellytubbyland. It sends out television signals that the teletubbies compete to receive on their bellies. Once a belly-screen is activated they all watch a short piece of real-life 'documentary' footage involving the activities of children; once finished the teletubbies insist on its instant repeat: 'Again! Again!' and the sequence is shown once more. According to Ragdoll, 'Teletubbies can receive pictures on their tummies. This is the most important moment in the programme. The pictures are of young children showing an aspect of their own experience in their world. The Teletubbies love each other and children very much' (ibid.).

The 'documentary' features show children doing various things, usually under adult supervision: looking at squirrels in the park, travelling on a ferry, drawing, painting, cooking and colouring, etc. The evident joy and excitement that the teletubbies manifest in watching the pictures is matched by the responses of another character, the Sun Baby, an infant face superimposed on an animated sun, that gurgles and giggles in excitement. Hence the programme internalises its range of target audiences – the pre-Oedipal, before-language baby, the proto-language and simple locomotive skills of the Teletubbies themselves and the slightly older children who narrate and take part in the 'documentary' segments. This is central to the innovative strategy of the show in foregrounding the child-centred experience above all. The makers conduct extensive research, taping and measuring the responses of child 'focus groups' while watching the show. For Davenport and Wood the success of *Teletubbies* is measured in the responses of children to it and is a product of the seriousness they bring to the design and lengthy production process. According to Davenport (ibid.):

> *If you are making a fantasy for a child you must work very hard to take it seriously: the colours, sets, voices, which character does what ... You can't expect a child to take a fantasy seriously if you have any cynical thinking. For us, Tellytubbyland has to be real; we believe in it absolutely.*

There is also the security provided by repetition, a tradition that is evident in older children's shows like *Camberwick Green* (BBC, 1966–9) and *Bagpuss* (BBC, 1974), but one that connects also to the world of nursery rhymes (Warner, 1998). The opening line of the show, 'Over the hills and far away, Teletubbies come to play!' signals the other-worldly quality of both the past and a magical land. Occasionally objects and creatures 'from far away' come to visit Tellytubbyland: a tap-dancing bear replete with boater and waistcoat, a scary lion and bear, a doll's house with the shadow of a man running about inside. Sometimes the references to the older past world of the nursery rhyme is oblique: the animal parade, a digitally created procession of giraffes, frogs, elephants, etc., seems to refer to the Noah's Ark story in the Old Testament; when Tellytubbyland fills with water and the teletubbies watch three giant liners manoeuvre in it, strains of the carol, 'I Saw Three Ships Come Sailing By' can be heard. In this way the technological/pastoral setting and the bright *mise-en-scène* is inflected with past traditions that adults can access as well. The success of *Teletubbies* did carry some surprising consequences, however, as David Buckingham notes (2002, 38):

> *...the bizarre day-glo figures of Tinky Winky, Dipsy, Laa-Laa and Po have... provoked a degree of outrage and irritation that is out of all proportion to their essentially mundane and harmless antics. Widely criticised by parents, politicians and journalists alike,* Teletubbies *seems to have become synonymous with the 'dumbing down' of contemporary childhood.*

The 'dumbing down' debate – which is essentially an anxiety about the perceived decline in the quality of contemporary culture – latched onto the success of *Teletubbies* as emblematic of the crass commercialism of the BBC and the celebration of creative infantilism by progressive educationalists. So, on the one hand, many criticised the show's baby talk – 'Eh-oh' for 'Hello', etc. – as setting a bad example for children, while, on the other, it was criticised for making money out of children's interests through its merchandise. In addition, as many critics noted, the BBC in the 1990s was attempting to realign itself as a public broadcaster that could compete in a global commercial media economy, for which it attracted considerable criticism for allegedly sacrificing standards on the altar of competitiveness. *Teletubbies* became a way into the discussion about the future of public service broadcasting in a highly competitive environment, one that was becoming alive to the value of the infant demographic.

The criticisms of the show reached epidemic proportions with fears about children getting addicted to the show or pulling the television sets on their heads in order to give the teletubbies a hug. Such criticism rapidly took on a predictable form of a war between self-appointed traditionalists and self-appointed progressives, so that US Reverend Jerry Falwell warned parents that Tinky-Winky (who is purple and likes his handbag) was homosexual, while media studies scholar Andy Medhurst claimed that the same character was the world's first pre-school gay icon. That the chosen terrain for battle was a show aimed at two to three year olds – at a time when news and current-affairs programmes were simplifying their formats and mode of address to be 'accessible' and focusing more on emotional human interest stories, and when documentaries chose increasingly sensationalist topics to the extent that some were faked – is indicative of the intellectual poverty of the debate.

Other critics pointed to the ways in which students and other adults had embraced *Teletubbies* as cult television, obsessing over supposed references to drug use and creating websites that detailed the structure of the Tubbytronic Superdome and the various waves each creature deployed to greet the viewers. Like many children's shows past and present, *Teletubbies* became available for all kinds of ironic and cult reappropriation. Certainly the adult interest in the show can be linked to the increasingly blurred boundaries between adult and childhood pleasures (a trend that has some history; see Calcutt, 1998), as evidenced by the popularity of the *Harry Potter* series and other fantasy products among adults. Some have argued that the world of *Teletubbies* is a sanitised adult fantasy of a safe, warm and comforting world where everyone loves each other 'very much'. Equally, it is tempting to draw parallels between the start of the show and the election of the (New) Labour Government in the UK in 1997 in order to critique the creation of a shiny shell built on marketing and focus groups but with little actual content.

But such crude comparisons would miss the charm of *Teletubbies* and its important innovations. Central to these is Anne Wood's commitment to television as a legitimate medium for education and entertainment and her belief that television is not inferior to books as a means for providing these things. The teletubbies' evident joy in watching television is clearly shared by millions of pre-school children as well.

QUESTIONS TO CONSIDER

- Evaluate *Teletubbies'* involvement in the 'dumbing down' debate in the national media.
- To what extent is *Teletubbies* innovative in its design and mode of address? What continuities does it exhibit in relation to traditional children's television?
- Examine the balance – or tension – between *Teletubbies'* aspirations as an educational programme and its desire to be entertaining for very young children.
- Consider the ways in which *Teletubbies* patterns repetition and variation in its structure.

RECOMMENDED READING

Buckingham, David (2002), 'Child-centred television: *Teletubbies* and the Educational Imperative' in David Buckingham (ed.), *Small Screens: Television for Children*, London and New York: Leicester University Press.

Televizion (special issue on the *Teletubbies*) (1999), No. 12, available at http://www.br-online.de/jugend/izi/english/12_1999_e.htm

Warner, Marina (1998), *No Go The Bogeyman: Scaring, Lulling and Making Mock*, London: Chatto and Windus.

Chapter Forty Three

Till Death Us Do Part and *All in the Family*

Brett Mills

Production Details

Till Death Us Do Part (BBC, 1965–75)

Writer: Johnny Speight
Producer: Dennis Main Wilson
Director: Douglas Argent and others

Cast includes:

Alf Garnett (Warren Mitchell)
Elsie 'Else' Garnett (Dandy Nichols)
Mike (Anthony Booth)
Rita (Una Stubbs)

All in the Family (CBS [Tandem Productions], 1971–9)

Executive Producers: Norman Lear, Bud Yorkin, Mort Lachman
Writers: Norman Lear, Susan Harris, Rob Reiner and others
Directors: Paul Bogart, John Rich and others

Cast includes:

Archie Bunker (Carroll O'Connor)
Edith Bunker (Jean Stapleton)
Michael Stivic (Rob Reiner)
Gloria Stivic (Sally Struthers)

Jonny Speight's *Till Death Us Do Part* originated as a pilot for the BBC's anthology *Comedy Playhouse* (1961–74) in 1965, beginning its first of seven series proper in 1966. Set in working-class London, this family sitcom centred on the Garnetts: patriarch Alf, his wife Elsie, their daughter Rita and her new husband Mike, both of whom lived with Alf and Elsie due to lack of funds. While maintaining the traditional sitcom premise of family life and generational conflicts, *Till Death Us Do Part* exploded the genre through its use of content not seen before in sitcom or, indeed, any popular television. Alf Garnett was 'an ill-educated, shockingly opinionated, loud-mouthed, appallingly tempered, deeply angry, Tory-voting, prudish, monarchist bigot, a deeply working-class man who nonetheless had no time for his kind and wouldn't hear a bad word said about the rich and privileged' (Lewisohn, 1998, 668). His son-in-law, in contrast, was a lazy liberal/'leftie', who represented all Alf found wrong with modern society. The bonds of family contrasted with the conflicts of politics in a series of debates, rows and arguments which made up much of the programme, and which allowed the series to use offensive – particularly racist – terms unheard on mainstream television before. Alf's invective against 'wops', 'coons', 'micks' and others gave public domain to debates and prejudices apparent all over Britain, but which had hitherto been steadfastly glossed over by the majority of broadcasting. The series was an instant hit, garnering audiences of up to 16 million (Husband, 1988, 160); it was, simultaneously, lambasted for its offensive nature and possible contribution towards, and justification of, prevalent racist attitudes.

If anything, the American version of the series – renamed *All in the Family* – intensified the applause and concomitant outrage. The sitcom writer Norman Lear bought the rights to the British version, renamed Alf Garnett Archie Bunker and set the programme in working-class New York. After spending three years trawling a succession of pilots around the networks, CBS, sensing a change in audience sympathies, resulting from a succession of pivotal news events (Staiger, 2000, 85), gambled on it. The first season gained notoriety but small audiences. Moved to the traditional family slot of Saturday evening in its second season, the programme's radicalism was more apparent and the audience rocketed: 'for five straight years Archie sat on top of the list' (Jones, 1992, 211), remaining one of America's most successful and popular sitcoms of all time.

On both sides of the Atlantic, the series are seen as responding to cultural developments of the 1960s in which conservatism grappled with liberalism, the young with the old, and the people with the state. So, while Alf and Archie wrestled with the rhetoric of social policy and the effects of changes within their countries, they did so firmly within the boundaries of their family, representing the distrust and incomprehension felt by many towards the establishment and government. In being only interested in how social changes affected themselves, Alf and Archie spoke to an older generation who had lost all they believed in, and a younger one who never had anything to believe in in the first place.

Debates – contemporary and recent – about both programmes centre squarely on whether they present Alf Garnett and Archie Bunker as objects of ridicule or sympathy, the former positioning the programmes as critiques of small-minded bigotry, the latter allowing audiences to identify with such racist beliefs, their justification apparent by their broadcast. Such debates latch on to concerns about the nature of humour as a whole and, since the so-called 'alternative comedy' movement in Britain in the 1980s, the possible effects of humour on a wider populace have been generally, if begrudgingly, accepted (see also *The Benny Hill Show* [ITV, 1969–89]). Because of this, much research has been carried out on audience responses to both programmes (Adler, 1979).

Husband (1998), for example, clearly sees the possibility of negative attitudes being reinforced by *Till Death Us Do Part*, undermining research conclusions reached by the BBC. He argues that there is a distinction to be made between rejecting Garnett/Bunker as a character, yet accepting his values as acceptable and worthy of a voice (165). Certainly there's a problem in that even if Garnett/Bunker is a bigot, he's a 'lovable bigot' (Staiger, 2000, 94). In addition, the fact that the representative of contemporary, liberal values – the son-in-law, Mike – is himself an unsympathetic, whinging layabout does little to suggest a viable, decent alternative. Indeed, the fact that rarely does either programme offer a concrete solution to the social problems they highlight, means that Alf/Archie, the literal voice of the series, becomes a set of values which audiences must identify with for the programme to remain in any way pleasurable. In that case, 'What are the social effects of loving someone whose beliefs you abhor?' (ibid.)

The programmes have also been criticised for their failure to offer effective central voices for anyone from the groups they purport to support. That is, a supposedly liberal programme still rests on heated debates between two white men. Also, 'the frequent tirades of Alf Garnett in *Till Death Us Do Part* are remembered for the virulence of their racism, but it must be remembered that insults to his wife, calling her "a silly moo", came thick and fast also' (Andrews, 1998, 52). Similarly, the programme suggests that the acceptance that black people are not the threat Garnett/Bunker perceives them to be rests on the protagonist defining them as such, rather than through those characters defining themselves.

Instead, it may be more valuable to see the programmes as a significant development in the portrayal of the white working class, the hardworking, poor majority who had rarely been depicted on television and whose confused voice, but hard-worn ideals, instead represent a failure of governments to adequately explain their role within society. Wagg sees *Till Death Us Do Part* as attempting to 'celebrate working class life and partly to ridicule the reactionary elements within it' (1998, 10). Because of this, the programme was often applauded for its attempt – flawed or otherwise – to engage with 'the real' (Staiger, 2000, 90). While this was sometimes understood in terms of the look of the programme, it also related to its engagement with many personal crises: impotence, redundancy, abortion and rape.

However, while it is tempting to see the two programmes as identical, it's apparent that significant differences exist between the two and these have been seen as representative of differences within British and American cultures. Jones maligns *All in the Family*'s sentimentality, 'that set it apart from its British inspiration' (1992, 208). He argues that the requirement for a happy ending in the American version not only demonstrates the kinds of stories acceptable to mainstream, mass US audiences, but also has significant consequences for the depiction of the characters. That is, the invoked emotional involvement with Archie Bunker is one of the ways in which the programme negates its attempt to present him as an ill-informed buffoon.

In addition, *Till Death Us Do Part* resonated with a history of British culture and its association with the working class, seen in soap operas like **Coronation Street** (ITV, 1960–), films like *A Taste of Honey* (Tony Richardson, 1961) and plays such as *Look Back in Anger* (John Osborne, 1956); that is, when *Till Death Us Do Part* began, Britain had already begun to wonder what it meant to be underprivileged, and had a film and television heritage which had developed generic conventions for their portrayal (see also **Monty Python's Flying Circus** [1969–74]).

In contrast, Miller finds that *All in the Family* plays down the role of class in a number of ways (2000, 145). The Bunkers' house, while less aspirational then the norm for American television, still represented a way of life which was clearly less difficult than was central to the British version. More importantly, Lear replaced the class tensions vital to *Till Death Us Do Part* with ones based instead around race, nation and religion. The family's neighbour, Michael, just another Cockney in the British version, became Polish for the American series, and in doing so highlighted the WASP nature of the Bunker family. Miller compares the first episodes of the two series, of which the American was a rewrite of the original British version (2000, 145–8). He finds that most of the targets for Garnett's attacks are social norms and politicians: for Bunker, though, the tirades range across a variety of cultural stereotypes, so that 'the French are virtually the only nationality or ethnic group left unscathed' (148). In this way, the American version not only latches on to concerns more visible in a confused, multi-ethnic America but also, subtly, prevents the programme from being the critique of authority and power which powers the original.

This can be seen as emblematic of American television and its stronger commercial forces, which had resolutely prevented it from dealing with the poor. Also, it symbolises the difference between British media that had traditionally attacked those in power and American media that had not. For American audiences, problems within the home and in society more generally can be traced to, and dealt with, within the domestic sphere. The change of the series' title once it crossed the Atlantic is no mere accident, for the series suggested that everything you need to know about America, its people and its society, could be found 'all in the family'.

The influence of both programmes is phenomenal, if only because of the repeated returns of the main characters and spin-offs from the main series. So far, Alf Garnett has returned on British Television in *The Thoughts of Chairman Alf at Christmas* (ITV, 1980), *Till Death …* (ITV, 1981) and *In Sickness and in Health* (BBC, 1985–92), meaning he has been a recurring television figure for almost three decades. In America, *All in the Family*, after the loss of a number of key characters, mutated into *Archie Bunker's Place* (CBS, 1979–83), in which Archie became the owner of his local bar. More significantly, a number of characters were spun off into their own series: *Maude* (CBS, 1972–8), *The Jeffersons* (CBS, 1975–86) and *Gloria* (CBS, 1982–3). These, along with other Lear series such as *Good Times* (CBS, 1974–9) and *Sanford and Son* (NBC, 1972–7) – itself a remake of the British series *Steptoe and Son* (BBC, 1962–74) – represented a glut of comedy programming containing issues of race, gender and politics, more realistic language and the return of comedy to its rightful position of questioning the social values of a culture. Indeed, the whole look, content and politics of sitcom on American television in the 1970s can be seen as emanating from *All in the Family*, and it is unlikely more modern series such as **The Cosby Show** (NBC 1984–92) and *Roseanne* (1988–98) would exist without its heritage.

QUESTIONS TO CONSIDER

- Is Alf Garnett/Archie Bunker racist? Do audiences sympathise with his opinions, or does the programme act as a critique of such views? How do the programmes attempt to signal to their audiences how they should respond?
- Look at the relationship between Alf/Archie and the other characters. How does the programme portray the female characters and Alf/Archie's interaction with them?
- How are the series different to other sitcoms around at the time? How are they different to contemporary sitcoms? Look at the acting style, the shooting style, the use of language and the jokes' targets. Why should these be different?
- Compare and contrast the British and American version of the series. What do the similarities and differences suggest about the respective television industries and audiences? Which do you prefer and why?
- Would either of these programmes be acceptable on television today? What changes would have to be made for audiences to find them acceptable and/or pleasurable?

RECOMMENDED READING

Adler, Richard P (ed.) (1979), *All in the Family: A Critical Appraisal*, New York: Praeger.

Husband, Charles (1988), 'Racist Humour and Racist Ideology in British Television, or I Laughed Till You Cried' in C Powell and GEL Paton (eds.), *Humour and Society: Resistance and Control*, Basingstoke: Macmillan.

Miller, Jeffrey S (2000), *Something Completely Different: British Television and American Culture*, Minneapolis and London: University of Minnesota Press.

Chapter Forty Four

Top of the Pops

KJ Donnelly

Production Details

(BBC, 1964–)

Producers have included: Johnnie Stewart (60s), Robin Nash (70s), Stan Dorfman (70s), Michael Hurll (80s), Stan Appel (90s), Ric Blaxill (90s), Chris Cowey (00s)

Presenters have included: Pete Murray, Alan Freeman, Jimmy Savile, David Jacobs, Emperor Rosco, Simon Dee, Tony Blackburn, Noel Edmonds, Gary Davies, Mike Smith, Janice Long, Peter Powell, Mike Read, Dave Lee Travis, John Peel, David 'Kid' Jensen, Anthea Turner, Jenny Powell, Andy Crane, Simon Parkin, Caron Keating, Toby Anstis, Dale Winton, Jayne Middlemiss, Zoe Ball, Jo Whiley

---

Top of the Pops (frequently abbreviated to *TOTP*) started at 6.35 on the evening of New Year's Day in 1964, with the words, 'It's number one; it's *Top of the Pops*'. These were spoken with characteristic enthusiasm by radio disc jockey Jimmy Savile and followed immediately by a studio performance from the Rolling Stones. Britain's most successful television pop music show, it was first broadcast from a converted church in Manchester and only intended to run for six weeks. In fact, it ran for 12, then was made continuous and still runs today. Broadcast in a prime-time slot, *TOTP* was precisely the sort of mass-culture show that embodied the newer brand of the BBC's public service broadcasting evident in the 1960s and 1970s. In particular, the development of *TOTP* was set against the background of the BBC's rather ineffectual competition with its new commercial rival. Although the BBC had a small tradition of pop music shows like *Six Five Special* (1957–9) and *Jukebox Jury* (1959–67), ITV's *Ready Steady Go!* (1963–6) was the top music show on British television in the early 1960s. However, *TOTP* helped establish and keep the BBC at the forefront of pop music at a time when it really needed to present itself as a more 'populist' institution.

As its title suggests, *Top of the Pops* has always been a version of 'pop' or popular music that is defined wholly by the sales of singles. It is a reflection of the charts, along with their weaknesses, such as the sameness of styles and questions over their veracity, etc. As a 'hit parade show', it was derived from the existing 'revue' form that had been prevalent among pop music films in Britain from the late 1950s to the mid-1960s. Indeed, the success of *TOTP* and other programmes showcasing a succession of acts was instrumental in the disappearance of this type of film (Donnelly, 2001b, 15). However, it has largely stayed with its basic blueprint of programme format. It is based on the pop singles chart and built around the principle of the chart countdown. The shifting roster of presenters mostly has been BBC Radio 1 DJs, whose celebrity has been magnified by having a face added to their radio persona. A central aspect of their hosting of the show is where they introduce acts, face-on to the camera, surrounded by members of the studio audience. The programme includes both live performances from groups and films/videos, while up until the 1980s it included dances to songs, by professional dancers and, in the early years, by members of the studio audience. The programme is of 25–30 minutes' duration and always culminates in the No. 1 record, while also featuring the highest new chart entry and highest climber. The No. 1 record is the only one that is able to feature on consecutive programmes.

TOTP's enduring popularity might be accounted for by its mixture of attractions. Primarily, it has offered the audience a high degree of intimacy with pop stars, allowing the sort of closeness to performers only available in the front row of live concerts. This intimacy is manifested in big close-ups of the singer's face, addressing words directly to the camera, as if singing specifically for and to an individual watching the television set. Alongside this, the studio audience, comprised of excited teenagers, works as a surrogate for the television audience sitting at home. Their prosaic 'ordinariness' not only doubles the viewers at home, but is a guarantee of the 'extraordinary' performers. Its 'liveness' is also very important and despite, the incursion of pop videos and lip-synching, still is premised upon the notion of the live performance, even in cases where artists never have recourse to perform live outside of the show. In fact, it was never far from controversy about lip-synching. From the beginning, it was apparent that the discs were mimed to by performers. The reason was the plenitude of sound available in the recording rather than simply a live rendition of the song. In 1966, however, the Musicians' Union's pressure made the show go completely live, although in the early 1970s, artists sang live to a recorded backing track, and by the late 1970s had reverted to miming completely again.

TOTP has included some fairly mild 'reinventing' over its considerable lifetime, but in reality has stuck with the same broad format. In the early 1970s there was a brief experiment whereby the programme was extended to 45 minutes. In the 1980s, new producer Michael Hurll radically changed the look of the show, especially the set, and included regular live broadcasts and Jonathan King's American chart slot. This was against a backdrop of it dropping in popularity and in competition with pop programmes on other channels. More recent innovations have included strange but unique occasional extras outside the bounds of the pop singles charts, including the reformed Sex Pistols performing (1996) and Coldplay performing two new songs from a forthcoming album (2002). As noted, for many years it was mostly presented by radio disc jockeys. It started with Pete Murray, Alan Freeman, David Jacobs and wrestling ex-miner Jimmy Savile. Over the years, it has included the most prominent DJs from BBC Radio 1, such as Tony Blackburn, Noel Edmonds and Mike Read. However, in 1989, a number of children's television presenters were co-opted for presenting, and in the mid-1990s it used celebrities such as British boxer Chris Eubank, jockey Frankie Dettori, and comedians Dennis Pennis (Paul Kaye) and Ardal O'Hanlon.

As a television institution running for nearly 40 years, *TOTP* has had more than its share of memorable moments, many of which have entered popular mythology. On February 5, 1970, John Lennon and the Plastic Ono Band performed 'Instant Karma', with Yoko Ono seated on a stool and blindfolded with a large sanitary towel. The unpredictability of such live moments added to the excitement of the programme. In 1980, on another live broadcast, All About Eve tried to perform their single 'Martha's Harbour', but with no audible playback on stage, singer Julianne Regan simply sat motionless on a stool. Hearing nothing of the lip-synching tape, she was unable to mime to her group's song. But perhaps the most famous incident on the programme was in September 1982, when Dexy's Midnight Runners performed *Jackie Wilson Said* in front of a large picture of Scottish darts player Jocky Wilson rather than the American soul singer in the song's title. Later producer Michael Hurll insisted it was an intentional joke rather than a stupid mistake (Simpson, 2002, 67). Memorably appalling moments were provided also by the programme's resident dance troupes, Pan's People (1968–76), who danced to Gilbert O'Sullivan's 'Get Down' on stage with some dogs ('You're a bad dog, baby'), and Legs & Co. (1976–81), who danced to The Clash's (who continually refused to appear on the show) 'Bankrobber' by pretending to rob a bank. Sometimes the presenters made the programme memorable. In May 1986, John Peel introduced Wah! with their song 'Sinful' by saying, 'If that doesn't make Number One, I'm going to come round and break wind in your kitchen' (Simpson, 2002, 72). Perhaps unsurprisingly, this inspired letters of complaint to the BBC, although probably not from teenage viewers.

Pop promos had been in use since the 1960s, and programmes from before then had used clips of groups from films. For many in Britain, however, the first notable exposure to pop video was Queen's 'Bohemian Rhapsody' (1976), which appeared on *TOTP* weekly during an extended occupation of the No. 1 singles spot. The opening and concluding segments simply were based on the 'live on stage' ethic, while the middle part became a dramatic and partially abstracted visual illustration of the quasi-operatic a capella section. Pop videos became more prominent in the early 1980s, with expensively filmed promos for Duran Duran's 'Rio' and Spandau Ballet's 'Paint Me Down', among others. At this time, *TOTP* instituted a large television screen in the corner of the studio for the videos. MTV beginning broadcasts in 1981 in the USA (but six years later in Europe) clearly became an influence on the look and format of *TOTP* as well as other television pop music shows at this time (Donnelly, 2001a, 90). Videos quickly became a regular slot, although in the 1990s, competition from video-based pop shows led to *TOTP* returning to an emphasis on its 'liveness'.

Record sales have always increased significantly for groups appearing on the programme, although *TOTP* has been less effective with the onset of 'faceless' dance culture since the early 1990s. Single sales dropped dramatically in the 1980s and 1990s, although they picked up in the early 2000s with massive British singles sales for **Pop Stars** (Screentime, 2001–) contestants Will Young and Gareth Gates. In the 1970s, according to Jeff Simpson, 'Record companies were making money like there was no tomorrow and *TOTP* was their main shop window' (Simpson, 2002, 48).

Significantly, *TOTP* marks an intersection of television and radio, thus constituting something of a heart of the BBC. Indeed, the programme was a clear influence in the inauguration of Radio 1, the BBC's pop music channel, in September 1967. *TOTP2* (which includes archive footage of 'classics', aimed at a more adult market) started in September 1994, first on Saturdays, then moving to Wednesdays (and then adding Tuesdays too), where it has managed to secure a significant audience. Not long after these developments, Radio 1 was radically reconfigured for the youth market, with almost all DJs either exiting or shifting across to Radio 2, which was remodelled for the baby-boomer generation. At the turn of the millennium, *Top of the Pops Plus*, a special version aimed specifically at children started at Sunday lunchtimes on BBC2 and *Top of the Pops Saturday* began on BBC1 in 2002 during Saturday morning. Meanwhile, BBC digital channel UK Play started *Top of the Pops@Play*. As a package, *Top of the Pops* has been sold by BBC Worldwide to other countries, where, with the same sets, local variation can be mixed with international acts from the British original.

QUESTIONS TO CONSIDER

- Is *TOTP* the important cultural event today that it was during the 1960s and 1970s? If no, then why not? If yes, then how does it manage to constantly remain relevant?
- Why do you think the format and general presentation of *TOTP* has changed so little over almost 40 years? How do you think it has managed to stay so popular despite only making minor changes to the way it looks?
- Who do you think the main audience for *TOTP* now is? Do you think the type of audience it attracts has changed over time?
- How did (and do) other television pop shows try to attract audiences away from *TOTP*? Can you think of other shows that have either copied their formula or tried deliberately to break away from it?
- Has (and does) *TOTP* adequately reflect all types of 'pop music'? Do you think it adequately reflects the contemporary music scene today?

RECOMMENDED READING

Cubitt, Sean (1986), 'Top of the Pops: the Politics of the Living Room' in Len Masterman (ed.), *Television Mythologies: Stars, Shows, Signs*, London: Comedia/MK Media Press, 46–8.

Donnelly, KJ (2001a), 'Music on Television' in Glen Creeber (ed.), *The Television Genre Book*, London: British Film Institute, 89–91.

Simpson, Jeff (2002), *Top of the Pops, 1964–2002*, London: BBC Books.

Chapter Forty Five

The Twilight Zone

Matt Hills

Production Details (original 1959–64 series only)

(Cayuga Productions/CBS, 1959–64, 1985–7, MGM/UA syndicated series, 1988–9, UPN, 2002–)

Creator: Rod Serling

Executive Producer: Rod Serling

Producers: Buck Houghton, Herbert Hirschman, Bert Granet, William Froug

Writers working on the series have included: Charles Beaumont, Ray Bradbury, Richard Matheson, Rod Serling

Directors have included: Richard Donner, Christian Nyby, Jacques Tourneur

Theme Music: Marius Constant

The Twilight Zone's status as a key TV text is almost ensured through its title alone, with the notion of entering 'the twilight zone' having become linked in popular consciousness with uncanny events. But the influence of this TV programme – four episodes of which were remade as segments of *Twilight Zone: The Movie* (Spielberg, Landis, Dante, Miller, 1983) – runs far beyond its titular connotations and its 'indelible, repetitive eight-note theme … still synonymous with eeriness' (Stark, 1997, 86). Pundits and academics have described *The Twilight Zone* as 'the best art-directed show in TV history and the most influential' (Wolfe, 1997, 1), and as 'notable for being almost everything that prime-time series television was not. It was a cerebral show: What other program promised to enter a "dimension of mind"?' (Stark, 1997, 87).

Clever, artistic and eerie, *The Twilight Zone*'s original 1959–64 incarnation (unless stated otherwise, all references are to this version) is thought of as 'classic television' thanks, in part, to its format, combining its status as 'strange TV' (Booker, 2002) with an anthology form. This format meant that each episode stood alone as a one-off drama, featuring original characters and premises. Linking aspects of the show's format, the programme title and its production crew gave *The Twilight Zone* its particular identity, but there were no ongoing characters to relate to and no continuing storylines to follow. As the seeming antithesis of TV seriality, *The Twilight Zone* avoided the narrative pitfalls of episodic series TV; it did not need to present invincible lead characters who would return in next week's adventure, nor did it need to return to a narrative status quo at the end of each episode so as to leave intact an established format. As Jeffrey Sconce comments in *Haunted Media*, the anthology format of 1950s/1960s shows like *The Twilight Zone* and *The Outer Limits* (ABC, 1963–5) meant that these programmes were 'unencumbered by the burden of continuing characters … [and] had the occasional license to destroy the centerpiece of both postwar life and episodic television – the nuclear family' (Sconce, 2000, 139). Allowing a narrative space where the certainties of comfortable seriality could be undercut, *The Twilight Zone*'s anthology format, therefore (ibid., 134):

> *served as the … always perverse 'unconscious' of television. It was a self-described 'zone' within the usually mundane procession of the broadcast schedules where the boundaries of televisual reality were the most ambiguous and where the typically cheerful world of television frequently found its ironic negation.*

The anthology format may therefore present writers with greater freedom to make political or ideological points through the wholesale destruction of certain characters and narrative worlds, and we might view this as one of the programme's more intriguing aspects. However, there are also disadvantages to this narrative structure, not the least of which is economic: basically, new sets could potentially need to be constructed for every episode. Where possible, *The Twilight Zone* made use of standing sets to get round this problem; for instance, the vast library steps in 'Time Enough at Last' (1959) were actually 'a standing set on the MGM backlot … These same steps can be seen in the episode *A Nice Place To Visit*' (Zicree, 1992, 70). Other narrative problems posed by the anthology format are the flipside of the format's possibilities: no recurring characters might mean greater narrative freedom, but it also means an absence of ongoing relationships and personalities for audiences to follow.

However, *The Twilight Zone* is not without its own recurring devices and themes, so to view it simply as a subversion of 'safe' formats and types of seriality occurring elsewhere in 1950s/1960s TV is somewhat disingenuous. While using uncanny and fantastic stories to address issues such as nuclear holocaust – in, for example, the episodes 'One More Pallbearer' (1962) and 'Time Enough At Last' (1959) – *The Twilight Zone* had its own points of formal continuity, the most significant of which was probably Rod Serling's opening and closing narration in every episode. It could be argued that rather than diegetic characters forming a point of familiarity for audiences, it was Serling himself who fulfilled this function.

Serling did not simply produce a voice-over; he actually appeared on-screen near the beginning of each episode, speaking directly to camera, yet seemingly appearing within the narrative world of the episode. This blurring of diegetic and extra-diegetic, often accompanied by a rapid, dizzying whip pan and/or cut from the diegetic action to Serling's narration, can be thought of as a postmodern textual device. It challenges the status of what we are seeing, suggesting that each episode is both constructed (it is a tale 'narrated' by Serling, the programme's creator, executive producer and frequent writer) as well as being an instance of realism, i.e. we become immersed in the narrative world, which observes the norms of continuity or invisible editing. By having Serling perform the narrator's role, it is not only diegetic and extra-diegetic spaces that are collapsed together in a 'postmodern' way (Booker, 2002); the show also blurs the line between 'on-screen' and 'behind-the-screen' personnel.

Rod Serling is both a performer – his reassuring on-screen presence functioning to unite different episodes under the banner and identity of *The Twilight Zone* – and the 'author'/creator of the show. Serling was reportedly not the original choice for the role of the narrator (that honour fell to Orson Welles, who was deemed too expensive; Zicree, 1992, 24–5). But his use in this role gave *The Twilight Zone* a visible and iconic author figure, working to sustain its interpretation as TV 'art'. Serling's appearances (akin to Hitchcock's film cameos and his own self-introduced television anthology series *Alfred Hitchcock Presents* [ABC, 1971–3]) certainly helped *The Twilight Zone* to blur the lines between devalued genre TV and culturally elevated forms such as the one-off and 'authored' teleplay. Serling had established a reputation as one of 'the hottest young scriptwriters of TV's so-called Golden Age (Gore Vidal, Reginald Rose, and Paddy Chayevsky [see **Marty** (NBC, 1953)] were the others)' (Wolfe, 1997, 1, 16) prior to his work on the fantasies of *The Twilight Zone*.

Blurring the lines between art and genre, diegesis and extra-diegesis, and on-screen and off-screen personnel, *The Twilight Zone* also repeatedly conveyed scepticism about the conformity of contemporary society. *The Monsters Are Due on Maple Street* (1960) portrays a neighbourhood tearing itself apart due to the paranoid fear that one family could be aliens disguised as down-home folks, and *Number Twelve Looks Just Like You* (1964) represents a future world where everybody is 'transformed' into a limited number of supermodel looks. Such critiques of social norms may have become more culturally acceptable by the time of 1990s shows like **The X-Files** (Fox, 1992–2002), but in the US of the late 50s and early 60s it was probably only *The Twilight Zone*'s use of fantasy that enabled it to code and convey such political parables and messages. The writing of Serling and others arguably smuggled social and cultural critiques past TV sponsors and advertisers who would have objected to these same ideas had they been rendered in a more conventionally realist mode. For example, Rex Brynen singles out *The Twilight Zone* for its prescient politics, noting that, 'The first shows to offer ... varied reflections on US foreign policy were the anthologies ... *The Twilight Zone* raised the possibility of US troops dying in Vietnam in 1963, a year before the Tonkin Gulf resolution formalised US entry into the war as an acknowledged combatant' (2000, 81).

As well as considering *The Twilight Zone* as politicised and artistic TV, acting as a landmark show in popular and fan narratives of US TV history (Stark, 1997 and Jenkins, 1992, 17), we can also consider it as a key TV text thanks to its use of generic conventions. Although sometimes characterised as TV science fiction (Brynen, 2000), *The Twilight Zone* can productively be thought of as an exercise in TV horror. The horror genre is often assumed to exist primarily in film and novels, as if the regulated production and domestic reception of television are both inimical to achieving the effects of horror. As JK Muir has observed, ' "Terror" and "television" are 2 words ... which ... do not appear to fit easily side by side. The word "terror" portends ... heightened emotions and heart-pounding horror. [T]hese elements seem at odds with the medium of television – a venue of the masses' (Muir, 1999, 1).

Although *The Twilight Zone* may not have achieved 'heart-pounding horror', its repeated emphases on disruptions of the familiar and on the intrusion of madness or delusion into everyday life, mark it out as a form of uncanny TV. Horror films and novels can be thought of as presenting at least two strands or traditions – the school of thought that emphasises graphic horror and its opponent, which stresses subtlety of effect and atmospheric spookiness or eeriness rather than graphic horror/ monstrosity. Unsurprisingly, *The Twilight Zone* favours the subtle approach, arriving at horrifying images through unsettling its audience rather than aiming for a 'gross-out' moment. Many *Twilight Zone* stories revolve around the possibility that their pro-tagonists are mad or deluded, so that the audience cannot be sure whether they are sharing in a narratively subjective delusion or an objective narrative world. 'A World of Difference' (1960) plays with this theme, representing an actor who may have over-identified with one of his roles. Where is narrative reality located here? Is the actor real, or his character? 'One More Pallbearer' also shifts its levels of diegetic reality, twisting assumed reality into delusion; and 'Nightmare at 20,000 Feet' (1963) con-cerns a man recovering from a mental breakdown who believes he can see a 'gremlin' on the wing of the plane he's flying in.

The Twilight Zone's status as a key TV text has also been attested to by its various remakes, all of which have traded on the show's brand recognition. Indeed, by the time of the second remake (the 1988–9 version), MGM/UA President of Tele-communications, Norman Horwitz, was quoted as saying that *The Twilight Zone* name 'gives us ... a genuine marketing advantage ... People would rather buy something they know, that gives them comfort, rather than something innovative and different' (cited by Muir, 2001, 575). The irony is that this statement sounds like something straight out of Rod Serling's original *Twilight Zone*; a potentially subversive social satire of mass-mediated sameness has, we might argue, become a branded part of that very conformity.

QUESTIONS TO CONSIDER

- Can *The Twilight Zone* be thought of as 'postmodern TV'? If so, in what ways might it be 'postmodern'?
- How does *The Twilight Zone* draw on conventions of the horror genre but make these conventions suitable for 1950s/1960s US network television?
- What are the economic and narrative advantages/disadvantages of an 'anthology show' like *The Twilight Zone*?

- Why do you think *The Twilight Zone* has been remade so frequently?
- Can certain political and ideological themes be perceived in different 1959–64 *Twilight Zone* stories? Is this programme 'subversive' and, if so, how?
- How did *The Twilight Zone* fantastically encode cultural anxieties and tensions of the 1960s in the US? Consider issues such as the Cold War, threats of nuclear holocaust and social conformity or alienation.

RECOMMENDED READING

Stark, Steven D (1997), '*The Twilight Zone*: Science Fiction as Realism' in *Glued To The Set: The 60 Television Shows That Made Us Who We Are Today*, New York: The Free Press, 85–9.

Wolfe, Peter (1997), *In the Zone: The Twilight World of Rod Serling*, Bowling Green: Bowling Green State University Popular Press.

Zicree, Marc Scott (1992), *The Twilight Zone Companion: Second Edition*, Los Angeles: Silman-James Press.

Chapter Forty Six

Twin Peaks

David Lavery

Production Details

(USA, ABC, 1990–1)

Writers: David Lynch, Mark Frost, Robert Engels, Harley Peyton, Scott Frost

Directors: David Lynch, Tim Hunter, Mark Frost, James Foley, Todd Holland, Duwaynne Dunham, Tina Rathone, Graehme Clifford, Lesli Linka Glatter, Caleb Deschanel

Producers: David Lynch, Mark Frost, Robert Engels, Marley Peyton, Gregg D Fienberg

Cast includes:

Annie Blackburne (Heather Graham)
Deputy Andy Brennan (Harry Goaz)
Bobby Briggs (Dana Ashbrook)
Major Garland Briggs (Don Davis)
Denis(e) Bryson (David Duchovny)
Gordon Cole (David Lynch)
Dale Cooper (Kyle MacLachlan)
Windom Earle (Kenneth Welsh)
Laura Palmer, Maddy Ferguson (Sheryl Lee)
Audrey Horne (Sherilyn Fenn)
Shelley Johnson (Madchen Amick)
The Log Lady (Catherine Coulson)
Man from Another Place (Michael J Anderson)
Catherine Martell (Piper Laurie)
Pete Martell (Jack Nance)
Lucy Moran (Kimmy Robertson)
Josie Packard (Joan Chen)
Leland Palmer (Ray Wise)
Sheriff Harry S Truman (Michael Ontkean)

With David Lynch's signature amalgamation of surrealism and Americana in mind, Mel Brooks once called the director of such bizarre films as *Eraserhead* (1977),

Elephant Man (1980), *Blue Velvet* (1986), *Lost Highway* (1997) and *Mulholland Drive* (2001), 'Jimmy Stewart from Mars'. *Twin Peaks*, Lynch's first foray into a broadcast medium, was weird, brilliant television from Mars. Co-created with Mark Frost, a TV veteran who had been a writer for **Hill Street Blues** (NBC, 1981–7), *Twin Peaks* had been labelled, before its much-ballyhooed April 8, 1990 premiere (which attracted 33 per cent of the American TV audience), 'the show that will change television' (Rodman, 1989). Indeed, in the late 1980s/early 1990s there was a strong feeling that, in the face of new challenges from the emergence of cable programming, TV *needed* changing.

Dreamy (it was lushly scored by Angelo Badalamenti), cinematic (rather than televisual) and slow-paced, *Twin Peaks* accentuated its subtext, indulged in extreme violence, emotional excess, disturbing sexuality, uncanny dream sequences, controversial subject matter and was ever reliant on 'a particular kind of irony where the very macabre and the very mundane combine in such a way as to reveal the former's perpetual containment in the latter' (Wallace, 1997, 161). As such, it demanded complete attention to its convoluted narrative from television viewers only too accustomed to distraction. Indeed, David Foster Wallace has described with great precision the distinctive characteristics of Lynch's style as a film-maker. For Wallace (ibid.), the term 'Lynchian' denotes:

> ... *the absence of linearity and narrative logic, the heavy multivalence of the symbolism, the glazed opacity of the characters' faces, the weird ponderous quality of the dialogue, the regular deployment of grotesques as figurants, the precise, painterly way scenes are staged and lit, and the over lush, possibly voyeuristic way that violence, deviance, and general hideousness are depicted.*

Seen in this light, *Twin Peaks* is unmistakably 'Lynchian'. Even though Lynch himself directed only a half-dozen episodes and received writing credit on only four, the series' directors took their lead from him. But the writer Mark Frost was a major contributor as well, and the nature of the Lynch/Frost collaboration remains the subject of a great deal of debate and conjecture. Writer-producer Harley Peyton observes on the DVD of the first season that, though Lynch's improvisations may have provided the creative impetus behind *Twin Peaks*, it was Frost who made it work as a TV series, Frost 'who kept the series inside his head' at all times, Frost who minded the details. According to Nochimson's Irigaray-influenced provocative analysis of Lynch's role in *Twin Peaks*, 'the complications of the extensively collaborative nature of television production had a deleterious effect on the series ...' (1997, 72). During Lynch's prolonged absence from the series (he was filming *Wild at Heart* [1992]), Nochimson argues, Frost seized control of the narrative and moved it away from Lynch's commitment to vision, feminine wisdom and 'the bounty of the subconscious' toward emphasis on male, verbal and rational control. Not surprisingly, neither Lynch nor Frost now remembers their partnership fondly.

Frost once described *Twin Peaks* as 'a moody, dark soap opera murder-mystery, set in a fictional town in the Northwest, with an ensemble cast and an edge' (cited by Pond, 1990, 54), but the series exhibited multiple generic allegiances. It was a mystery

('Who killed Laura Palmer?') and a soap opera (it even contained within it another soap opera called *Invitation to Love*), but it was also an FBI drama (Malach, 1994), a sitcom (particularly the antics of Deputy Andy and Lucy), a detective story (Hague, 1994), a sensation novel (Huskey, 1993), a western (complete with a 'Doc' right out of *Gunsmoke* [CBS, 1955–75] and a sheriff in a cowboy hat) and a coffee commercial (Reeves et al., 1994). Seen by many as thoroughly 'postmodern' (Collins, 1992 and Reeves et al., 1994), it sampled innumerable other texts, connected (through overt and implicit references and the presence of consciously cast actors) in its intertext to movies like *Laura* (Preminger, 1944), *Double Indemnity* (Wilder, 1944), *The Searchers* (Ford, 1956), *Vertigo* (Hitchcock, 1958), *One-Eyed Jacks* (Brando, 1961), *West Side Story* (Wise, 1961); television shows like *The Flintstones* (CBS, 1960–6), *The Mod Squad* (ABC, 1968–73), *Then Came Bronson* (NBC, 1969) and *Mister Ed* (CBS, 1961–6); as well us literature from the Arthurian legends to Spenser's *The Fairie Queene* to Charles Brockden Brown's *Wieland* (Carroll, 1993) and Hawthorne's *The Scarlet Letter*.

It is certainly arguable that no television series has been more carefully studied. A decade of work by the fanzine *Wrapped in Plastic* has examined virtually every facet of the series' creation and production, interviewing many of the writers and directors and almost all of the key performers and comparing scripted and televised versions of whole episodes. As a result of the efforts of Craig Miller and John Thorne (2001a and 2001b), we now possess unsurpassed behind-the-scenes knowledge about *Twin Peaks* and understand better how much of the genius of the series was intended and how much a lucky accident. The many commentaries on the first season DVD of the series (by the director of photography, writers and directors) add much to this knowledge base. As a result, *Twin Peaks* has been subjected to a televisual version of textual criticism – debate about authorial intent, internal and external evidence, etc. – normally associated with literature. The series even provided an aberrant text, the 'European version' of the pilot: a complete *Twin Peaks* narrative, released as a feature film, including Cooper's famous dream sequence from the second episode in which Laura's murderer is found and killed.

Critics and scholars have likewise illuminated the series' subject matter and themes, examining (a partial list only) its quintessentially postmodern music (Kalinak, 1994), its use of doubling (Kuzniar, 1994), its failed challenge to commercial television (Dienst, 1994), its politics (Rosenbaum, 1994), its nature as a cult (as defined by Eco, 1986) television program (Lavery, 1994), Laura Palmer as a television saint (Desmet, 1994), its strategic use of the fantastic in order to depict the unthinkable subject of child sexual abuse (Stevenson, 1994), the series as an exemplar of Foucauldian disorder (Telotte, 1994), its depiction of women (George, 1994), its translation of Gothic conventions to television (Ledwon, 1993), its role as 'difficult viewing' (Chisholm, 1991), its implications for understanding the complex nature of serial storytelling (Dolan, 1994) and its revisioning of Oedipal themes (Kimball, 1993).

Such various (and sometimes contradictory) readings perhaps partly suggest why *Twin Peaks* was one of the first television series to really inspire *obsessive* fan participation and investment. At water-coolers around America, at *Twin Peaks* parties featuring 'joe' (coffee), cherry pie and doughnuts, and on alt.tv.twinpeaks, avid followers of the show speculated endlessly about the significance of minute visual details (often captured and rewatched on their VCRs) and narrative developments in the series (Jenkins, 1994). Between the first and second seasons, buzz about who shot Agent Cooper in the cliffhanger ending of the final episode was comparable to that occasioned by the infamous shooting of JR in **Dallas** (CBS, 1978–91). And interest in the series was not limited to the US: *Twin Peaks* was a cultural phenomenon in Europe and, especially, Japan. Even after the show's cancellation, Japanese tourists flocked to the Pacific Northwest to see the 'actual' sites of the series: the Double R Cafe, the Great Northern Hotel, the location where Laura Palmer's body was found, 'dead, wrapped in plastic'.

Fueling the conjectures of the interpretive community of *Twin Peaks* were the commodity intertexts (Collins, 1992, 341–2) that began to appear in the first season. Revelations about the identity of Laura's killer and the secret backstory of the series' hero in books like *The Secret Diary of Laura Palmer* (1990), written by Lynch's daughter Jennifer, and *The Autobiography of F.B.I. Special Agent Dale Cooper: My Life, My Tapes* (1991), authored by Scott Frost (Mark's brother), became part of *Twin Peaks'* already formidably complicated narrative skein. Those who read the former were not completely surprised to learn that it was Laura's father, Leland Palmer, under the control of the parasitic supernatural being BOB, who had killed her. Those who had read the latter knew that Cooper had a dark side not yet revealed in *Twin Peaks'* narrative, but were as shocked as anyone at the series' final scene. (According to Nochimson [1994, 75–7], the final episode, as it aired on June 10, 1991, was the somewhat botched result of a creative clash between the series' co-creators, with Lynch tossing out much of the screenplay by Frost, Engels and Peyton and extemporising his own version of the finale.)

Having plummeted in the ratings, routinely ranked among the bottom five shows in the Nielsens, *Twin Peaks* was cancelled by ABC in the spring of 1991 after a confusing sequence of events in which the series was temporarily suspended, then shifted to a new night and time and finally axed, and Lynch/Frost were given no opportunity to bring their narrative to an end. The forever frozen-in-time final image of the series – a bloody Cooper staring into a bathroom mirror he has just smashed with his head and seeing BOB as his reflection – will forever be 'The End'. In 1992 Lynch delivered the feature film *Twin Peaks: Fire Walk with Me*, but the prequel, dealing with the last seven days in the life of Laura Palmer, was a critical and financial disaster and did little to provide closure for the series' narrative.

Though *Twin Peaks* did not, as predicted, radically alter television, it has had a lasting influence. *Northern Exposure* (CBS, 1990–5), *Picket Fences* (NBC, 1992–6) and **The X-Files** (Fox, 1993–2002) – whose star David Duchovny played a transvestite Drug Enforcement Administration agent in *Twin Peaks* – colonised television territory *Twin Peaks* had opened up, as did, less successfully, *Eerie, Indiana* (NBC, 1991–2), *American Gothic* (CBS, 1995–6) and *Murder One* (ABC, 1995–7). Though post-*Twin Peaks* television has often seemed designed for a viewership with Attention Deficit Disorder (Peyton, 2002), some of the medium's most important contemporary creators now think of the series as a television touchstone: both Joss Whedon (***Buffy the Vampire Slayer*** [WB, 1997–2001, UPN, 2001–]) and David Chase (***The Sopranos*** [HBO, 1999–]) speak of *Twin Peaks* in hushed tones. And the name itself has become part of the language – to evoke 'Twin Peaks' in relation to any narrative or any sequence of events in the 'real' world is to label it as fantastic, inexplicable and unmistakably unique.

QUESTIONS TO CONSIDER

- In what ways was *Twin Peaks* a radical departure from standard television?
- *Twin Peaks* has been described as more cinematic than televisual. In what respects is the series indebted to the movies?
- Can you make the case for identifying *Twin Peaks* as a soap opera?
- Can you identify the presence of other genres in *Twin Peaks?* What is the purpose of such narrative fragmentation and intertextuality?
- Using Eco's (1986) description of the cult movie, is it possible to characterise *Twin Peaks* as cult TV?
- Why did *Twin Peaks* acquire such a devoted fan base? What is there about the series which seems to solicit active fan involvement?
- Can you spot characteristics of *Twin Peaks* evident in today's television?

RECOMMENDED READING

Lavery, David (ed.) (1994), *Full of Secrets: Critical Approaches to Twin Peaks*, Detroit: Wayne State University Press.

Lavery, David (ed.) (1993), 'Peaked Out!' *Twin Peaks* Special Issue, *Literature/Film Quarterly*, Vol. 21, No. 4, 238–306.

Nochimson, Martha P (1997), *The Passion of David Lynch: Wild at Heart in Hollywood*, Austin: University of Texas Press.

Chapter Forty Seven

Walking With Dinosaurs

KJ Donnelly

Production Details

(BBC/Discovery Channel/TV Asahi co-production, in association with ProSieben and France 3)

Series Producer: Tim Haines
Executive Producer: John Lynch
Narrator: Kenneth Branagh
Music: Ben Bartlett
Photography: John Howarth
Animatronics Supervision: Jez Harris
Computer Animation and Post-production: Framestore
Director of Computer Animation: Mike Milne

In the same way that television series regularly spin off from films, it might easily be argued that *Walking With Dinosaurs* was the TV spin off from Steven Spielberg's *Jurassic Park* (1993). However, the television miniseries, made by BBC Science, was more educational than its celluloid counterparts. A BBC-Discovery Channel co-production, it was a landmark in television, its mixture of computer-generated dinosaurs and authoritative narrative commentary proving popular with audiences and programmers worldwide. The original 6 part miniseries was broadcast on the BBC, starting on October 4, 1999, with the same 30-minute programme being repeated 6 days later as a lead-in to the following episode the next night. Since then there have been additional special episodes: *A Walking With Dinosaurs Special: The Ballad of Big Al* (December 25, 2000) and two further episodes broadcast at New Year 2003, *A Walking With Dinosaurs Special: The Giant Claw* and *A Walking With Dinosaurs Special: Land of Giants*. The success of the initial series has certainly left it open to intermittent 'special' sequels, of which we can expect more.

Walking With Dinosaurs was one of the first major television programmes to benefit from new technological developments, and indeed, the use of CGI (computer graphics images [Cubitt, 2002, 17–29]) was central to the programme to the point where *The Making of Walking With Dinosaurs* documentary spent a significant proportion of its time recounting how the images were obtained using digital animation over a two-year period. The CGI processing, which was achieved by the production company Framestore (led by Mike Milne), involved making a drawing, then a clay model, then a resin cast. This was scanned and a skeleton constructed in the computer, which allowed movement. The location shot consisted only of a man in a rubber suit or sticks where the dinosaur would later be animated onto the shot. The film was then sent to Framestore's 'tracking department', where the precise relation of lens and camera movement to the object was painstakingly worked out, the dinosaur could be put in and, finally, the lighting worked out and the animation matched accordingly. In tandem with these techniques, the programme also used Animatronics, including both mechanical and glove puppetry.

Walking With Dinosaurs showcased the possibilities for computer-based animated 'resurrections' of extinct animals, but also evinced the science-fiction possibilities of representing seemingly alien worlds. The programme was conceived as an upmarket product, educational and scientific as well as visually gripping. It was expensive and aimed at being an international product, embodying precisely the kind of 'quality' with which the BBC has tried to be associated for overseas sales. A key sign of this was the sumptuous orchestral score that was available instantly on CD, as well as the expensive glossy-pictured hardback book tied to the series. It was certainly a revolutionary programme in the way that it realised the dreams of many (and not only young children), to be able to experience the world of dinosaurs. It emphasised this in the implied personal involvement of the title, to be 'walking with' rather than simply watching. Its desire to animate the television viewer was doubtless less successful than its reanimation of long-dead beasts. It explicitly engaged with age-old wishes to commune with dead and mythological creatures, and indeed, it might be argued that the dinosaurs on-screen were closer to mythical chimeras than they were to reality. The accompanying programme *Making of Walking With Dinosaurs* and book demonstrate how little information actually formed the basis of reconstructing (or rather reimagining) some of the creatures that ended up on-screen. For example, the Arizona Cinodont in episode one could not be based purely on the fossils of two molar teeth that were found where the episode was set. Instead, the animal had to be extrapolated from a much smaller South African version of the Cinodont, a 'Thrinaxodon', of which a skeleton existed (Haines, 25).

Despite these problems, the use of CGI certainly brought state-of-the-art screen effects out of the cinema and onto television's small screen. The startling effect of bringing the extinct back to life was cemented by animating dinosaurs against a background of actual landscapes, thus mixing in the real with the animated. But the programme crucially went further, wearing the mantle of the television natural history programme. As a *faux* documentary, it made the audience believe, if only for a moment, that they were watching footage shot stealthily by the BBC natural history unit. The key to this was the use of an authoritative 'Voice of God' narration (by Kenneth Branagh), added to a 'dramatisation' of events on-screen. To induce empathy in the audience, certain dinosaur 'characters' were established and then followed through a series of adventures, much as can happen in recent nature documentaries like *Big Cat Diary* (BBC, 1996–), which follows named individuals in the Masai Mara.

Each episode of *Walking With Dinosaurs* was self-contained, being based on a particular character or set of characters. Its time-frame was wide: it spanned the period when dinosaurs ruled the earth – 185 million years (the Triassic, Jurassic and Cretaceous periods). So while the episodes were tens of millions of years apart, there was still a sense of continuity in that the creatures on-screen largely were unfamiliar but the format was familiar. Aesthetic unity was achieved through the voice-over declaring a 'scientific' analysis of the activities on-screen – although not in two final special episodes, where a presenter (Nigel Marven, who described himself as 'a zoologist and adventurer') appeared on-screen, relating his 'safari' through the dinosaur world. Masquerading as a natural history programme turned out to be one of the most striking aspects of the programme, a touch of genius. This had the net effect of asserting the power of television, while also keeping the viewers in a state of awe as well as informing them.

To some, this might be a fair description of the essence of public service broadcasting, and *Walking With Dinosaurs* certainly can be seen as a central tenet of the BBC's attempts to reinvent its beleaguered public service remit. It perhaps should be seen to embody one very particular kind of 'infotainment', one that comes from the angle of making entertaining illustration of educational discourses. In fact, one thing that television can do well is present complex and affecting ideas in seemingly less profound situations. However, critics argue that conveying complex ideas in 'entertainment' sometimes proves to be a garb that detracts from their significance or effect, seeming to deny them any 'weight'. One review of *Walking With Dinosaurs* noted that '… some viewers have crossly declared it irresponsible, for coming over all factual about events 350 million years or so ago when much of it is merely informed speculation'. According to theses pedants, 'Branagh [the narrator] cannot possibly know for sure …' (Viner, 1999, 6). According to Neil Postman, television (what he calls visual) culture is merely entertainment, whereas the literary and theatrical tradition (verbal/print culture) is discursive, rational and debates things. Postman declares the television ' … is devoted entirely to supplying the audience with entertainment … [and] has made entertainment itself the natural format for the representation of all experience' (1987, 88–9). So, the language of televisual entertainment, such as the technique of television drama, shapes all discourses and our abilities to discuss them. Seen in this light, in *Walking With Dinosaurs*, science and the representation of dinosaurs had been forced into a form derived less from its own material than from television convention in existing programmes.

In fact, the programme makes a point of using more recent theories to do with dinosaurs. For example, it shows stiff-necked diplodoci and dimetrodons whose back sails change colour. The relatively recent evolutionary theory of 'convergence' clearly has had a significant influence on the programme. This theory suggests that due to similar environmental situations, different species will evolve towards a similar form.

This allows certain dinosaurs to bear striking similarity to familiar animals of the present. For example, the Icthyosaurs in episode three are based on dolphins, and the Cinodont in episode one is very similar to a dog.

While viewers watched gigantic predators on-screen, they found it difficult to escape the predatory commercial exploitation of *Walking With Dinosaurs*. One review noted: 'The cliché clanking commentary described in the simplest terms how a baby diplodocus may have survived various Jurassic dangers like an Allosuarus attack ('Saved by the huge tail of a larger diplodocus!') I began to think the whole thing is geared to selling chocolate dinosaur eggs to five-year-olds' (Banks-Smith, 1999, 22). The most prominent tied-in products were the sell-through video, the music soundtrack CD, the glossy hardback book, a small illustrated magazine and a *Radio Times* special issue. But there was more, aimed specifically at young children: a children's sticker book, a children's 3-D book and a children's guide called *How Big is a Dinosaur?*, among other items. Significantly, *Walking With Dinosaurs* was used to bolster the fledgling digital television channels and Internet capacity of the BBC. Digital channel BBC Knowledge broadcast *Meet the Dinosaurs* in December 1999, just after the series finished. It included all of *Walking With Dinosaurs*, mixed with discussions on television and forums online. The BBC website included 'how to collect fossils' and information presented as 'Live from Dinosaur Island', while the Discovery Channel's website had 'The Dinosaur Survival Game' and 'Meet Big Al, the Allosaur'.

The publicity for *Walking With Dinosaurs* used the catchphrase, 'the biggest thing on television in 160 million years'. The programme certainly was a signpost to the future capabilities of television. Its mixture of exciting CGI and informative natural history could be seen as the absolute definition of a particular type of television 'infotainment'. It includes spectacle for children and erudition for adults, or perhaps it is the other way round. However, it is hard not to watch it and think of the 'active' museums that are now dominant, where everything is aimed at children, and information and knowledge merely inhabit the edges of the 'experience'. It was hard to watch *Walking With Dinosaurs* without thinking of Ray Harryhausen's ground-breaking model work for films like *King Kong* (Cooper and Schoedsack, 1933), both his genius and how far technology has changed. *Walking With Dinosaurs* has certainly supplied audiences with some extremely enduring images, such as the line of Diplodoci walking away into the distance, and the Tyrannosaurus rex turning and spitting on the camera as it roars.

It has also inspired its own loose sub-genre of dramatic reconstructions of the distant past, including BBC-Discovery's sequel, *Walking With Beasts* (sometimes called *Walking With Prehistoric Beasts*) (2001), which moved the time-frame forward to look at prehistoric animals after dinosaurs. This palaeontological drama-documentary strand has proved successful, with programmes such as *Neanderthal* (BBC, 2000) and *Walking With Cavemen* (BBC, 2003), which followed a group of prostheticised *Homo sapiens* acting as earlier species, and *Extinct* (Channel Four, 2001), which investigated dead species such as the dodo and the Tasmanian tiger, through a mixture of documentary techniques and computer graphics. And this is possibly only the beginning of a whole new breed of television genres.

QUESTIONS TO CONSIDER

- How far is *Walking with Dinosaurs* a traditional wildlife documentary?
- What are the limits of (and downside to) CG visuals?
- What if these dinosaurs did not exist in this form? Should speculation be presented as fact in this manner?
- Is 'infotainment' an effective form of education?
- What future developments in television programmes might follow from *Walking with Dinosaurs*?

RECOMMENDED READING

Donnelly, KJ (2001), 'The Discovery Channel and *Walking With Dinosaurs*' in Glen Creeber (ed.), *The Television Genre Book*, London: British Film Institute, 138.

Haines, Tim (1999), *Walking With Dinosaurs: A Natural History*, London: BBC Worldwide.

Martill, David and Naish, Darren (2000), *Walking with Dinosaurs: The Evidence, How Did They Know That?*, London: BBC Consumer Publishing.

Chapter Forty Eight

Who Wants to be a Millionaire?

Glen Creeber

Production Details

(UK, Celador, ITV, 1998–)
(The original British version)

Creators: David Briggs, Mike Whitehall, Steve Knight
Directors: Paul Kirrage/Patricia Mordecai
Director of Production: Steve Springfield
Master of Ceremonies: Chris Tarrant
Producers: Guy Freeman, Colman Hutchinson, David Briggs
Composers: Keith Strachan, Matthew Strachan
Lighting Director: Brian Pearce

Who Wants to be a Millionaire? is one of the most successful television quiz shows of all time, the original British series gaining as much as 72 per cent of the television audience when it first aired. Started in 1998, by the end of 2000 it was on air in 35 countries and sold as a format to 45 more. In America, it lifted ABC from third to first place in network competition for the first time ever in US television history, while in India its 87 per cent audience share immediately catapulted Rupert Murdoch's Star Plus satellite channel from third to first place across the country (Boddy, 2001, 81). The unprecedented decision to run the show on consecutive evenings has also rewritten the TV rule-book, taking the quiz show away from the relative obscurity of daytime television and temporarily making it the jewel in the crown of prime-time schedules around the globe. Although in Britain the show was finally reduced to once a week (Saturday night) as audience figures dropped from its peak of 19.2 million in 1999 to between 7 and 8 million in 2003, the show is still considered to be one of the most influential examples of its kind.

The phenomenal success of *Millionaire* is all the more surprising when one considers that Celador, an English company, produced it. Historically, Britain always looked to America for quiz shows, their more commercially minded broadcasting system appearing to provide the perfect breeding ground for new and original formats. In contrast, Britain's public service ethos tended to view the genre with great suspicion.

232

The Pilkington Committee argued in 1962 that these types of shows simply played on the 'acquisitiveness, snobbery, fear' and 'uncritical conformity' of ordinary viewers (cited by Sales, 1986, 68). It is arguable that such a condescending attitude towards the genre stunted the creation and development of original British game shows for decades to come, consistently importing but rarely exporting its own formats. Even when successful American quiz and game shows were transferred to Britain, prizes and prize money had to be considerably lowered in order to satisfy the strict regulations of the British broadcasting authorities. When, for example, America's phenomenally successful *$64,000 Question* (CBS, 1955–6) – where even the loser won a Cadillac – was replicated for British television, the title was changed to simply *The 64,000 Question* (ITV, 1956–8) and the contestants won prize units of a sixpence!

It was not until the arrival of the Peacock Committee into broadcasting in 1986 that a more commercially driven broadcasting system became increasingly possible within the UK. One of the recommendations of a White Paper that followed in 1988 was to replace ITV's regulatory body the IBA (The Independent Broadcasting Authority) with the ITC (The Independent Television Commission). As well as introducing programme sponsorship for the first time in Britain, the more lenient ITC relaxed the strict regulations concerning prize money on quiz shows. As a result, the environment for a show like *Millionaire* was created. Sponsored originally by the *Sun* newspaper (a lucrative deal that involved a tie-in game), the huge amount of money it offered to contestants (generated by viewers phoning premium-rate telephone lines hoping to take part [see also **Big Brother** [Endemol, 1999–]]) could now finally compete with American television.

Critics like Mike Wayne bemoan this type of development in British broadcasting, interpreting the arrival of a quiz show like *Millionaire* as symbolic of the sad decline in British public service television as a whole. Wayne argues that while earlier British quiz and game shows such as *It's a Knockout* (BBC, 1966–82), *The Generation Game* (BBC 1971–), *Mastermind* (BBC, 1972–97) and *University Challenge* (ITV, 1962–87 and BBC, 1994–) promoted 'physical/problem solving skills' and values such as 'camaraderie', *Millionaire*'s success is built on little but personal greed (Wayne, 2000, 200). Despite the programme connecting itself with the trappings of community and family values (for example, a family member or friend of the contestant is usually singled out in the audience), Wayne argues that it is simply market orientated, biased towards middle-class male contestants and excludes younger members of the family. For Wayne, 'the more exchange value permeates television, the more we can expect consumerism, consumer goods, individualism and hard cash to be at the centre of the game show' (ibid.).

Yet, despite the unusually high prize money at the heart of *Millionaire* (in fact, it was to be originally called *Cash Mountain* but the title was changed to make the show appear more 'classy' and 'aspirational' [Wayne, 2000, 201]), the format is surprisingly traditional. Indeed, the 'double or quit' formula of *Millionaire* (risking everything you've already won to accumulate more) can clearly be found in TV quiz shows as far back as *Double Your Money* (ITV, 1955–64) and *The $64,000 Question*. This creates a time-honoured form of suspense that helps to keep viewers on the edge of their seats, the tension building as the stakes get increasingly higher. As in *Double Your Money*, the easier questions at the beginning of a contestant's monetary ascendance clearly gives everyone (even small children) the opportunity to get some questions right. As in shows such as *Jeopardy* (NBC, 1964–75) and *The Sale of the Century* (Network 9, 1980–), the careful mixture of general knowledge and popular culture (including subjects such as sport, pop music, television, film, etc.) also enables those not traditionally educated to become and remain involved. As the questions get tougher so the multiple-choice selection of four answers on the screen also gives most viewers the chance to have a guess, a traditional way of maintaining viewer involvement as the difficulty gradually increases.

Millionaire also continues the tradition of presenting itself as if live (although it is actually recorded in advance), a technique that allows the audience at home to feel part of the action, as if the drama is unfolding there and then in their very living room. As John Fiske puts it, ' "liveness" or "nowness" is crucial as it positions the viewer as the equal of the characters in the narrative. The narrative appears unwritten, the resolution is as much a mystery to the characters as to their viewer...' (Fiske, 1987, 272). In fact, *Millionaire* simply heightens traditional audience involvement by giving a contestant the opportunity to 'Ask the Audience' or 'Phone a Friend', perhaps symbolically increasing the viewer's sense of participation in the game. Indeed, this form of interactivity has a long historical tradition in the genre, encouraging the viewer at home to actually shout out answers or commands at the TV screen. As Garry Whannel (1990, 106) puts it:

> the more populist quizzes have always actively mobilized audience participation – from the cries of 'take the money/open the box' on Take Your Pick, to the shouts of 'higher/lower' on Play Your Cards Right, and the general freestyle yelling of The Price is Right.

Audience involvement also clearly relies on the fact that contestants are generally perceived as 'ordinary' members of the public. While well-educated or highly knowledgeable participants populated programmes such as *University Challenge* and *Mastermind*, *Millionaire*'s populist approach seems to be partly based on the audience's emotional identification with the contestants in the hot seat. How crucial a component of the show's success this is was actually made transparently clear when Judith Keppel (the first British contestant to win a million pounds) was discovered to be a friend of the British Royal Family and a relatively wealthy woman. Accusations of 'fixing' were rife and although the programme-makers vehemently denied it, no doubt they would have preferred the crucial first winner to have been slightly less well-heeled. Things became even worse in Britain when Celador had to take three people to court when it was claimed that they had won the top prize of a million pounds dishonestly. Major Charles Ingram, his wife Diana and college lecturer Tecwen Whittock were later found guilty of attempting to defraud the programme (Vasagar, 2003, 11).

It is, then, not its structure that makes *Millionaire* so different from earlier quiz shows, but in the way that the formula is rearticulated and redefined for a contemporary audience. While the format may be familiar, the programme-makers produced a radically new environment in which the drama could be played out. The set design – apparently inspired by the Riddler's lair in *Batman Forever* (Schumacher, 1995), the courtroom scene in *Judge Dredd* (Cannon, 1995) and the incubation room in *Jurassic Park* (Spielberg, 1993) – helps to create a 'postmodern' coliseum, a gladiatorial arena that clearly enhances the action (McGregor, 1999, 30). The overwhelming intensity of electric blue in the set (more usually found in 'serious' news programmes) also adds a seriousness to the proceedings not commonly associated with the game show – but now blatantly 'borrowed' by shows such as the BBC's *The Weakest Link* (BBC, 2000–). A camera on a crane high above the heads of the studio audience – frequently swooping down towards the podium and getting within inches of the perplex floor – also heightens the dramatic urgency of the game, while another seven cameras continually capture, in close-up, the expressions of the audience and the contestant.

Millionaire's use of music also adds a crucial element to its dramatic intensity. Consciously attempting to differentiate itself from the rather jolly, light-hearted music of earlier daytime game or quiz shows, its composers wanted it to be 'big, bold and almost orchestral in style. Something like a John Williams score for a Spielberg movie ... *ET* or *Raiders of the Lost Ark*' (cited by ibid., 32). In fact, there are 140 different pieces of music in total (each cued to a precise moment in the show) and played with very few breaks, almost subliminally building up the intensity of the action. To compliment the music, the studio lights cascade down into the audience at moments of high drama. Originally developed by the rock group Genesis for their live concerts, these lights (known as 'Varilites') instantly change the atmosphere on the set, gradually getting dimmer as the questions are answered correctly (ibid., 35).

It is these subtle but important changes to the basic formula of the traditional quiz show that initially distinguished *Millionaire* from other shows of its kind. With its sci-fi inspired set, big movie score and swooping camera angles and lights, it introduced an almost 'cinematic' dimension to the quiz show – interestingly, after the first two series the British moved the original set to a film studio in Elstree where *Star Wars* (Lucas, 1977) was originally made (ibid., 30). Perhaps, then, the show has simply modernised the genre, meeting the needs of a contemporary audience that have come to expect the small screen to increasingly replicate the drama and spectacle of the big. Seen in this light, perhaps *Millionaire* is not so much a symbol of British television's sad decline, as proof that, given the right environment, it can now triumphantly beat American television at its own game.

QUESTIONS TO CONSIDER

- Compare and contrast the basic structure of *Millionaire* with other game or quiz shows you are familiar with. Are you surprised at the similarities or differences between the basic formula of these programmes?

- How do you think the studio lighting and background music add to the dramatic tension of *Millionaire?* Do you think the show could have been so successful without these elements?

- If *Millionaire* represents the commercialisation of British broadcasting, do you think *The Weakest Link* better represents the public service ethos of the BBC?

- Despite having the Lottery prize as an enormous audience draw, the BBC's Saturday night prime-time Lottery show has never come near to equalling the success of *Millionaire*. How do you account for these differences?

- According to recent figures the audience for *Millionaire* has continued to fall since 1999. How do you account for its recent decline?

RECOMMENDED READING

Boddy, William (2001), 'The Quiz Show & *Who Wants to be a Millionaire?*' in Glen Creeber (ed.), *The Television Genre Book*, London: British Film Institute.

McGregor, Tom (1999), *Behind the Scenes at Who Wants to be a Millionaire?*, Basingstoke: Macmillan.

Wayne, Mike (2000), '*Who Wants to be a Millionaire?*: Contextual analysis and the endgame of public service television' in Dan Fleming (ed.), *Formations: A 21st Century Media Studies Textbook*, Manchester: Manchester University Press.

Chapter Forty Nine

World in Action

Peter Goddard

Production Details

(Granada Television [ITV], 1963–5, 1967–98)

Editors/Executive Producers have included: Tim Hewat, Derek Granger, Alex Valentine, David Plowright, Jeremy Wallington, Leslie Woodhead, John Birt, Gus Macdonald, David Boulton, Brian Lapping, Ray Fitzwalter, Allan Segal, Stuart Prebble, Nick Hayes, Diane Nelmes, Charles Tremayne, Steve Boulton, Jeff Anderson

---

Like *Panorama* (BBC, 1953–) and *This Week* (Associated-Rediffusion/Thames, 1955–92), *World in Action* was a major, prime-time current-affairs series that helped to develop and sustain regular and serious television journalism on British screens throughout its most settled 'public service' era. As such, it became a cornerstone of the British television schedule, contributing to wider understanding and scrutiny of social and public affairs, and helping to produce a more or less standardised formula for current-affairs television. Removed from the daily topicality of news, current-affairs series were able to look behind existing news events, to anticipate the news agenda and, by developing a strand of investigative journalism on television (a particular strength of *World in Action*), to expose wrongdoing. A key element in the public significance of the current-affairs series lay in its regular presence: like its two competitors, *World in Action* was scheduled for 39 or more weeks of the year, enabling it to employ a substantial team of journalists, to research several stories simultaneously – over long periods if required – and yet to respond to breaking news by pre-empting planned programmes for swiftly compiled topical background reports.

World in Action is best understood as having three distinct phases. In the earliest of these, from 1963 to 1965, it was innovative in form and technique and avowedly populist in orientation. It owed much of its distinctiveness to its creator and first executive producer, Tim Hewat, an iconoclastic Australian who had moved to Granada Television after a successful career at the *Daily Express*. Hewat aimed to create a series that avoided the formulaic studio discussions and magazine items that were then normal in current affairs, exploiting instead television's ability to show events 'on the spot' and to explain them with a directness and urgency partly derived from the popular press. But this approach was matched from the start by an emphasis on meticulous background research, making *World in Action* 'as informed as the main story in *The Economist* but as briskly and interestingly written as the cover story of *Time*' (Barrie Heads, 1964, cited by Goddard et al., 2001).

The series was innovative in several important ways and the main elements of its style were to remain relatively constant until the 1990s, although by then its novel aspects had become commonplace as part of a standard current-affairs rhetoric. *World in Action* rejected the hitherto common devices of the presenter/reporter as front-person and the studio as core location, reflecting Hewat's belief that such mediating factors inhibited viewers' direct engagement with subjects. Instead, it was the first current-affairs series to employ only voice-over narration and to be made entirely on film. From the start, each half-hour programme devoted itself to a single subject, and *World in Action* was made on 16 mm film, taking advantage of the availability of new lightweight cameras – the first series of its kind to do so. This made it cheaper and more flexible than its competitors – which were still burdened with Outside Broadcast units or 35 mm film – and able to use much smaller crews. Initially, established documentary film-makers as well as journalists were recruited, but the hybrid 'current-affairs producer', often a journalist with print experience supplemented by training in television production, soon emerged as a new television occupation.

Another innovative – and markedly populist – aspect of the series' style was its willingness to use memorable visual devices and 'stunts' to capture viewers' attention and aid their understanding. One famous example, in a 1965 programme about bronchitis, saw coffins emerging from the doors of houses in a Salford street, each one representing a death from the disease. Finally, *World in Action* adopted a fresh, classless 'voice', a world away from the cosy patrician tone of its predecessors. '*World in Action* was actually a very well-informed person in a pub, and the other guys were having dinner parties', Brian Winston, a researcher on the series, recalls (cited by Goddard et al., 2001).

World in Action's subject agenda was wide-ranging, if not strikingly different from its competitors. Its mixture of 'profiles, inquiries and exposés', at times examining the broad background to news stories but at others focusing on specific cases to show the effects of events or policy in microcosm, included a range of international stories. 'Serious' topics were interspersed periodically with lighter pop culture or personality-based programmes. But an avowedly liberal approach to stories was a distinctive characteristic of the series, reflecting Granada's own liberalism and concern with socially controversial topics. Accusations of one-sidedness and 'left-wing bias' were frequent and continued through later phases of the series' history, resulting in regular clashes with regulators. A programme on arms spending, only the ninth in the first series, became the first of six that were banned or deferred by television authorities, the most recent in 1989.

World in Action went off the air in August 1965 and Granada developed new current-affairs formats in its place. The series that returned in June 1967 bore the same title but was not strictly its successor, Granada having considered at least 280 titles before settling again on *World in Action*. By now Hewat had left and the new series was the creation of David Plowright, with a brief to produce swiftly made reports on 'the arguments and controversies of the moment', research-led enquiries and observations that revealed social trends. With occasional exceptions, however, the characteristic style was retained – half-hour location films with voice-over narration.

Reflecting the spirit of the times, this series was challenging from the outset, with fewer lighter topics than before. When, in only its sixth programme, it persuaded Mick Jagger to be interviewed in an English garden by the editor of *The Times*, and the Bishop of Woolwich following his acquittal on drugs charges, this was justly regarded as a journalistic coup. Many other remarkable programmes followed: Vietnam War refuseniks, sanctions-busting arms sales, the hippie movement and various manifestations of the civil rights movement were part of its topical and notably international agenda over the next few years. Topics such as Northern Ireland and, later, torture, the secret state and food safety were the subject of regular examination over long periods. 1967 also saw the commencement of a serious commitment to investigations, and thus began the series' long-lasting role as a pioneer of British television investigative journalism, devoted to exposing corruption and wrongdoing amongst individuals, businesses and public authorities. Over the years, its investigations have helped to expose the web of corruption surrounding Reginald Maudling and John Poulson (1971–4), political manipulation of a steel industry strike (a 1980 programme which led to new legal safeguards over the protection of journalistic sources), the wrongful conviction of the Birmingham Six (1985–91), Jonathan Aitken's involvement in arms sales whilst a cabinet minister (1995–7), and countless other examples of wrongdoing in business, industry, law enforcement, politics and sport, at home and abroad.

In other areas, too, new approaches to current-affairs television were tried. A 1968 programme on the Grosvenor Square anti-Vietnam demonstration, shown the following day, included a 10-minute observational sequence without commentary showing the riots that ensued (Corner, 1996) and, in the same year, an experimental political interview was conducted by disembodied voices in a darkened studio, empty but for the Liberal Party leader. The 'stunts' continued, too, including a 1971 experiment in which an entire village was persuaded by producers to quit smoking and a 1984 programme showing an MP's attempt to live for a week on social benefits. And from 1970, under Leslie Woodhead, *World in Action* pioneered drama-documentary, often as a means of illustrating Eastern European stories to which its cameras could not gain access. These programmes prioritised documentary values, involving meticulous research; speech based on first-hand accounts of participants and no invention for dramatic purposes. Thus began a Granada specialism that has continued to the present day.

By the mid-1970s, the series had settled down, losing some of its inventive freshness but continuing to produce challenging, well-researched programmes and to contribute prominently to the public agenda. Under Ray Fitzwalter, its longest-serving editor (1976–87), it maintained a remarkable standard and fine viewing figures for a current-affairs series. Although no longer regularly in the top 20, as it had been in 1967, *World in Action* continued substantially to outscore the BBC's *Panorama*, a direct competitor for its time-slot. As late as 1991, no longer competing directly with *Panorama*, it was still averaging a respectable 6.5–7 million viewers. This second phase, from 1967 to the late 1980s, represented the heyday of *World in Action* as it continued to break major stories and to embody many of the values of the British public service broadcasting tradition.

As the public service ethos of British television came under threat from more market-orientated models by the end of the 1980s, so did the prominence given to prime-time current affairs by Independent Television. The third phase of *World in Action* involved a rearguard action against ITV schedulers keen to move or cancel the series so as to maximise the returns from its time-slot. One result of this was that *World in Action* was increasingly torn between imperatives, on the one hand, to maintain the standard of its programmes and the public significance of its subject matter and, on the other, to maximise its audience. Many strong and worthwhile subjects continued to be tackled, but the series showed a detectable increase in programmes featuring or fronted by members of the public, often observing their experiences in confronting challenges involving health, crime, public policy or the service industries. This represented a partial refocusing of the series away from journalistic and 'expert' voices and in favour of public or consumer testimony. *House of Horrors* (Granada/ITV, 1998–), in which cowboy tradespeople were trapped by hidden cameras, was a series that originated in *World in Action* programmes of the late 1990s, embodying this new brand of 'consumer populism'.

The cancellation of *World in Action* in 1998 followed from three events at the beginning of the decade: the passage of the 1990 Broadcasting Act, in which ITV's public service responsibilities were relaxed, the centralisation of the control and scheduling of ITV and the institution of a new commercial focus at Granada whereby senior executives schooled in television production were replaced by those drawn from the world of business. On appointment as the first ITV Chief Executive in 1992, Charles Allen announced that current affairs could only be sustained in prime time if it could consistently attract eight million viewers. This was always likely to be an impossible threshold for a traditional current-affairs series, even one as popular as *World in Action*. At the same time, with the departure of David Plowright as Chairman, the series lost the unstinting support of Granada that it had always enjoyed. Throughout its history, Granada had seen *World in Action* as one of the series of which it was most proud, lending enormous prestige to the company and demonstrating irrefutably its public service credentials. It had always benefited from the robust protection of senior executives against attacks from regulators and schedulers, and

Granada's policy of promoting internally had meant that many of its senior figures had formerly worked on the series. Most of these departed quickly in Plowright's wake, leaving the series to stand or fall solely on its commercial merits. The end came in December 1998, in the face of press criticism of the 'dumbing down' of ITV. *Tonight with Trevor McDonald* (Granada/ITV, 1999–), journalistically softer and with greater emphasis on human stories, was commissioned as a direct replacement.

QUESTIONS TO CONSIDER

- Explain the benefits of regular scheduling and a long run in producing current-affairs television.

- Examine the difficulties involved in producing television journalism that is both socially valuable and attractive to viewers.

- To what extent can *World in Action* be said to embody the values of public service broadcasting?

- Why do you think *World in Action* was replaced by *Tonight with Trevor McDonald*? Do you think this new programme will focus on similar subjects to the earlier programme? If not, why not?

RECOMMENDED READING

Buscombe, Ed (ed.) (1981), BFI Dossier 9: *Granada: The First 25 Years*, London: British Film Institute.

Corner, John (1996), *The Art of Record*, Manchester: Manchester University Press.

Goddard, Peter, Corner, John and Richardson, Kay (2001), 'The Formation of *World in Action*', *Journalism*, Vol. 2, No. 1, 73–90.

alien species supported by 'The Syndicate' and an ultra-secret, sinister NGO, whose members once included Mulder's own father. Indeed, it had been the abduction of Mulder's sister Samantha (while, as children watching the Watergate coverage on television) which had originally inspired his interest in UFOs and led to his assignment by the FBI to take charge of 'the X-Files' (those cases deemed outside the Bureau's definition of 'normal').

At least since the actual Roswell incident in 1947, 'The Syndicate', it seems, has had prior knowledge about a coming alien invasion of the planet, a future conquest (it is apparently scheduled for 2012) with which they seem to have been cooperating. However, they have bargained for time by offering to first perfect (with the help of medical scientists recruited from the Axis powers after World War II) a slave race of alien-human hybrids to be used by the invaders (Syndicate members' wives and children, including Samantha Mulder, were offered up as guinea pigs for this research), while secretly developing an antidote to the Black Oil, a pathogenic substance, present on earth since prehistory, instrumental to the coming 'viral holocaust'. 'Survival', the Well-Manicured Man (a key conspirator) tells Mulder in *Fight the Future* (a 1998 feature film which extended and explored the series' Mythology), 'is the ultimate ideology', and The Syndicate are ideologues. The malevolent Cigarette-Smoking Man (who appears to be Mulder's real father and may, as we learn in the season four episode, 'Musings of a Cigarette-Smoking Man', have assassinated both JFK and Martin Luther King) is their chief enforcer, though his motives are never entirely clear. If this all-too-brief summary of *X-Files* Mythology appears confusing, part of the blame must be placed on the narrative itself. By the end of the series, at least one admirer had begun to wonder 'whether the mythos storyline had become so complicated and so muddled that even Carter couldn't untangle it' (Kelsey, 2002, 29).

Devoted fans (known as 'X-Philes') turned their obsession with the series into inspired websites that helped newcomers to the series get caught up and acclimatise themselves to the *X-Files* universe. One ambitious, meticulous *X-Files* time-line, to cite but one example, provides a chronology of the series' Mythology that runs to over 70 pages in length (Marek, 2002). Some prominent fans even came to write for the show: cyberpunk founder William Gibson wrote two episodes and horror master Stephen King one. Meanwhile, websites like The David Duchovny Estrogen Brigade (DDEB) and Gillian Anderson Testosterone Brigade (GATB) promoted the show's stars as sex symbols. Slash fan-fiction also coupled Mulder and Scully (in the show's actual nine-year run, the partners never did more than kiss, and the series' UST – Unresolved Sexual Tension – was never relieved) and even Mulder and Skinner. Fans did more than write and talk about the series, of course; thanks to Fox's skilful vertical integration of their franchise show, they would have the opportunity to spend millions of dollars a year on official books, novels, trading cards, coffee mugs, T-shirts, DVDs and action figures.

In season seven's 'X-Cops', Mulder and Scully even find themselves in the middle of an episode of the Fox reality show *Cops* (1989–) in what becomes a kind of *X-Files* 'mockumentary'. In the same season's 'Hollywood A.D.', the partners become consultants on a movie version of an X-File, in which comic Garry Shandling plays Mulder and Tea Leoni (Duchovny's wife) does Scully. However, such send-ups and tour-de-force episodes, like 'Triangle' (season six), inspired by Alfred Hitchcock's experiment in shooting without cuts in *Rope* (1948), helped to give the series new creative energy. As Kinney (2002) notes on the web:

> ... *every time you pronounce it creatively dead, it comes back to life like the ghouls that Mulder and Scully have been investigating these eight odd years. Every time you think the show has fallen into irreparable self-parody, Chris Carter has a marijuana-induced epiphany, rolls off his chaise on some remote Hawaiian beach, and videophones in an idea that shakes new life into it.*

In 2001, *The X-Files* produced its one and only spin-off, the short-lived *The Lone Gunmen* (Fox, 2001) which featured the three conspiracy-nerds, Langly, Frohike and Byers, who had often aided Scully and Mulder in their investigations. (After the demise of their show, Carter would have the Gunmen heroically killed off in the 'Jumping the Shark' episode of *X-Files*' final season). Many series, however, attempted to mine the vein *X-Files* had opened up. *Millennium* (Fox, 1996–9) and *Harsh Realm* (Fox, 1999) – both created by Chris Carter – *Dark Skies* (NBC, 1996), *Roswell* (UPN, 1999–2002) and *Dark Angel* (Fox, 2000–2) all owed a substantial debt to *The X-Files*, though none arguably matched its success.

Not surprisingly, then, the series has inspired a good deal of critical attention. Both Graham (1996) and Knight (2001), for example, find it a revealing example of late twentieth-century 'conspiracy culture'. Delasara (2000) has exhaustively catalogued how the series is indebted to and imbedded in popular culture. Wilcox and Williams (1996) and Parks (1996) see it as an important 'feminist' text, with Scully, both a scientist and a courageous FBI agent, serving as an important new role model. Badley (1996) examines it as a Foucauldian revelation about contemporary attitudes concerning the body. Clerc (1996) considers its fandom, Kubek (1996) offers a Lacanian, psychoanalytic reading of the series, while both Burns (2001) and McLean (1998) engage in 'paranoid criticism' that appears to mirror the series' own obsessional sense of paranoia (Lavery, 1996b).

The philosopher Nietzsche once observed, through his mouthpiece Zarathustra, that the great secret of life is to 'die at the right time'. Though its nine-year run as a television series was governed by the faith that 'the truth is out there', some argue that *The X-Files* could not claim to have understood Zarathustra's truth; it lived on for two or three seasons too long, its ratings halved from their peak and it may not be dead yet. Having already spun off one feature film (*The X-Files* [1998]), additional movies are possible, and it will likely continue to be one of the most popular shows in syndication. For a time, however, it was an international cultural phenomenon, an entertainment that both shaped and reflected, and finally confirmed, American sensibility in the pre-millennium, pre-9/11 decade. It was not *Law and Order* (NBC, 1990–), recycling cases from contemporary headlines; it borrowed from the zeitgeist, not the front page. Though it remained a series that never really took itself that seriously, *The X-Files* made sublime paranoia the stuff of network television and 'drastically raised the bar on this particular genre', as contributor William Gibson would observe in a dialogue with Chris Carter. 'It's a genre without a name', Gibson insisted, 'but there's a lineage. The next time somebody approaches this genre, the bar is *The X-Files*' (cited by McIntyre, 2002, 6).

QUESTIONS TO CONSIDER

- How did *The X-Files* develop from a cult show into a mainstream hit? What particular factors do you think secured both its cult credibility and its widespread popularity?
- *The X-Files* has often been referred to as 'subversive television'. But what exactly did it subvert and do you think it managed to subvert itself as well?
- How did the series' 'unresolved sexual tension' between Mulder and Scully contribute to its ongoing narrative and the popularity of *The X-Files* as a whole?
- After inspecting some fan sites, as well as the official *X-Files* website (http://www. x-files.com/), how would you characterise the contributions of the Internet to our understanding and appreciation of the series?
- How do you think *The X-Files* learnt from the narrative 'mistakes' made by earlier shows like **Twin Peaks**? Why do you think both these shows have been labelled as 'postmodern'?

RECOMMENDED READING

Delasara, Jan (2000), *Poplit, Popcult and The X-Files: A Critical Explanation*, Jefferson: McFarland and Co.

Knight, Peter (2001), *Conspiracy Culture: From Kennedy to The X-Files*, London: Routledge.

Lavery, David, Hague Angela and Cartwright Marla (eds.) (1996a), *Deny All Knowledge: Reading The X-Files*, Syracuse: Syracuse University Press.

Bibliography

Abele, B (2001), 'TV rights are too expensive IOC told', *Daily Nation*, July 14.

Allen, Robert C (ed.) (1992), *Channels of Discourse, Reassembled: Television and Contemporary Criticism*, London: Routledge.

Alters, Diane F (2003), '"We Hardly Watch that Rude, Crude Show": Class and Taste in *The Simpsons*' in Carol Stabile and Mark Harrison (eds.), *Prime-Time Animation: Television Animation and American Culture*, London and New York: Routledge.

Amory, Cleveland (1975), 'Review: *Monty Python's Flying Circus*', *TV Guide*, May 17, 32.

Andrews, D (1998), 'Feminizing Olympic reality. Preliminary dispatches from Baudrillard's Atlanta'. *International Review for the Sociology of Sport*, 33(1), 5–18.

Ang, Ien (1985), *Watching Dallas: Television and the Melodramatic Imagination*, London: Routledge.

Arlidge, J (2000), 'Battered BBC Wins Olympic Race', *Observer*, October 1.

Arrowsmith, SMJ (1981), 'Peter Watkins', in George Brandt (ed.), *British Television Drama*, Cambridge: Cambridge University Press, 217–30.

Auster, Albert (2002), 'The Sopranos: The Gangster Redux' in David Lavery (ed.) (2002), *This Thing of Ours: Investigating The Sopranos*, New York: Columbia University Press, 10–17.

Badley, Linda (1996), 'The Rebirth of the Clinic: The Body as Alien in *The X-Files*' in David Lavery, Angela Hague and Marla Cartwright (eds.), *Deny All Knowledge: Reading The X-Files*, Syracuse: Syracuse University Press, 148–67.

Bailey, Steve (2001), '"Professional Television": Three (Super) Texts and a (Super) Genre', *The Velvet Light Trap*, No. 47.

Baiocchi, G (2002), 'Media Coverage of 9/11 in Brazil' in *Television and New Media*, Vol. 3, No. 2.

Baker, Glenn A (1986), with Tom Czarnota and Peter Hogan, *Monkeemania*, London: Plexus.

Bakhtin, Mikhail (1984), *Rabelais and his World*, Bloomington: Indiana University Press.

Balio, Tino (1997), 'Fred Coe' in H Newcomb (ed.), *Encylopedia of Television*, Chicago and London: Fitzroy Dearborn.

Banham, Martin (1981), 'Jeremy Sanford' in George W Brandt (ed.), *British Television Drama*, London and New York: Cambridge University Press.

Banks, Morwenna and Swift, Amanda (1987), *The Joke's On Us: Women in Comedy from Music Hall to the Present*, London: Pandora.

Barnouw, Erik (1992), *Tube of Plenty: The Evolution of American Television*, second revised edition, New York: Oxford University Press, 422–8.

Barr, Charles (1996), '"They Think It's All Over": The Dramatic Legacy of Live Television' in John Hill and Martin McCloone, *Big Picture, Small Screen: The Relations Between Film and Television*, Luton: John Libbey.

Barrett, Michèle and Barrett, Duncan (2001), *Star Trek: The Human Frontier*, Cambridge: Polity Press.

Bates, Alden (2002), 'Not-so-civil war', Timelines in *Doctor Who Magazine* No. 324, 11.

Bazalgette, C et al (1983), *Teaching Coronation Street*, London: British Film Institute.

Bennett, Tony et al (eds.) (1981), *Popular Television and Film*, London: British Film Institute/Open University.

Bernardi, Daniel (1998), *Star Trek and History: Race-ing Toward a White Future*, New Brunswick and London: Rutgers University Press.

Bernstein, Alina (2002), 'Gender and the Media: The Representation of Men, Masculinity(ies), Gays and Lesbians' in Chris Newbold, Oliver Boyd-Barret and Hilde Van Den Buulk (eds.), *The Media Book*, London and New York: Arnold.

Bhattacharya, Sanjiv (2000), 'Homer's Odyssey', *Observer*, Review Magazine, August 6, 17–23.

Binaculli, David (1992), *Teleliteracy: Taking Television Seriously*, New York: Continuum.

Bishop, David (2001), *Bright Lights, Baked Ziti: The Sopranos – An Unofficial and Unauthorised Guide*, London: Virgin.

Bishop, Ellen (1990), 'Bakhtin, Carnival and Comedy: The New Grotesque in *Monty Python and the Holy Grail*', *Film Criticism*, Vol. 15, No. 1, 49–64.

Boddy, William (2001), 'The Quiz Show & *Who Wants to be a Millionaire?*' in Glen Creeber (ed.), *The Television Genre Book*, London: British Film Institute.

Bodroghkozy, Aniko (1993), '"We're the Young Generation and We've got Something to Say": A Gramscian Analysis of Entertainment Television and the Youth Rebellion of the 1960s' in *Critical Studies in Mass Communication*, June.

Bogdanovich, Peter (interview with David Chase) (2002), *The Sopranos: The Complete First Season*, DVD, New York: HBO-Time-Warner Production.

Bondebjerg, Ib (1992), 'Intertextuality and Metafiction: Genre and Narrative in the Television Fiction of Dennis Potter' in M Shormand and KC Schroder (eds.), *Media Cultures: Reappraising Transnational Media*, London: Routledge.

Borcila, A (2000), 'Nationalizing the Olympics around and away from "vulnerable" bodies of women: The NBC coverage of the 1996 Olympics and some moments after', *Journal of Sport and Social Issues*, Vol. 24, No. 2, 118–47.

Bordwell, David and Thompson, Janet (1986), *The Classical Hollywood Cinema*, London: Routledge.

Bordwell, David and Thompson, Kristin (1986), *Film Art: An Introduction*, New York: Alfred Knopf.

Boyd, Andrew (1990), *Broadcast Journalism: Techniques of Radio and TV News*, Oxford and London: Heinemann Professional Publishing Ltd.

Brandt, George W (ed.) (1993), *British Television Drama in the 1980s*, Cambridge: Cambridge University Press.

Broadcasting Standards Commission (1998), *Codes of Guidance June 1998*, London: Broadcasting Standards Commission.

Broadcasting Standards Commission (2001), *Brass Eye Special Finding*, <http://www.bsc.org.uk/pdfs/bulletin/brasseyespecialfinding.htm>

Brooker, M Keith (2002), *Strange TV: Innovative Television Series from The Twilight Zone to The X-Files*, Connecticut and London: Greenwood Press.

Brooker, Peter (2002), *A Glossary of Cultural Theory*, Oxford and New York: Arnold.

Brookes, Rod (2001), 'Sport' in Glen Creeber (ed.), *The Television Genre Book*, London: British Film Institute.

Brosnan, John and Nicholls, Peter (1979), 'Dr. Who' in Peter Nicholls (ed.), *The Encyclopedia of Science Fiction*, London: Granada Books.

Brown, Rob (2001), 'I never saw *Queer as Folk* as a gay drama' (interview with producer Nicola Shindler), April 9, 2001, *Guardian*.

Brunsdon, Charlotte (1997), 'Problems of Quality' in *Screen Tastes: Soap Opera to Satellite Dishes*, London and New York: Routledge.

Brunsdon, Charlotte (1998), 'Structure of anxiety: recent British television crime fiction', *Screen*, Vol. 39 No. 3, Autumn, 1998, republished in Edward Buscombe (ed.) (2000), *British Television: A Reader*, London and New York: Oxford University Press, 195–218.

Bruzzi, S (2000), *New Documentary: A Critical Introduction*, London and New York: Routledge.

Brynen, Rex (2000), 'Mirror, Mirror? The Politics of Television Science Fiction' in David A Schultz (ed.), *It's Show Time! Media, Politics and Popular Culture*, New York: Peter Lang, 73–99.

Buckingham, David (1993), *Children Talking Television: The Making of Television Literacy*, London: Falmer Press.

Buckingham, David, Davies, Hannah, Jones, Ken and Kelley, Peter (1999), *Children's Television in Britain*, London: British Film Institute.

Buckingham, David (2000), 'Creating the Audience' in Edward Buscombe (ed.), *British Television: A Reader*, Oxford: Oxford University Press.

Burns, Christy L (2001), 'Erasure: Alienation, Paranoia, and the Loss of Memory in *The X-Files*', *Camera Obscura*, Vol. 15, No. 3, 194–219.

Buscombe, Ed (ed.) (1981), BFI Dossier 9, *Granada: The First 25 Years*, London: British Film Institute.

Buxton, David (1990), *From The Avengers to Miami Vice: Form and Ideology in Television Series*, Manchester and New York: Manchester University Press.

Calcutt, Andrew (1998), *Pop Culture and the Erosion of Adulthood*, London: Cassell.

Caldwell, John Thornton (1995), *Televisuality: Style, Crisis, and Authority in American Television*, New Brunswick, NJ: Rutgers University Press.

Caldwell, John (1997), 'Steadicam' in Horace Newcomb (ed.), *Encylopedia of Television*, Chicago and London: Fitzroy Dearborn.

Carpenter, Humphrey (1998), *Dennis Potter: The Authorized Biography*, London: Faber & Faber.

Carpenter, Humphrey (2000), *That Was Satire That Was: The Satire Boom of the 1960s*, London: Phoenix.

Carrazé, Alain and Oswald, Hélène (1990), *The Prisoner: A Televisionary Masterpiece*, London: Virgin.

Carroll, Michael (1993), 'Agent Cooper's Errand in the Wilderness: *Twin Peaks* and American Mythology' in David Lavery, *Literature/Film Quarterly*, 51–9.

Caughie, John (2000), *Television Drama: Realism, Modernism, and British Culture*, Oxford: Oxford University Press.

Cauldry, N (2002), 'Playing for Celebrity: *Big Brother* as Ritual Event' in *Television and New Media*, Vol. 3, No. 3, 283–93.

Chaikin, Andrew (1994), *A Man on the Moon: The Voyages of the Apollo Astronauts*, New York: Viking.

Channel Four (2000), *What the Folk?* (documentary on *Queer as Folk*) included in Channel Four/Red Productions, *Queer as Folk 2: Same Men, New Tricks*, DVD.

Chapman, James (2002), *Saints and Avengers: British Adventure Series of the 1960s*, London and New York: IB Tauris.

Chase, David (2002), 'Introduction' in *The Sopranos: Selected Scripts from Three Seasons*, New York: Warner Books, vii–x.

Chisholm, A (1999), 'Defending the nation: national bodies, US borders, and the 1996 US Olympics women's gymnastics team', *Journal of Sport and Social Issues*, 23, 126–39.

Chisholm, Brad (1991), 'Difficult Viewing: The Pleasure of Complex Narratives' in *Critical Studies in Mass Communication*, Vol. 8, No. 4, 389–403.

Chomsky, Noam (2001), *9–11*, New York: Seven Stories Press.

Clarke, Alan (1986), ' "This is not the boys scouts": Television police series and definitions of law and order' in Tony Bennett et al. (eds.), *Popular Culture and Social Relations*, Buckingham: Open University.

Clerc, Susan J (1996), 'DDEB, GATB, MPPB, and Ratboy: *The X-Files*' Media Fandom, Online and Off' in David Lavery, Angela Hague and Marla Cartwright (eds.), *Deny All Knowledge: Reading The X-Files*, Syracuse: Syracuse University Press, 36–51.

Cohen, S (1980), *Folk Devils and Moral Panics*, Oxford: Martin Robertson.

Collins, Jim (1992, second edition), 'Television and Postmodernism' in Robert C Allen, *Channels of Discourse, Reassembled*, Chapel Hill, NC: University of North Carolina Press, 327–53.

Collins, Michael (2000), 'Sing if you're glad to be gay (and cute)', *Observer*, 'Television', January 30, 6–7.

Cook, John R (1995), 'Singing for Your Supper' in *Dennis Potter: A Life on Screen*, Manchester and New York: Manchester University Press.

Corner, John (ed.) (1991), *Popular Television in Britain: Studies in Cultural History*, London: British Film Institute.

Corner, John (1996), *The Art of Record: A Critical Introduction to Documentary and New York*, Manchester: Manchester University Press.

Corner, John (2002), 'Performing the Real: Documentary Diversions' in *Television and New Media*, Vol. 3 No. 3, 255–69.

Creeber, Glen (1998), 'Mothers and Mistresses: Women, Sexuality and the Male Unconscious' in *Dennis Potter: Between Two Worlds, A Critical Reassessment*, London and New York: Macmillan.

Creeber, Glen (2001), '"Taking our personal lives seriously": intimacy, continuity and memory in the television drama serial' in *Media, Culture & Society*, Vol. 23, 439–55.

Creeber, Glen (2001), 'Cigarettes and Alcohol: Investigating Gender, Genre, and Gratification in *Prime Suspect*', *Television & New Media*, Vol. 2, No. 2, May.

Creeber, Glen (ed.) (2002), *The Television Genre Book*, London: British Film Institute.

Creeber, Glen (2002), '"TV Ruined the Movies": Television, Tarantino, and The Intimate World of The Sopranos' in David Lavery (ed.), *This Thing of Ours: Investigating The Sopranos*, New York: Columbia University Press, 124–34.

Creeber, Glen (forthcoming, 2004), '*Queer as Folk*' in *Next Week On ...: Television Drama in the Age of Serial Fiction*, London: British Film Institute.

Cripps, Thomas (1995), 'Historical Truth: An Interview with Ken Burns', *American Historical Review*, Vol. 100 No.3, June, 741–64.

Crisell, Andrew (1997), *An Introductory History of British Broadcasting*, London and New York: Routledge.

Croft, Karen (accessed 2002), 'Made Women. *The Sopranos* Deals with Female Emotional and Sexual Desire Better than Any Other Show on TV' on <http://www.salon.com/sex/feature/2001/04/09/mob_women/index.html>

Crofts, Stephen (1995), 'Global Neighbours?' in Robert C Allen (ed.), *To Be Continued... Soap Operas Around the World*, London and New York: Routledge.

Cubitt, Sean (1986), 'Top of the Pops: the Politics of the Living Room' in Len Masterman (ed.), *Television Mythologies: Stars, Shows, Signs*, London: Comedia/MK Media Press, 46–8.

Cubitt, Sean (1997), 'Peter Watkins', in Horace Newcombe (ed.), *The Encyclopaedia of Television, Volume 3: Q-Z*, Chicago and London: Fitzroy Dearborn, 1807–8.

Cubitt, Sean (2002), 'Digital Filming and Special Effects' in Dan Harries (ed.), *The New Media Book*, London: British Film Institute.

Cull, Nicholas J (2001), 'Bigger on the inside...: *Doctor Who* as British cultural history' in Graham Roberts and Philip M Taylor (eds.), *The Historian, Television and Television History*, Luton: University of Luton Press, 95–111.

Cunningham, Stuart and Miller, Toby (1994), *Contemporary Australian Television*, Sydney, Australia: University of New South Wales Press.

Cunningham, Stuart and Jacka, Elizabeth (1996), *Australian Television and International Mediascapes*, Melbourne, Australia: Cambridge University Press.

D'Acci, Julie (1993), *Defining Women: Television and the Case of Cagney and Lacey*, Chapel Hill: University of North Carolina Press.

Davies, Máire Messenger (1989), *Television is Good for your Kids*, London: Hilary Shipman.

Davies, Máire Messenger (1997), *Fake, Fact and Fantasy: Children's Interpretations of Television Reality*, Mahwah, NJ: Lawrence Erlbaum.

Davies, Russell T (1999), *Queer as Folk: The Scripts*, Basingstoke and Oxford: Channel Four Books/Macmillan.

Day-Lewis, Sean (1998), *Talk of Drama: Views of the Television Dramatist Now and Then*, Luton: University of Luton Press.

Delasara, Jan (2000), *Poplit, Popcult and The X-Files: A Critical Explanation*, Jefferson: McFarland and Co.

Desmet, Christy (1994), 'The Canonization of Laura Palmer' in David Lavery (ed.), *Full of Secrets: Critical Approaches to Twin Peaks*, Detroit: Wayne State University Press, 93–108.

Dienst, Richard (1994), 'Magic and Commerce in Twin Peaks' in *Still Life in Real Time: Theory After Television*, Durham, NC: Duke University Press, 89–99.

Dolan, Marc (1994), 'The Peaks and Valleys of Serial Creativity: What Happened to/on *Twin Peaks*' in David Lavery (ed.), *Full of Secrets: Critical Approaches to Twin Peaks*, Detroit: Wayne State University Press, 30–50.

Dolenz, Micky and Bego, Mark (1993), *I'm A Believer: My Life of Monkees, Music, and Madness*, New York: Hyperion.

Donatelli, Cindy and Alward, Sharon (2002), '"I dread you"?: Married to the Mob in *The Godfather, Goodfellas*, and *The Sopranos*' in David Lavery (ed.), *This Thing of Ours: Investigating The Sopranos*, New York: Columbia University Press, 58–69.

Donnelly, KJ (2001a), 'Music on Television' in Glen Creeber (ed.), *The Television Genre Book*, London: British Film Institute, 89–91.

Donnelly, KJ (2001b), *Pop Music in British Cinema: A Chronicle*, London: British Film Institute.

Dougherty, Anne Millard (2002), 'Just a Girl: Buffy as Icon' in Roz Kaveney (ed.) (2002), *Reading the Vampire Slayer: An Unofficial Critical Companion to Buffy and Angel*, London: IB Tauris, 148–66.

Dovey, Jon (2000), *Freakshow: First Person Media and Factual Television*, London: Pluto Press.

Downing, J (1988), '*The Cosby Show* and American Racial Discourse' in G Smitherman-Donaldson and T van Dijk (eds.), *Discourse and Discrimination*, Michigan: Wayne State University Press.

Dugdale, John (1994), 'Taped Up for Auntie', *Guardian*, July 25, 16–17.

Dyer, Richard, Geraghty, Christine, Jordan, Marion, Lovell, Terry, Paterson, Richard, Stewart John, et al (eds.) (1981), *Coronation Street*, London: British Film Institute.

Dyson, M (1989), 'Bill Cosby and the Politics of Race', *Zeta*, September.

Eastman, ST and Billings, A (1999), 'Gender parity in the Olympics. Hyping women athletes, favoring men athletes', *Journal of Sport and Social Issues*, Vol. 23, No. 2, 140–70.

Eaton, Mary (1995), 'A Fair Cop? Viewing the Effects of the Canteen Culture in *Prime Suspect* and *Between the Lines*' in David Kidd-Hewitt and Richard Osborne (eds.), *Crime and the Media: The Postmodern Spectacle*, London: Pluto Press.

Eco, Umberto (1986), '*Casablanca:* Cult Movies and Intertextual Collage' in *Travels in Hyper Reality*, translated by William Weaver, New York: Harcourt, Brace Jovanovich, 197–211.

Edgerton, Gary R (2001), *Ken Burns's America*, New York: Palgrave for St. Martin's Press.

Edgerton, Gary R (1993), '*Ken Burns's America*: Style, Authorship, and Cultural Memory', *Journal of Popular Film and Television*, Vol. 21 No. 2, 50–62.

Edgerton, Gary R (1992), 'Ken Burns's Rebirth of a Nation: Television, Narrative, and Popular History', *Film & History*, Vol. 22 No. 4, 118–33.

Edgerton, Gary R, and Rollins, Peter C (eds.) (2001), *Television Histories: Shaping Collective Memory in the Media Age*, Lexington: University Press of Kentucky.

Edwards, Lynne (2002), 'Slaying in Black and White: Kendra as Tragic Mulatto' in David Lavery and Rhonda V Wilcox (eds.), *Fighting the Forces: What's at Stake in Buffy the Vampire Slayer*, Lanham, MD: Rowman and Littlefield, 85–97.

Eliot, George (1871–2, reprinted 1965), *Middlemarch: A Study of Provincial Life*, (ed.) WJ Harvey, Harmondsworth: Penguin.

Elsaesser, Thomas (1996), 'Subject positions, speaking positions: from *Holocaust, Our Hitler*, and *Heimat* to *Shoh* and *Schindler's List*' in Vivian Sobchack (ed.), *The Persistence of History: Cinema, Television and the Modern Event*, London: Routledge.

Erickson, Gregory (2002), '"Sometimes You Need a Story" American Christianity, Vampires, and Buffy' in David Lavery and Rhonda V Wilcox (eds.), *Fighting the Forces: What's at Stake in Buffy the Vampire Slayer*, Lanham, MD: Rowman and Littlefield, 108–19.

Erickson, Hal (1995), *Television Cartoon Shows: An Illustrated Encyclopedia 1949 Through 1993*, Jefferson: McFarland and Company.

Evensen, Bruce J, 'Moon Landing' in Michael D Murray (ed.) (1999), *Encyclopedia of Television News*, Phoenix, AR: Oryx Press, 153–5.

Farley, Rebecca (2003), 'From Fred and Wilma to Ren and Stimpy: What Makes a Cartoon "Prime-Time"?' in Carol Stabile and Mark Harrison (eds.), *Prime-Time Animation: Television Animation and American Culture*, London and New York: Routledge.

Ferguson, Euan (2001a), 'Bold as Brass', *Observer*, July 22, 23.

Ferguson, Euan (2001b), 'Why Chris Morris Had to Make *Brass Eye*', *Observer*, August 5, 13.

Feuer, Jane et al (eds.) (1984), *MTM 'Quality Television'*, London: British Film Institute.

Feuer, Jane (1995), *Seeing Through the Eighties: Television and Reaganism*, London: British Film Institute.

Fiske, John (1987), 'Quizzical Pleasures' in *Television Culture*, London: Routledge.

Fiske, John (1987), *Television Culture*, London: Routledge.

Flew, Terry (1994), 'The Simpsons: Culture, Class and Popular TV', *Metro*, 97, 14–19.

Freeman, Nick (1999), 'See Europe with ITC: Stock Footage and the Construction of Geographical Identity' in Deborah Cartmell, IQ Hunter, Heidi Kaye and Imelda Whelehan (eds.), *Alien Identities: Exploring Differences in Film and Fiction*, London: Pluto Press.

Freud, Sigmund (1960), *Jokes and Their Relation to the Unconscious*, London: Penguin.

Frost, Scott (1991), *The Autobiography of F.B.I. Special Agent Dale Cooper: My Life, My Tapes. A Twin Peaks Book*, New York: Pocket Books.

Furniss, Maureen (1998), *Art in Motion: Animation Aesthetics*, London: John Libbey.

Gamman, Lorraine (1988), 'Watching the Detectives: The Enigma of the Female Gaze' in Lorraine Gamman and Margaret Marshment (eds.), *The Female Gaze: Women as Viewers of Popular Culture*, London: The Women's Press, 8–26.

Gardner, Carl and Young Robert (1981), 'Science on TV: A Critique' in Tony Bennett et al (eds.), *Popular Television and Film*, London: British Film Institute, 171–93.

Gates, HL (1989), 'TV's Black World Turns – But Stay's Unreal', *New York Times*, November 12.

Gauntlett, David (2002), *Media, Gender and Identity: An Introduction*, London and New York: Routledge.

George, Diana Hume (1994), 'Lynching Women: A Feminist Reading of *Twin Peaks*', in David Lavery, *Full of Secrets: Critical Approaches to Twin Peaks*, Detroit: Wayne State University Press, 109–19.

'Georgina', '*Alternative 3*, The UK Anglia Television Programme', *Alternative 3* <http://www.conspiracy-net.com/archives/articles/alienufo/alt3/CNAf0003.txt> (accessed March 26, 2002).

Geraghty, Christine (2000), 'The Construction of a Community' in Edward Buscombe (ed.), *British Television: A Reader*, Oxford: Oxford University Press.

Gibberman, Susan R (1991), *Star Trek: An Annotated Guide to Resources on the Development, the Phenomenon, the People, the Television Series, the Films, the Novels and the Recordings*, North Carolina: McFarland.

Gibberman, Susan R (1997), 'Delbert Mann' in H Newcomb (ed.), *Encylopedia of Television*, Chicago and London: Fitzroy Dearborn.

Gibson, Janine (1999), 'Channel Four glad to pioneer the first gay drama on British TV', *Guardian*, February 24.

Gitlin, Todd (1983, revised and reprinted 1994), *Inside Prime Time*, London: Routledge.

Glynn, Kevin (1996), 'Bartmania: the Social Reception of an Unruly Image', *Camera Obscura*, 38, 61–90.

Goddard, Peter, Corner, John and Richardson, Kay (2001), 'The Formation of *World in Action*', *Journalism*, Vol. 2, No. 1, 73–90.

Godwell, D (2000), 'The Olympic branding of aborigines' in K Schaffer and S Smith (eds.), *The Olympics at the Millennium*, Piscataway, NJ: Rutgers University Press.

Gomez, Joseph A (1979), *Peter Watkins*, Boston: Twayne.

Goodwin, A et al (eds.) (1983), *Drama-Documentary: BFI Dossier*, 19, London: British Film Institute.

Goostree, Laura (1988), 'The Monkees and the Deconstruction of Television Realism', *Journal of Popular Film and Television*, Vol. 16, No. 2, Summer, 50–8.

Gordon, S and Sibson, R (1998), 'Global television: the Atlanta Olympics opening ceremony', in D Rowe and G Lawrence (eds.), *Tourism, Leisure, Sport: Critical Perspectives*, Sydney: Hodder.

Graef, Roger (1974), 'Skeletons on the Box', *New Society*, June 27, 1974, 772–3.

Graham, Allison (1996), '"Are You Now or Have You Ever Been?": Conspiracy Theory and *The X-Files*', in David Lavery, Angela Hague and Marla Cartwright (eds.), *Deny All Knowledge: Reading The X-Files*, Syracuse: Syracuse University Press, 52–62.

Gray, Frances (1994), *Women and Laughter*, Basingstoke: Macmillan.

Gray, H (1995), *Watching Race: Television and the Struggle for Blackness*, Minneapolis: University of Minnesota Press.

Gregory, Chris (1997), *Be Seeing You... Decoding The Prisoner*, Luton: University of Luton Press.

Gregory, Chris (2000), *Star Trek: Parallel Narratives*, London: Macmillan.

Gripsrud, Jostein (1995), *The Dynasty Years: Hollywood Television and Critical Media Studies*, London: Routledge.

Gunter, Barrie, and McAleer, Jill (1997, second edition), *Children and Television*, London and New York: Routledge.

Gurevitch, Michael (1991), 'The globalisation of electronic journalism' in James Curran and Michael Gurevitch (eds.), *Mass Media and Society*, London and New York: Edward Arnold.

Hacker, A (1992), *Two Nations: Black and White, Separate, Hostile, Unequal*, New York: Scribner.

Hague, Angela (1994), 'Infinite Games: the Derationalization of Detection in *Twin Peaks*' Lavery, *Full of Secrets: Critical Approaches to Twin Peaks*, Detroit: Wayne State University Press, 130–44.

Haines, Tim (2001), *Walking With Beasts*, London: BBC Worldwide.

Halliwell, Leslie (1987), *Double Take and Fade Away*, London: Grafton Books.

Hanley, Richard (1997), *The Metaphysics of Star Trek*, New York: Basic Books.

Hargreaves, Ian and Thomas, James (2002), *New News, Old News*, London: Independent Television Commission and Broadcasting Standards Commission.

Harrison, Jackie (2000), *Terrestrial TV News in Britain*, Manchester: Manchester University Press.

Harrison, Jackie (2001), 'Constructing News Values' in Glen Creeber (ed.), *The Television Genre Book*, London: British Film Institute.

Harrison, Taylor, Projansky, Sarah, Ono, Kent A and Helford, Elyce Rae (eds.) (1996), *Enterprise Zones: Critical Positions on Star Trek*, Boulder, CO: Westview Press.

Hartley, John (1999), *The Uses of Television*, London and New York: Routledge.

Hartsough, D (1989), '*The Cosby Show* in Historical Context', paper presented to the Ohio University Film Conference.

Haskell, Molly (1973), *Reverence to Rape: The Treatment of Women in the Movies*, Harmondsworth: Penguin.

Hayward, Anthony and Rennert, Amy (eds.) (1996), *The Prime Suspect Book*, London: Carlton Books.

Heaton, AJ and Wilson, NL (1995), *Tuning in Trouble; Talk Show's Destructive Impact on Mental Health*, San Francisco: Jossy-Bass Inc.

Heider, Karl G (ed.) (1993), 'Was It Not Real? Democratizing Myth Through Ken Burns's *The Civil War*', *Images of the South: Constructing a Regional Culture on Film and Video*, Athens: University of Georgia Press, 112–23.

Helford, Elyce (2002), '"My Emotions Give Me Power": The Containment of Girls' Anger in *Buffy*' in David Lavery and Rhonda V Wilcox (eds.), *Fighting the Forces: What's at Stake in Buffy the Vampire Slayer*, Lanham, MD: Rowman and Littlefield, 18–34.

Henderson, Brian (1991), '*The Civil War*: "Did It Not Seem Real?"' *Film Quarterly*, Vol. 44, No. 3, 2–14.

Herf, Jeffrey (1980), 'The "Holocaust" Reception in West Germany: Right, Centre and Left', *New German Critique*, 19, Winter, 30–52.

Hey, Kenneth (1983), '*Marty*: Aesthetics vs. Medium in Early TV Drama' in Leslie Fishbein (ed.), *American History/American Television: Interpreting the Video Past*, New York: Frederick Ungar.

Heywood, L (2000), 'The Girls of Summer: social contexts for the year of the woman at the '96 Olympics', in K Shaffer and S Smith (eds.), *The Olympics at the Millennium*, Piscataway, NJ: Rutgers University Press.

Hill, Annette and Palmer, Gareth (eds.) (2002), 'Special Issue: Big Brother', *Television & New Media*, Vol. 3, No. 3, August.

Hill, Annette (2002), '*Big Brother*: The Real Audience' in *Television and New Media*, Vol. 3, No. 3, 323–40.

Hill, Annette and Palmer, G (2002), 'Editorial' in *Television and New Media*, Vol. 3, No. 3, 251–4.

Hill, John (1986), *Sex, Class and Realism: British Cinema 1956–63*, London: British Film Institute.

Hill, John (1991), 'Television and Pop: the Case of the 1950s' in John Corner, (ed.), *Popular Television in Britain: Studies in Cultural History*, London: British Film Institute.

Hills, Matt (2000), 'To boldly go where others have gone before...? *Star Trek* and (academic) narratives of progress' in *Scope: An On-line Journal of Film Studies*, November 2000 edition, available at http://www.nottingham.ac.uk/film/journal/bookrev/star-trek.htm

Hills, Matt (2002), *Fan Cultures*, London and New York: Routledge.

Hilton-Morrow, Wendy and McMahan, David T (2003), '*The Flintstones* to *Futurama*: Networks and Prime Time Animation' in Carol Stabile and Mark Harrison (eds.), *Prime-Time Animation: Television Animation and American Culture*, London and New York: Routledge.

Hobson, Dorothy (2003), *Soap Opera*, Oxford: Polity Press.

Hockley, Luke (2001), 'Science Fiction' in Glen Creeber (ed.), *The Television Genre Book*, London: British Film Institute, 26–31.

Hodgson, Jessica (2002), 'ITN Newsreader Loses *Brass Eye* Case', *Guardian*, March 5, 5.

Holden, Stephen (2000), introduction to *The New York Times on The Sopranos*, New York: ibooks.

Holland, Patricia (1997), *The Television Handbook*, London and New York: Routledge.

Home, Anna (1991), *Into the Box of Delights: a History of Children's Television*, London: BBC Books.

Horne, J and Manzenreiter, W (eds.) (2002), *Japan, Korea and the 2002 World Cup*, London: Routledge.

Horowitz, Susan (1997), *Queens of Comedy: Lucille Ball, Phyllis Diller, Carol Burnett, Joan Rivers, and the New Generation of Funny Women*, Amsterdam: Gordon and Breach.

Housham, D (1994), 'Primetime', *Are We Having Fun Yet? The Sight and Sound Comedy Supplement*, Vol. 4, No. 3, 10–13.

Howe, David J and Walker, Stephen James (1998), *Doctor Who: The Television Companion*, London: BBC Worldwide.

Hunningher, Joost (1993), '*The Singing Detective*: Who done it?' in George W Brandt (ed.), *British Television Drama in the 1980s*, Cambridge and New York: Cambridge University Press.

Hurd, Geoffrey (1981), 'The Television Presentation of the Police' in Tony Bennett et al. (eds.), *Popular Film & Television*, Buckingham: Open University.

Huskey, Melynda (1993), '*Twin Peaks*: Re-writing the Sensation Novel' in David Lavery, *Literature/Film Quarterly*, 12–18.

Independent Television Commission (2001a), *The ITC Programme Code*, London: Independent Television Commission.

Independent Television Commission (2001b), *Press Release 46/01: ITC Publishes Findings on Channel 4's 'Brass Eye'*, September 6.

Irwin, William, Conard, Mark T and Skoble, Aeon J (eds.) (2001), *The Simpsons and Philosophy: the D'oh! of Homer*, Chicago and La Salle: Open Court.

Jacka, Elizabeth and Johnson Lesley (1995), 'Australia' in, Anthony Smith (ed.), *Television, An International History*, Oxford: Oxford University Press.

Jacobs, Jason (2000), *The Intimate Screen: Early British Television Drama*, Oxford: Oxford University Press.

Jacobs, Jason (2001), 'Issues of Judgement and value in television studies', in *International Journal of Cultural Studies*, Vol. 4, No. 4, December.

Jacobs, Jason (2003), *Body Trauma TV: The New Hospital Dramas*, London: British Film Institute.

Jeffries, Stuart (2002), 'Grange Hill Heads North', *Guardian*, G2, April 9, 2–3.

Jenkins, Henry (1992), *Textual Poachers: Television Fans and Participatory Culture*, New York and London: Routledge.

Jenkins, Henry (1994), '"Do You Enjoy Making the Rest of Us Feel Stupid?" alt. tv. twinpeaks, the Trickster Author, and Viewer Mastery' in David Lavery (ed.), *Full of Secrets: Critical Approaches to Twin Peaks*, Detroit: Wayne State University Press, 51–69.

Jennings, Ros (1997), 'Prime Suspect' in Horace Newcomb (ed.), *Encyclopaedia of Television*, Chicago and London: Fitzroy Dearborn.

Jhally, S and Lewis, J (1992), *Enlightened Racism: The Cosby Show, Audiences, and the Myth of the American Dream*, Boulder: Westview.

Johnson, Catherine (2001), '*Buffy the Vampire Slayer*' in Glen Creeber (ed.), *The Television Genre Book*, London: British Film Institute, 42.

Johnston, Dawn Elizabeth B (2002), 'Way North of New Jersey: A Canadian Experience of *The Sopranos*' in David Lavery (ed.), *This Thing of Ours: Investigating The Sopranos*, New York: Columbia University Press, 32–41.

Jones, Gerard (1992), *Honey, I'm Home! Sitcoms: Selling the American Dream*, New York: St. Martin's Press.

Jordan, Marion (1981), 'Realism and convention' in Richard Dyer et al. (eds.), *Coronation Street*, London: British Film Institute, 27–39.

Joseph-Witham, Heather R (1996), *Star Trek Fans and Costume Art*, Jackson: University Press of Mississippi.

Joyner, Priest (1995), *Public Intimacies: Talk Show Participants and Tell-All TV*, New Jersey, Hampton Press.

Kaes, Anton (1989), 'Germany as Memory' in *From Hitler to Heimat: The Return of History as Film*, Massachusetts and London: Harvard University Press.

Kalinak, Kathryn (1994), "Disturbing the Guests with This Racket": Music and *Twin Peaks*' in David Lavery (ed.), *Full of Secrets: Critical Approaches to Twin Peaks*, Detroit: Wayne State University Press, 82–92.

Kaplan, E Ann (1978, revised edition 1998), *Women in Film Noir*, London: British Film Institute.

Katz, Elihu and Liebes, Tamar (1986), 'Mutual Aid in the Decoding of *Dallas*: Preliminary Notes from a Cross-cultural study' in P Drummond and R Patterson (eds.), *Television in Transition*, London: British Film Institute, 187–98.

Katz, Elihu, Peters, John Durham, Libebes, Tamar and Orloff, Avril (2003), 'Introduction: Shoulders to Stand on' in Elihu, Katz John Durham Peters, Tamar Libebes and Avril Orloff (eds.), *Canonic Texts in Media Research*, Cambridge and Malden: Blackwell Publishing, 4.

Kaveney, Roz (ed.) (2002), *Reading the Vampire Slayer: An Unofficial Critical Companion to Buffy and Angel*, London: IB Tauris.

Kawakami, A (2002), 'Japan? Not quite', *Guardian*, G2 June 12.

Keller, James R (2002), *Queer (Un) Friendly Film and Television*, Jefferson, NC and London: McFarland & Company Inc.

Kellner, D (2002), 'September 11, the Media and War Fever' in *Television and New Media*, Vol. 3, No. 2.

Kelsey, Rick (2002), '*X-Files*: An Appreciation', *Wrapped in Plastic* I (59) June, 29.

Kilborn, R and Izod, J (1997), *Introduction to Television Documentary*, Manchester University Press.

Kimball, Samuel (1993), '"Into The Light, Leland, Into The Light": Emerson, Oedipus, And The Blindness Of Male Desire in *Twin Peaks*', *Genders*, 16, Spring, 17–35.

King, Geoff (2002), *Film Comedy*, London: Walflower Press.

Kingsley, Hilary (1989), *Soap Box: The Australian Guide to Television Soap Operas*, South Melbourne, Australia: Sun Books.

Kinney, Aaron (accessed 2002), 'The Truth is, Um, Where Exactly?' *Salon.com*

Knight, Peter (2002), *Conspiracy Culture: From Kennedy to The X-Files*, London: Routledge.

Koeniger, A Cash (1991), 'Ken Burns's "*The Civil War*": Triumph or Travesty?' *The Journal of Military History*, Vol. 55, April, 225–33.

Krugman, P (2001), 'Taking Care of Business', *The New York Times*, October 28.

Kubek, Elizabeth B (1996), '"You Only Expose Your Father": The Imaginary, Voyeurism, and the Symbolic Order in *The X-Files*' in David Lavery, Angela Hague and Marla Cartwright (eds.), *Deny All Knowledge: Reading The X-Files*, Syracuse: Syracuse University Press, 168–206.

Kuzniar, Alice (1994), 'Double Talk in *Twin Peaks*' in David Lavery, *Full of Secrets: Critical Approaches to Twin Peaks*, Detroit: Wayne State University Press, 120–9.

Lajtha, Terry (1981), 'Brechtian Devices in Non-Brechtian Cinema: *Culloden*', *Literature/Film Quarterly*, Vol. 9 No. 1, 9–14.

Landy, Marcia (ed.) (2001), *The Historical Film: History and Memory in Media*, New Brunswick, NJ: Rutgers University Press.

Larbalestier, Justine (2002), 'Buffy's Mary Sue is Jonathan: Buffy the Vampire Slayer Acknowledges the Fans' in David Lavery and Rhonda V Wilcox (eds.), *Fighting the Forces: What's at Stake in Buffy the Vampire Slayer*, Lanham, MD: Rowman and Littlefield, 227–38.

Lauzen, Martha (2001), 'Don't Forget the Brutalized Women behind *The Sopranos*', *Los Angeles Times*, April 16, http://www.sicilianculture. com/news/sopranoswomen. htm

Lavery, David (ed.) (1993), 'Peaked Out!' *Twin Peaks* Special Issue, *Literature/Film Quarterly*, Vol. 21, No. 4, 238–306.

Lavery, David (1994), '"The Semiotics of Cobbler": *Twin Peaks*' Interpretive Community' in David Lavery (ed.), *Full of Secrets: Critical Approaches to Twin Peaks*, Detroit: Wayne State University Press, 1–21.

Lavery, David (ed.) (1994), *Full of Secrets: Critical Approaches to Twin Peaks*, Detroit: Wayne State University Press.

Lavery, David, Hague, Angela and Cartwright, Marla (eds.) (1996a), *Deny All Knowledge: Reading The X-Files*, Syracuse: Syracuse University Press.

Lavery, David, Hague, Angela Cartwright Marla (1996b), 'Generation X: *The X-Files* and the Cultural Moment' in David Lavery, Angela Hague and Marla Cartwright (eds.), *Deny All Knowledge: Reading The X-Files*, Syracuse: Syracuse University Press, 1–21.

Lavery, David (2002), 'The Genius of Joss Whedon' in David Lavery and Rhonda V Wilcox (eds.), *Fighting the Forces: What's at Stake in Buffy the Vampire Slayer*, Lanham, MD: Rowman and Littlefield, 251–56.

Lavery, David and Thompson, Robert J (2002), 'David Chase, *The Sopranos*, and Television Creativity' in David Lavery (ed.), *This Thing of Ours: Investigating The Sopranos*, New York: Columbia University Press, 18–25.

Lavery, David (2002), 'Coming Heavy: The Significance of *The Sopranos*' in David Lavery (ed.), *This Thing of Ours: Investigating The Sopranos*, New York: Columbia University Press, xi–xviii.

Lavery, David (2003), '*The X-Files*', *Encyclopedia of American Conspiracy Theories*, (ed.) Peter Knight, London: ABC-Clio.

Leavis, FR (1948), *The Great Tradition: George Eliot, Henry James, Joseph Conrad*, London: Chatto and Windus.

Ledwon, Lenora (1993), '*Twin Peaks* and the Television Gothic' in David Lavery, *Literature/Film Quarterly*, 24–34.

Leigh, Jacob (2002), '*Cathy Come Home*: Fictional Journalism' in *The Cinema of Ken Loach: Art in the Service of the People*, London and New York: Walflower Press.

Leonard, John (1990), 'The Quirky Allure of *Twin Peaks*', *New York*, May 7, 32–9.

Levinson, Paul (2002), 'Naked Bodies, Three Showings a Week, and No Commercials: *The Sopranos* as a Nuts-and-Bolts Triumph of Non-Network TV' in David Lavery (ed.), *This Thing of Ours: Investigating The Sopranos*, New York: Columbia University Press, 26–31.

Lewis, Justin (1985), 'Decoding Television News' in P Drummond and R Paterson, (eds.), *Television in Transition*, London: British Film Institute.

Lewis, Jon E and Stempel, Penny (1993), *Cult TV: The Essential Critical Guide*, London: Pavilion Books.

Lewis, Justin (2001), *Constructing Public Opinion: How Elites Do What They Like and Why We Seem To Go Along With It*, New York: Columbia University Press.

Lewis, Justin, Maxwell, R and Miller, Toby (eds.) (2002), special issue of *Television and New Media*, Vol. 3, No. 2.

Lewis, Justin (2002), 'Speaking of Wars' in *Television and New Media*, Vol. 3, No. 2.

Lewisohn, Mark (1998), *The Radio Times Guide to TV Comedy*, London: BBC.

Lewisohn, Mark (2002), *Funny, Peculiar: The True Story of Benny Hill*, London: Sidgwick and Jackson.

Lurie, Karen (2001), *British Youth Television: Cynicism and Enchantment*, Oxford: Oxford University Press.

Little, Daran (1995), *The Coronation Street Story*, London: Andre Deutsch Ltd.

Livingstone, Sonia and Lunt, Peter (1994), *Talk on Television: Audience Participation and Public Debate*, London and New York: Routledge.

Lord, Lewis (1990), 'The Civil War, unvarnished', *U.S. News & World Report*, September 24, 74–75.

Lynch, Jennifer (1990), *The Secret Diary of Laura Palmer*, New York: Pocket Books.

Mack, John E (1994), *Abduction: Human Encounters with Aliens*, New York: Scribner.

Maconie, Stuart (2002), 'It's Still No. 1 … It's Top of the Pops' in *Radio Times*, September 7–13, 14–16.

Malach, Michele (1994), '"You Better Dust Off Your Own Black Suit": Agent Cooper, *Twin Peaks*, and the Rewriting of the FBI Agent', *Wrapped in Plastic* 1(14), 2–7.

Marc, David and Thompson Robert J (1992), *Prime Time, Prime Movers: From* I Love Lucy *to L.A. Law – America's Greatest TV Shows and the People Who Created Them*, Boston: Little, Brown.

Mann, Chris (1997) '*Charlie's Angels*' in Horace Newcomb (ed.), *The Encyclopedia of Television*, London and Chicago: Fitzroy Dearborn.

Marc, David (1989), *Comic Visions: Television Comedy and American Culture*, Winchester: Unwin Hyman.

Marek, Michael (accessed, 2002), *X-Files* Conspiracy Timeline http://www.themareks.com/xf/conspiracy.shtml

Maxwell, R (2002), 'Honor Among Patriots' in *Television and New Media*, Vol. 3, No. 2.

McCarthy, Anna (2001), 'Realism and Soap Opera' in Glen Creeber (ed.), *The Television Genre Book*, London: BFI.

McChesney, R (2002), 'The Zillionth Time as Tragedy' in *Television and New Media*, Vol. 3, No. 2.

McGrath, John (1983), 'The Boys are Back' *The Listener*, January 13, 1983.

McGregor, Tom (1999), *Behind the Scenes at Who Wants to be a Millionaire?* Basingstoke: Macmillan.

McIntyre, Gina (2002), 'Science Faction: Sci-fi Guru William Gibson and *X-Files* Mastermind Chris Carter Ponder the Versatility of Genre Storytelling', *Hollywood Reporter*, May 10, 5–6.

McKee, Alan (2001), 'Which is the best *Doctor Who story*? A case study in value judgements outside the academy' in *Intensities: The Journal of Cult Media*, issue 1, available at www.cult-media.com/issue1/Amckee.htm

McKee, Alan (forthcoming), 'How to tell the difference between production and consumption: a case study in *Doctor Who* fandom' in Sara Gwenllian Jones and Roberta E Pearson (eds.), *Essays on Cult Television*, Minneapolis: University of Minnesota Press.

McKee, Alan (2002), 'Interview with Russell T Davies', *Continuum: Journal of Media and Cultural Studies*, Vol. 16, No. 2, July, 235–44.

McLean, Adrienne L (1998), 'Media Effects: Marshall McLuhan, Television Culture, and *The X-Files*', *Film Quarterly*, Vol. 51, No. 4, 2–11.

Mellencamp, Patricia (1992), *High Anxiety: Catastrophe, Scandal, Age, and Comedy*, Bloomington and Indianapolis: Indiana University Press.

Milius, John (1990), '*Reliving the War Between Brothers*', *New York Times*, September 16, Sec. 2, 1, 43.

Miller, Craig and Thorne, John (2001a), 'Half the Man He Used to Be: Dale Cooper and the Final Episode of *Twin Peaks*', *Wrapped in Plastic* 1.53, 2–11.

Miller, Craig and Thorne, John (2001b), 'Strolling Through the Red Room', *Wrapped in Plastic* 1(54), 2–12.

Miller, Jeffrey S (2000), *Something Completely Different: British Television and American Culture*, Minneapolis and London: University of Minnesota Press.

Miller, MC (1986), 'Deride and Conquer' in Todd Gitlin (ed.), *Watching Television*, New York: Pantheon.

Miller, Toby, Lawrence, Geoffrey A, McKay, Jim, and Rowe, David (eds.) (2001), *Globalization and Sport: Playing the World*, London: Sage.

Millington, Bob (1993), '*Boys from the Blackstuff* (Alan Bleasdale)' in George W Brandt, (ed.) (1993), *British Television Drama in the 1980s*, Cambridge University Press.

Millington, Bob and Nelson, Robin (1986), *'Boys from the Blackstuff': The Making of TV Drama*, London: Comedia.

Moragas Spa, M de, Rivenburgh, NK and Larson, JF (1995), *Television in the Olympics*, London: John Libbey.

Moran, Albert (1993), *Moran's Guide to Australian TV Series*, North Ryde, New South Wales, Australia: Allen and Unwin and the Australian Film Television and Radio School.

Morley, D and Robins, K (1995), *Spaces of Identity*, London: Routledge.

Morris, Chris and Iannucci, Armando (2002), 'Absolute Atrocity Special', *Observer*, March 17.

Muir, John Kenneth (1999), *A Critical History of Doctor Who on Television*, Jefferson, NC: McFarland.

Muir, John Kenneth (1999), *Terror Television: American Series, 1970–1999*, Jefferson, NC and London: McFarland.

Myers, Greg (2001), ' "I'm Out of It; You Guys Argue": Making an Issue of It on *The Jerry Springer Show*' in Andrew Tolsen (ed.), *Television Talk Shows: Discourse, Performance, Spectacle*, New Jersey and London: Lawrence Erlbaum Associates, Publishers.

Neale, Steve and Krutnik, Frank (1990), *Popular Film and Television Comedy*, London and New York: Routledge.

Nelson, Robin (1997), *TV Drama in Transition: Forms, Values and Cultural Change*, Basingstoke and New York: Macmillan and St. Martin's Press.

Newman, Anne Waldron (1996), '*The Simpsons*', *Quadrant*, Vol. 40, No. 12, 25–9.

Nightingale, V (1996), *Studying Audiences: The Shock of the Real*, London and New York: Routledge.

Nochimson, Martha (1994), 'Desire Under the Douglas Firs: Entering the Body of Reality in *Twin Peaks*' in David Lavery (ed.) (1995), *Full of Secrets: Critical Approaches to Twin Peaks*, Detroit: Wayne State University.

Nochimson, Martha P (1997), *The Passion of David Lynch: Wild at Heart in Hollywood*, Austin: University of Texas Press.

Novick, Jeremey (2000), *Benny Hill: King Leer*, London: Carlton Books.

O'Regan, Tom (1987), 'The Historical Relations between Theatre and Film: *The Summer of the Seventeenth Doll*', *Continuum: The Australian Journal of Media and Culture*, Vol. 1, No. 1.

O'Regan, Tom (1993), *Australian Television Culture*, Sydney: Allen and Unwin.

Osgerby, Bill, Gough-Yates, Anna and Wells, Marianne (2001), 'The Business of Action: Television History and the development of the action TV series' in Bill Osgerby and Anna Gough-Yates (eds.), *Action TV: Tough Guys, Smooth Operators and Foxy Chicks*, London and New York: Routledge.

Overbey, Karen Eileen and Preston-Matto, Lahney (2002), 'Staking in Tongues: Speech Act as Weapon in *Buffy*', David Lavery and Rhonda V Wilcox (eds.), *Fighting the Forces: What's at Stake in Buffy the Vampire Slayer*, Lanham, MD: Rowman and Littlefield, 73–84.

Paget, Derek (1998), *No Other Way to Tell it: Dramadoc/Docudrama on Television*, Manchester: Manchester University Press.

Paglia, Camille (2001), 'The Energy Mess and Fascist Fays', *Salon,* May 23, http://www.salon.com/people/col/pagl/2001/05/23/oil/index2.html.

Palmer, Jerry (1994), *Taking Humour Seriously,* London: Routledge.

Parkin, Lance (2002), 'Postmodernism: Nudge Nudge, Wink Wink' in *Doctor Who Magazine,* #323, November 13, 2002, 10–16.

Parks, Lisa (1996), 'Special Agent or Monstrosity?: Finding the Feminine in *The X-Files*' in David Lavery, Angela Hague and Marla Cartwright (eds.), *Deny All Knowledge: Reading The X-Files,* Syracuse: Syracuse University Press, 121–34.

Paterson, Richard (1981), 'The Production Context of *Coronation Street*' in Richard Dyer et al., *Coronation Street,* London: British Film Institute.

Paterson, Richard (1984), BFI Dossier 20, '*Boys from the Blackstuff*', London: British Film Institute.

Pattie, David (2002), 'Mobbed Up: *The Sopranos* and the Intertextual Gangster' in David Lavery (ed.), *This Thing of Ours: Investigating The Sopranos,* New York: Columbia University Press, 135–45.

Pender, Patricia (2002), ' "I'm Buffy and You're History": The Postmodern Politics of *Buffy*', in David Lavery and Rhonda V Wilcox (eds.) *Fighting the Forces: What's at Stake in Buffy the Vampire Slayer,* Lanham, MD: Rowman and Littlefield, 35–44.

Perry, George (1983), *Life of Python,* London: Pavilion Books.

Perry, Jeb H (1991), *Screen Gems: A History of Columbia Pictures Television from Cohn to Coke, 1948–1983,* Portland: Scarecrow, 136–8, 306–7.

Peyton, Harley (2002), Audio Commentary on *Twin Peaks: The First Season Special Edition DVD,* Artisan Entertainment.

Pinsky, Mark (2001), *The Gospel According to the Simpsons: The Spiritual Life of the World's Most Animated Family,* Westminster: John Knox Press.

Playden, Zoe-Jane (2002), ' "What you are, what's to come": Feminisms, Citizenship and the divine' in Roz Kaveney (ed.), *Reading the Vampire Slayer: An Unofficial Critical Companion to Buffy and Angel,* London: IB Tauris, 120–47.

Pond, Steve (1990), 'Naked Lynch', *Rolling Stone,* March 22, 51–4, 120.

Poniewozik, James (2002), 'Back in Business: Next Month *The Sopranos* Gives Some Bada-Bing to a Too Safe Fall TV Season', *Time,* September 2, 2002, 56–7.

Porter, Jennifer and McLaren, Darcee L (eds.) (1999), *Star Trek and Sacred Ground: Explorations of Star Trek, Religion and American Culture,* New York: State University of New York Press.

Porter, Loraine (1998), 'Tarts, Tampons and Tyrants: Women and Representation in British Comedy' in Stephen Wagg (ed.), *Because I Tell a Joke or Two: Comedy, Politics and Social Difference*, London and New York: Routledge.

Postman, Neil (1987), *Amusing Ourselves to Death*, London: Methuen.

Potter, Dennis (1986), *The Singing Detective* (the script), London and Boston: Faber & Faber.

Potter, Jeremy (1990), 'Independent Television News' in *Independent Television in Britain*, Vol. 4, London and New York: Macmillan.

Pounds, Michael C (1999), *Race in Space: The Representation of Ethnicity in Star Trek and Star Trek: The Next Generation*, Maryland: The Scarecrow Press.

Press, Andrea (1991), *Women Watching Television: Gender, Class and Generation in the American Television Experience*, Philadelphia: University of Pennsylvania Press.

Putterman, Barry (1995), *On Television and Comedy: Essays on Style, Theme, Performer and Writer*, Jefferson: McFarland.

Ramaeker, Paul B (2001), ' "You Think They Call Us Plastic *Now...*": The Monkees and *Head*' in Pamela Robertson Wojcik and Arthur Knight (eds.), *Soundtrack Available: Essays on Film and Popular Music*, Durham: Duke University Press.

Reeves, Jimmie L et al. (1994), 'Postmodernism and Television: Speaking of *Twin Peaks*' in David Lavery (ed.), *Full of Secrets: Critical Approaches to Twin Peaks*, Detroit: Wayne State University Press, 173–95.

Reeves, Jimmie L, Rodgers, Mark C and Epstein, Michael (1996), 'Re-Writing Popularity: The Cult Files' in David Lavery, Angela Hague and Marla Cartwright (eds.), *Deny All Knowledge: Reading The X-Files*, Syracuse: Syracuse University Press, 22–35.

Remnick, David (2001), 'Is this the End of RICO? With *The Sopranos* the Mob Genre is on the Brink', *New Yorker*, April 2; 38–44.

Riggs, M (1991), *Color Adjustment*, San Francisco: California Newsreel.

Roberts, Robin (1999), *Sexual Generations: Star Trek: The Next Generation and Gender*, Urbana: University of Illinois Press.

Rodgers, Marc C, Epstein, Michael and Reeves, Jimmie (2002), '*The Sopranos* as HBO Brand Equity: The Art of Commerce in the Age of Digital Reproduction', in *This Thing of Ours: Investigating The Sopranos*, New York: Columbia University Press, 42–57.

Rodman, Warren (1989), 'The Series that Will Change TV', *Connoisseur*, September, 139–44.

Roscoe, J (2001a), '*Big Brother*: Performing the real 24 hours a day', *International Journal of Cultural Studies*, Vol. 4, No. 4, December.

Roscoe, J (2001b), 'Real Entertainment: new factual hybrid television', *Media International Australia*, No. 100, August.

Roscoe, J (2002), 'Interview with Peter Abbott', *Continuum*, Vol. 16, No. 2, 225–34.

Rosenbaum, Jonathan (1994), 'Bad Ideas: The Art and Politics of *Twin Peaks*' in David Lavery (ed.), *Full of Secrets: Critical Approaches to Twin Peaks*, Detroit: Wayne State University Press, 22–9.

Ross, Robert (1999), *Benny Hill: Merry Master of Mirth*, London: BT Batsford.

Rothkerch, Ian (2002), 'A day in the life', www.salon.com, February 5, an interview with creator, producer and writer of *24*, Joel Surnow.

Rowe, Kathleen (1990), 'Roseanne: Unruly Woman as Domestic Goddess', *Screen*, 31 (4), 408–19.

Rowe, Kathleen (1995), *The Unruly Woman: Gender and the Genres of Laughter*, Austin: University of Texas Press.

Rucker, Allen (2000, expanded edition, covering all three seasons, 2001), *The Sopranos: A Family History*, New York: New American Library.

Rucker, Allen (2002), *The Sopranos Cookbook*, New York: Warner.

Rugaber, Walter (1969), 'Nixon Makes Most Historic Telephone Call Ever', *The New York Times*, July 21, 2.

Ruoff, Jeffrey (2002), *An American Family: A Televised Life*, Minneapolis: University of Minnesota Press.

Russell, David (2000), 'A Cinema of Repression: De Niro and Depardieu', *Movie*, No. 36.

Sales, Roger (1986), 'An Introduction to Broadcasting History' in David Punter (ed.), *Introduction to Contemporary Cultural Studies*, London and New York: Longman.

San Martin, Nancy (2003), 'Must See TV: Programming Identity on NBC Thursdays' in Mark Jancovich and James Lyons (eds.), *Quality Popular Television: Cult TV, Industry and Fans*, London: British Film Institute.

Sangster, Jim (2002), *24: The Unofficial Guide*, London: Contender.

Scannell, Paddy (1979), 'The Social Eye of Television, 1946–1957', *Media, Culture and Society*, Vol. 1, No. 1, 65–80.

Scannell, Paddy (2002), '*Big Brother* as Event Television', *Television and New Media*, Vol. 3, No. 3, 271–82.

Schaffer, K and Smith, S (eds.) (2000), *The Olympics at the Millennium*, Piscataway, NJ: Rutgers University Press.

Schatz, Thomas (1997), 'Workplace Programs' in Horace Newcomb (ed.), *The Encyclopedia of Television*, Chicago: Fitzroy Dearborn.

Schwichtenberg, Cathy (1981), 'A Patriarchal Voice in Heaven', *Jump Cut*, No. 24/25.

Sconce, Jeffrey (2000), *Haunted Media: Electronic Presence from Telegraphy to Television*, Durham and London: Duke University Press.

Seiter, Ellen (1985), 'The Hegemony of Leisure: Aaron Spelling Presents *Hotel*' in Phillip Drummond and Richard Paterson, *Television in Transition: Papers from the First International Television Studies Conference*, London: British Film Institute.

Selby, Keith and Cowdery, Ron (1995), 'Analysing a TV news broadcast: *News at Ten*' in *How to Study Television*, London and New York: Macmillan.

Selby, Keith and Cowdery, Ron (1995), 'The TV Soap: *Neighbours*' in *How to Study Television*, London and New York: Macmillan.

Semati, M (2002), 'Imagine the Terror', *Television and New Media*, Vol. 3, No. 2.

Serge Denisoff, R and Romanowski, William (1991), *Risky Business: Rock in Film*, New York: Transaction.

Shattuc, Jane (1997), *The Talking Cure: TV Talk-shows and Women*, London: Routledge.

Shattuc, Jane (2001), 'The Confessional Talk Show' in Glen Creeber (ed.), *The Television Genre Book*, London: British Film Institute.

Sheehan, Helena (2002), '*Hill Street Blues*: an analysis of text and context', www.comms.dcu.ie.sheehanh/tv/hillstbl.html

Shubik, Irene (1975), *Play for Today: The Evolution of Television Drama*, London: Davis Poynter.

Siemann, Catherine (2002), 'Darkness Falls on the Endless Summer: Buffy as Gidget for the Fin de Siecle' in David Lavery and Rhonda V Wilcox (eds.), *Fighting the Forces: What's at Stake in Buffy the Vampire Slayer*, Lanham, MD: Rowman and Littlefield, 120–9.

Silverstone, Roger (1984), 'Narrative Strategies in Television Science: A Case Study', *Media, Culture and Society*, Vol. 6, No. 4, 337–410.

Simon, Ron (1992), 'The Flow of Memory and Desire in The Television Plays of Dennis Potter', a brochure that accompanied the Museum of Television and Radio's retrospective of Potter's work in New York, January 23 to May 31.

Simpson, Jeff (2002), *Top of the Pops, 1964–2002*, London: BBC Books.

Smith, Nancy-Banks (1999), 'A Bone to pick', *Guardian*, October 11.

Smith, Nancy-Banks (1999), 'Last Night's TV', *Guardian*, section 2, Tuesday, October 12, 22.

Sparks, Colin (2000), 'Introduction: the Panic Over Tabloid News' in Colin Sparks and John Tulloch (eds.), *Tabloid Tales: Global Debates Over Media Standards*, Lanham: Rowman and Littlefield.

Springer, Jerry and Morton, Laura (1999), *Ringmaster*, New York: St. Martin's Press.

Stabile, Carol and Harrison, Mark (eds.) (2003), *Prime-Time Animation: Television Animation and American Culture*, London and New York: Routledge.

Staiger, Janet (2000), *Blockbuster TV: Must See Sitcoms in the Network Era*, New York: New York University Press.

Stanley, David (1999), *News at Ten: A Celebration of 32 Years of Television News*, London: Macmillan.

Stark, Steven D (1997), '*The Twilight Zone*: Science Fiction as Realism' in *Glued To The Set: The 60 Television Shows That Made Us Who We Are Today*, New York: The Free Press, 85–9.

Statistical Research Incorporated, Westfield, NJ (1990), '1990 Public Television National Image Survey', commissioned by PBS Station Independence Program, September 28, 2.1–2.8.

Steele, S (1990), *The Content of Our Character*, New York: Harper Perennial.

Stevenson, Diane (1994), 'Family Romance, Family Violence, and the Fantastic in *Twin Peaks*' in David Lavery (ed.), *Full of Secrets: Critical Approaches to Twin Peaks*, Detroit: Wayne State University Press, 70–81.

Strate, Lance (2002), 'No(rth Jersey) Sense of Place: The Cultural Geography (and Media Ecology) of *The Sopranos*' in David Lavery (ed.), *This Thing of Ours: Investigating The Sopranos*, New York: Columbia University Press, 178–91.

Sturken, Frank (1990), *Live Television: The Golden Age of 1956–1958 in New York*, Jefferson, NC: McFarland.

Swanson, Gillian (1981), '*Dallas*, part 1', *Framework*, No. 14, spring, 62.

Sugden, J and Tomlinson, A (1998), *FIFA and the Contest for World Football*, Cambridge: Polity Press.

Talen, Julie (2002), '24: split screen's big comeback', *www.salon.com*, May 14.

Taylor, Charles (1994), 'Truth Decay: Sleuths After Reagan', *Millenium Pop*, 1 summer.

Taylor, Charles (accessed, 2002), 'The WB's Big Daddy Condescension', *Salon.com*, http://www.salon.com/ent/log/1999/05/26/buffy_rant/index.html

Telotte, JP (1994), 'The Dis-order of Things in *Twin Peaks*' in David Lavery (ed.), *Full of Secrets: Critical Approaches to Twin Peaks*, Detroit: Wayne State University Press, 160–72.

Thelen, David (1994), 'The Movie Maker as Historian: Conversations with Ken Burns', *Journal of American History*, Vol. 81, No. 3, December, 1031–50.

Thomson, David (1990), 'History Composed with Film', *Film Comment*, Vol. 26, No. 5, September/October, 12–16.

Thompson, John O (1982), *Monty Python: Complete and Utter Theory of the Grotesque*, London: British Film Institute.

Thompson, Robert J (1996), *Television's Second Golden Age: From Hill Street Blues to ER*, New York: Continuum.

Tibbetts, John C (1996), 'The Incredible Stillness of Being: Motionless Pictures in the Films of Ken Burns,' *American Studies*, Vol. 37, No. 1, Spring, 117–33.

Tomc, Sandra (1995), 'Questing Women: The Feminist Mystery after Feminism' in Glenwood Irons (ed.), *Feminism in Women's Detective Fiction*, Toronto, Buffalo and London: University of Toronto Press.

Tomlinson, A (1996), 'Olympic spectacle: opening ceremonies and some paradoxes of globalization', *Media Culture and Society*, 18, 583–602.

Tomlinson, A (2000), 'Carrying the torch for whom? Symbolic power and Olympic ceremony' in K Schaffer and S Smith (eds.), *The Olympics at the Millennium*, Piscataway, NJ: Rutgers University Press.

Toohey, K (1997), 'Australian television, gender and the Olympic Games', *International Review for the Sociology of Sport*, Vol. 32, No. 1, 19–29.

Toplin, Robert Brent (ed.) (1996), *Ken Burns's The Civil War: Historians Respond*, New York: Oxford University Press.

Topping, Keith (2003), *A Day in the Life: The Unofficial and Unauthorized Guide to 24*, Tolworth: Telos.

Tudor, A (1975), 'The Panels' in E Buscombe (ed.), *Football on Television*, London: British Film Institute.

Tuggle, C and Owen, A (1999), 'A descriptive analysis of NBC's coverage of the centennial Olympics: the "Games of the Woman"?' *Journal of Sport and Social Issues*, Vol. 23, No. 2, 171–82.

Tulloch, John and Alvarado, Manuel (1983), *Doctor Who: The Unfolding Text*, London: Macmillan.

Tulloch, John and Jenkins, Henry (1995), *Science Fiction Audiences: Watching Doctor Who and Star Trek*, London and New York: Routledge.

Tulloch, John (2000), *Watching Television Audiences: Cultural Theories and Methods*, London and New York: Arnold.

271

Tumber, Howard (2001), '10 pm and all that: The battle over UK TV news' in Michael Bromley (ed.), *No News is Bad News: Radio, Television and the Public*, London and New York: Longman.

Turner, Graeme (2001), 'Genre, Hybridity and Mutation' in Glen Creeber (ed.), *The Television Genre Book*, London: British Film Institute, 6.

Vasagar, Jeevan (2003), 'Guilty: trio who cheated their way to a million', *Guardian*, April 8, 11.

Verba, Joan Marie (1996), *Boldly Writing: A Trekker Fan and Zine History, 1967–1987*, Minnesota: FTL Publications.

Viner, Brian (1999), 'Old Predators on the Warpath', *Independent on Sunday*, 'Culture' section, October 10, 6.

Vint, Sheryl (accessed 2002), 'Killing us Softly'? A Feminist Search for the 'Real' Buffy, *Slayage* No. 6, http://www.slayage.tv/essays/slayage5/vint.htm.

Vowell, Sarah (accessed 2002), 'Please Sir May I Have a Mother?' Salon.com. http://www.salon.com/ent/col/vowe/2000/02/02/vowell_wb/index.html.

Vitaris, Paula (1995), 'The Making of *The X-Files*', *Cinefantastique*, October, 17–89.

Wagg, Stephen (1998), 'You've Never Had it so Silly: the Politics of British Satirical Comedy from *Beyond the Fringe* to *Spitting Image*' in D Strinati and S Wagg (eds.), *Come on Down? Popular Media Culture in Post-War Britain*, London and New York: Routledge.

Wagner, Jon and Lundeen, Jan (1998), *Deep Space and Sacred Time: Star Trek in the American Mythos*, Connecticut: Praeger.

Wallace, David Foster (1997), *A Supposedly Fun Thing I'll Never Do Again: Essays and Arguments*, Boston: Little Brown.

Ward, Geoffrey C, with Ric Burns and Ken Burns (1990), *The Civil War: An Illustrated History*, New York: Knopf.

Warshow, Robert (1962), *The Immediate Experience: Movies, Comics, Theatre and Other Aspects of Popular Culture*, New York: Doubleday and Co. Inc, 127–33.

Watters, Harry F (1990), 'An American Mosaic', *Newsweek*, September 17, 68–70.

Watkins, Peter, 'The Films of Peter Watkins', *Peter Watkins: Filmmaker and Media Critic*, http://www.peterwatkins.lt, accessed March 22, 2002.

Wayne, Mike (2000), '*Who Wants to be a Millionaire?*: Contextual analysis and the endgame of public service television' in Dan Fleming (ed.), *Formations: a 21st Century Media Studies Textbook*, Manchester: Manchester University Press.

Wells, M (2000), 'BBC staff to outnumber British athletes at Sydney Olympics', *Guardian*, August 17.

Wells, Paul (1998a), 'Where Everybody Knows Your Name: Open Convictions and Closed Contexts in the American Situation comedy', in Stephen Wagg (ed.), *Because I Tell a Joke or Two: Comedy, Politics and Social Difference*, London and New York: Routledge.

Wells, Paul (1998b), *Understanding Animation*, London and New York: Routledge.

Wells, Paul (2002), *Animation and America*, Edinburgh: Edinburgh University Press.

Werts, Diane (2002), 'Nervous Ticks', *Newsday*, October 27.

Wexman, Virginia Wright (1984), 'The Television Love Goddess: Defining Female Beauty within the Family', unpublished conference paper, International Television Conference, London.

Whannel, Garry (1990), 'Winner Takes All: competition' in Andrew Goodwin and Garry Whannel (eds.), *Understanding Television*, London and New York: Routledge.

Whannel, Gary (1992), *Fields of Vision: Television Sport and Cultural Transformation*, London and New York: Routledge.

Wheatley, Helen (2002), 'Mystery and Imagination: Anatomy of a Gothic anthology series' in Janet Thumim (ed.), *Small Screens, Big Ideas: Television in the 1950s*, London and New York: IB Tauris, 165–80.

Whedon, Joss (interview with), accessed 2002a, BBC Online, http://www.bbc.co.uk/buffy/reallife/jossinterview.shtml.

Whedon, Joss (interview with), accessed 2002b, *The Onion*, AV Club, September 5, 2001, http://www. theonionavclub. com/avclub3731/avfeature_3731.html.

White, Matthew and Jaffer, Ali (1988), *The Official Prisoner Companion*, New York: Warner Books.

White, Mimi (1992), *Tele-advising: Therapeutic Discourse in American Television*, Chapel Hill: University of North Carolina Press.

Wilcox, Rhonda V and Williams JP (1996), ' "What to You Think?" *The X-Files*, Liminality, and Gender Pleasure' in David Lavery, Angela Hague and Marla Cartwright (eds.), *Deny All Knowledge: Reading The X-Files*, Syracuse: Syracuse UP, 99–120.

Wilcox, Rhonda V (1999), 'There Will Never Be a "Very Special" *Buffy: Buffy* and the Monsters of Teen Life', *Journal of Popular Film and Television*, 27 (2), 16–23, republished in *Slayage: The Online International Journal of Buffy Studies*, No. 2 (March 2001), http://www.slayage.tv/essays/slayage2/wilcox.htm.

Wilcox, Rhonda V and David Lavery (eds.) (2002), Introduction in *Fighting the Forces: What's at Stake in Buffy the Vampire Slayer*, Lanham, MD: Rowman and Littlefield, xvii–xxix.

Will, George F (1990), 'A Masterpiece on the Civil War', *Washington Post*, September 20, section A, 23.

Williams, Raymond (1974), *Television, Technology and Cultural Form*, London: Collins.

Williams, Raymond (1977) 'A lecture on Realism', *Screen*, spring Vol. 18, No.1, 61–74.

Willis, Paul (1990), *Common Culture*, Buckingham: Open University Press.

Willis, Ellen (2002), 'Our Mobsters, Ourselves', *This Thing of Ours: Investigating The Sopranos*, New York: Columbia University Press, 2–9, originally published in *The Nation*, April, 2, 2001.

Wilmut, Roger (1980), *From Fringe to Flying Circus: Celebrating a Unique Generation of Comedy 1960–1980*, London: Methuen.

Wilmut, Roger and Rosengard, Peter (1989), *Didn't You Kill my Mother-in-Law?* London: Methuen.

Wilson, WJ (1987), *The Truly Disadvantaged*, Chicago: University of Chicago Press.

Winston, Brian (1995), *Claiming the Real*, London: British Film Institute.

Wolcott, James (2000), 'HBO's Singular Sensation', *Vanity Fair*, February, 24–7.

Wolfe, Peter (1997), *In the Zone: The Twilight World of Rod Serling*, Bowling Green: Bowling Green State University Popular Press.

Yacowar, Maurice (2002), *The Sopranos on the Couch: Analyzing Television's Greatest Series*, New York: Continuum.

Zelizer, Barbie and Allan, Stuart (eds.) (2002), *Journalism After September 11*, London and New York: Routledge.

Zicree, Marc Scott (1992), *The Twilight Zone Companion: Second Edition*, Los Angeles: Silman-James Press.

Zoglin, Richard (1990a), 'Like Nothing on Earth: David Lynch's *Twin Peaks* May Be the Most Original Show on TV', *Time*, April 9, 96–7.

Zoglin, Richard (1990b), 'A Sleeper with a Dream: After the Eerie *Twin Peaks*, TV May Never be the Same Again', *Time*, May 21, 86–7.

Zoglin, Richard (1990c), 'The Terrible Remedy', *Time*, September 24, 73.

Zweerink, Amanda and Gatson, Sarah H (2002), 'www.buffy.com: Cliques, Boundaries, and Hierarchies in an Internet Community' in David Lavery and Rhonda V Wilcox (eds.), *Fighting the Forces: What's at Stake in Buffy the Vampire Slayer*, Lanham, MD: Rowman and Littlefield, 239–49.

Index

Television programme titles appear in italics, those in bold type have articles within the text of the book